T...laan
... y but
my ... to
make a statement
about the 20th
Century.

Thanks for all
you do for
the University!

Jim

Jan. 2016

MAKING SENSE OF HISTORY
Studies in Historical Cultures
General Editor: Stefan Berger
Founding Editor: Jörn Rüsen

Bridging the gap between historical theory and the study of historical memory, this series crosses the boundaries between both academic disciplines and cultural, social, political and historical contexts. In an age of rapid globalization, which tends to manifest itself on an economic and political level, locating the cultural practices involved in generating its underlying historical sense is an increasingly urgent task.

VIKTOR FRANKL'S SEARCH FOR MEANING

An Emblematic 20th-Century Life

Timothy E. Pytell

berghahn
NEW YORK · OXFORD
www.berghahnbooks.com

First published in 2015 by
Berghahn Books
www.berghahnbooks.com

Library of Congress Cataloging-in-Publication Data

Pytell, Timothy, author.
 Viktor Frankl's search for meaning : an emblematic 20th-century life / Timothy
E. Pytell. — First edition.
 pages cm. — (Making sense of history ; volume 23)
 Includes bibliographical references and index.
 ISBN 978-1-78238-830-2 (hardback : alk. paper) —
 ISBN 978-1-78238-831-9 (ebook)
 1. Frankl, Viktor E. (Viktor Emil), 1905-1997. 2. Psychologists—Austria—
Biography. 3. Holocaust, Jewish (1939-1945)—Psychological aspects. I. Title.
 BF109.F695P95 2015
 150.19'5092—dc23

 2015003131

British Library Cataloguing in Publication Data

A catalogue record for this book is available from the British Library

ISBN: 978-1-78238-830-2 hardback
ISBN: 978-1-78238-831-9 ebook

Contents

Preface

The origins of this book stem from my attempt to understand how Western culture went from Freud's postulation of a death instinct in 1922 to the contemporary Kervorkianism or medicalization of death. Influenced by the French philosopher Michel Foucault, I originally aspired to write a genealogy of the last of the human sciences—thanatology. My friend, the late Lawrence Birken, suggested I investigate Viktor Frankl. Since Frankl had been influenced by Freud, and late in his life had made critical comments on Kervorkian, I thought his intellectual production might be the anchor for the study that I was then formulating as the desublimation of the death instinct in Western civilization. Although embers of that initial quest remain, I quickly realized that an intellectual biography of Viktor Frankl was an ideal stand-alone topic.

This book project has left me indebted to a plethora of family, friends, and institutions. It is impossible to acknowledge them all so I will attempt a short list. I am grateful to Günter Bischopf for suggesting I contact Marion Berghahn. The good people of Berghahn Books are producing top-notch and groundbreaking historical works. I am honored to be a part of the team.

Over the years I have received a great deal of institutional support. A Mellon Foundation grant provided initial seed money. Social science research grants provided by Colorado College allowed me to further my understanding of Holocaust survival issues. I presented my initial research to the Richardson History of Psychiatry Seminar at Cornell University in New York, and I am particularly grateful to George Makari, Aaron Esman, and Joseph Reppen for both the opportunity and feedback. Participation in the Silbermann Seminar and participation in the Hess Seminar at the United States Holocaust Memorial Museum led by Mark Roseman, Jurgen Matthaus, Donald Bloxham, and John Roth were the most profoundly rewarding professional development experiences of my career. The museum's mission of Holocaust education, genocide prevention, and advanced research is being achieved at the highest level because of the exceptional people working there. The *world* owes them gratitude.

For the last twelve years my home institution of California State University San Bernardino has provided both financial support and a working environment that was central in bringing the book to fruition. I am especially appreciative of the warm welcome offered by Professor Lawrence "Laurie" Baron upon my arrival in California and subsequent support and friendship over the years. I also owe my "immediate" family a word of gratitude. My mother Honora and her late husband Wayne Anzick opened their home for the initial writing. Similarly, my sister and brother-in-law, Katie and Mike Boone, loaned their alpine retreat, and also discussed issues relating to the history of psychology. Finally my great friend John Rice provided recreation time as we four-wheeled and biked around Colorado when I was taking breaks from writing. For the last twelve years my wife Lucy and our two children Alexandra and Sebastian have kept life full of reward and emotion. Thanks for giving me the time away to finish this project!

I owe a special acknowledgement to Alexander Batthyány. In the famous Viennese cafés "Sperl" and "Schwarzenberg," amid coffee and clouds of smoke, Alex took me through a page by page critical reading of my manuscript. I did my very best to incorporate his opinions and criticisms, and the manuscript is the better for it. Although his training as a philosopher and Logotherapist, in contrast with my training as a European intellectual historian, led us to some perhaps "irreconcilable" disagreements, I appreciate his good humanity and his willingness to agree to disagree.

My circle of close comrades in Vienna, Wolfgang Maderthaner, Siegfried Mattl, Karl Fallend, and Gerhard Benetka, made this book possible. Thank you! My research was also enhanced by Wolfgang Neugebauer, Elisabeth Klamper, Gerhard Botz, Oliver Rathkolb, Karin Holzer, Joachim Widder, Wilfried Pototsnig, Ernst Kreishler, Richard Mitten, Walter Manoschek, Rüdiger Stix, Judy Podilipnik, Peter Malina, Karl Pfeifer, Ernest Seinfeld, Lydia Marinelli, Helwig Leibinger, Anna Hájková, Camilla Nielsen, Peter Mauer, and Herbert Kuhner. In New York, my colleagues at New York University, Ed Zupcic, Nicole Dombrowski-Risser, and John Savage helped me survive the ups and downs of graduate school. At Cooper Union, Peter Buckley and David Weir kept my spirits and humor up while I was working as an adjunct. Along with being a great friend, Mark Durkin provided generous editorial assistance with my writing. Other close friends and patrons in New York include Roger Mullarkey, Tom Howes, Scott Driggers, Andrew Collins, Barry Pailet, and Rob Morea, along with Barbra Dixon, Tom and Jeanne Hill, Alice Geller, Lorig Yekhairparin, and David Rentschler. So many others have had a profound impact on my life. Thanks for enhancing the ride.

The stars literally aligned for me at NYU in the late 1980s and early 1990s. NYU already had an excellent faculty that included Molly Nolan when three outstanding European intellectual historians, the late Tony Judt, Anson Rabinbach, and Jerrold Seigel, arrived on the scene. Each in their own unique way

made a profound impact on me, and made my life so much more worth living. Early on I came in contact with the work of Geoffrey Cocks. We became friends and the reader will easily see the debt I owe him. The late Lawrence "Larry" Birken spent countless hours discussing not only Frankl but intellectual life in general and was a great "intellectual" friend to me. I miss him. I am deeply appreciative of the direction of Jerry Seigel. He forced me to become a better writer, thinker, and scholar. Finally I owe my greatest debt to Andy Rabinbach. I learned to teach under his tutelage at Cooper Union, he established all my initial contacts in Vienna that made the research for this book possible, he read the initial draft, and most importantly he has been the ideal mentor, steady, inspiring, and the epitome of a "gut mensch." He has my and many other students' deepest admiration and appreciation.

It has been my great fortune in life to have encountered exceptional teachers. From the nuns in my grammar school that first sparked my interest in the past, to the exceptional group of extraordinary professors at Colorado College that gave me the foundation and confidence to pursue a Ph.D., to the brilliant minds I encountered at NYU, I owe my deepest gratitude. The oft-quoted line from Yeats that "Education is not the filling of a pail, but the lighting of a fire" is undoubtedly true. But to teach is in essence nurturing and coaxing that "fire" into form through writing, speaking, and critical thinking. Subsequently, to the teachers and especially "Susan" Ashley at Colorado College, who taught me to never stop asking "so what," this book is dedicated.

Finally for those who find *Viktor Frankl's Search for Meaning* disturbing for any reason I offer "all apologies."

Timothy Pytell
So-Cal February 2015

Introduction

Viktor Frankl and Man's Search for Meaning

Viktor Frankl was born on 26 March 1905 in the Jewish district of Leopold-stadt in Vienna. After living a remarkable life that was shaped by the major intellectual and cultural trends of the twentieth century, he died at the age of ninety-two of heart failure on 2 September 1997 in Vienna. Frankl is best known for writing the highly acclaimed Holocaust testimony *Man's Search for Meaning*, and he is also recognized as the founder of his own school of psychotherapy—logotherapy. As the proclaimed successor to Freud's psychoanalysis and Adler's individual psychology, logotherapy is promoted as the "third Viennese school of psychotherapy."[1] Defined succinctly, logotherapy is a form of existential psychotherapy that is conceived as "therapy through meaning."[2] Frankl's third school of Logotherapy therefore complements the Freudian will to pleasure, and the Adlerian will to power, by considering the primary motivational force in humans to be the will to meaning. In Freudian and Adlerian therapies the focus is on personal introspection, uncovering character structures, and remembering significant (often traumatic) events in the past. In contrast, logotherapy focuses on concrete life conditions and guides the patient to find what is considered the unique and specific meaning to their existence.

Since his death, three biographies of Frankl have been published. In Vienna, Frankl's disciple Alfred Längle published *Viktor Frankl Ein Porträt* in 1998. Längle, the head of the International Society for Logotherapy and Existential Analysis, was Frankl's right-hand man from 1982 until 1991. In 1991 Frankl severed ties with Längle over the latter's psychotherapeutic revisions that incorporated elements of depth psychology, personal introspection, and significant

Notes for this section begin on page 12.

experiences. According to Frankl, these revisions were "anti-logo-therapeutic."[3] Despite the rejection, Längle's biography is full of praise and admiration. This is not surprising since Längle conceived of Frankl as a "fatherly friend" during their association and claimed that he was one of only two friends Frankl had in his life, and the "one who knew him best."[4] This intimate friendship allowed Längle to rely on personal stories and anecdotes, along with an extended version of Frankl's autobiography that Frankl had entrusted to him, to paint a glowing portrait.

The second biographer, the American psychologist Haddon Klingberg, Jr., was a professor of psychology at North Park University in Chicago. Klingberg originally studied with Frankl in Vienna in 1962. Although they had little to no contact over the years, Frankl chose Klingberg in the early 1990s to become his official biographer. Based on hundreds of hours of interviews Klingberg provides an "unabashedly sympathetic rendering of their story as Viktor and Elly [Frankl's second wife] told it to me."[5] Similar to Längle's, Klingberg's book is conceived in a hagiographic mode that is profoundly flattering. I published the third biography, *Viktor Frankl: Das Ende eines Mythos?* in 2005. The objective of my biography was to provide a critical reflection that focused on Frankl's intellectual struggle for meaning. This substantially revised English version includes two chapters not originally published in German, and also incorporates the insights of Längle and Klingberg. In addition I respond to criticisms that head of the Frankl archive and university Professor Alexander Batthyány expressed in his response to my critical view of Frankl, entitled *Mythos Frankl? Geschichte der Logotherapie und Existenzanalyse 1925-1945, Entgegnung auf Timothy Pytell.*

All biographers agree that Frankl's biography is fascinating. In his long and productive life Frankl wrote over thirty books and dozens of articles. As a neurologist and self-proclaimed founder of existential analysis, Frankl addressed in his writings subjects ranging from therapeutic and social concerns to scientific research.[6] His renowned Holocaust memoir, *Man's Search for Meaning*, is a worldwide best seller, and was once ranked by "Library of Congress in Washington ... as one of the ten most influential books in America."[7] *Man's Search for Meaning* has also sold millions of copies in the English version alone, and has been chosen five times by American colleges as "the book of the year."[8] Indeed, the impact of the book has been global because it has been translated into twenty languages, including Chinese and Japanese, and sold over ten million copies worldwide. Touting his success to Robert Leslie, the curator of the Viktor Frankl Library and Memorabilia in Berkeley, Frankl proclaimed, "*Man's Search for Meaning* was Number One on a new list called Longseller. This list refers to those bestsellers which throughout decades, do not stop bestselling."[9]

The success of *Man's Search for Meaning* has also served to promote logotherapy because Frankl included a theoretical synopsis of his brand of analysis as a postscript. The synopsis, entitled "Logotherapy in a Nutshell," was included at the suggestion of the renowned Harvard psychologist, Gordon Allport. Allport

was an early supporter of Frankl when he came to America in the late 1950s, and he wrote a preface for the first English translation of Frankl's testimony. During the 1960s the success of *Man's Search for Meaning* enabled Frankl to steadily build a broad base of support for logotherapy in America, and, from the 1970s on, globally. Currently there are numerous logotherapeutic institutes and societies that literally span the globe.

Along with his Holocaust testimony, Frankl's broad popular appeal stems from the fact that his intellectual work focused on what is arguably the central question of Western culture in the twentieth century: nihilism and the problem of human meaning.[10] Besides asking this essential question, Frankl also claimed that his existential psychology provided ways to answer to this profound dilemma. His brand of existentialism certainly does offer a straightforward and quite popular answer to the problem of human meaning. As a doctor and psychiatrist Frankl took a practical and humanistic approach to the problem of human meaning. He therefore developed "dimensional ontology" that allowed him to diagnose patients as beset with either a somatogenic (physical), psychogenic (psychological), or noogenic (spiritual) malady. Logotherapy focuses primarily on the latter category as it helps patients to triumph over the psychosomatic by allowing them to muster "the defiant power of the human spirit" and derive meaning from their problems/conditions. As praxis, logotherapy is very eclectic and open to almost any therapeutic technique from hypnosis to lobotomy. However, Frankl developed two logotherapeutic techniques—paradoxical intention and dereflection—based on the noological dimension's ability to disassociate. The origins of paradoxical intention are discussed in chapter 4 and dimensional ontology is covered in chapters 8 and 10.

Logotherapy also provided a theory of values that pointed to three possibilities for the fulfillment of the will to meaning: (1) a deed or creative work; (2) an experience, especially love; and (3) the attitude we take toward an unalterable fate.[11] This latter category of attitudinal values is key to logotherapy because it helps individuals derive meaning from the most tragic and "meaningless" circumstances of human suffering. Undeniably, Frankl and his movement of logotherapy provide a great deal of solace and comfort for those in emotional and spiritual need. On the other hand a more critical view argues that by offering hope and consolation rather than intellectual challenge, logotherapy is a "surface psychology." In this view logotherapy is an early example of the "self-help" movement that fits into the genre of "retail psycho-spirituality."

The effectiveness or ineffectiveness of logotherapy as a *therapy* is not a primary concern of this book and instead the focus is on a biographical history of Frankl's intellectual struggle to find meaning as it unfolded in the dynamic twentieth century. The development of logotherapy and in particular the logotherapeutic conception of humanity is central to this story.

The secondary literature on Frankl is constantly expanding, and often consists of tributes of resounding praise. There is also a significant body of literature

on the therapeutic aspects and strategies of logotherapy being developed by the Viktor Frankl Institute.[12] Frankl and his intellectual production have been overlooked by academic historians for a variety of reasons. Most academics have focused on the arguably more sophisticated work of Martin Heidegger, Ludwig Binswanger, and Medard Boss. However, when Frankl reflected on his rejection by academia he was fond of stating "that the really big ones," i.e., Heidegger, Jaspers, Binswanger, and Allport, showed appreciation for his work.[13] Part of the rejection undoubtedly also stemmed from Frankl's character. For example, in their biographies both Längle and Klingberg describe Frankl as a genius, but also suggest Frankl's personal style might have led some to reject or overlook the significance of his ideas. According to Klingberg, Frankl could appear to "be demanding, impatient, too quick and tart in debate… At times he sounded boastful, self-congratulatory."[14] On the other hand Klingberg claims Frankl's characteristics of self-absorption, self-promotion, and disregard for others are attributable to his "creative genius."[15] Längle asserts a similar view of Frankl but uses the term "narcissistic" to capture Frankl's character and to explain why he was rejected by many of his contemporaries.[16] These assessments are confirmed by the renowned scholar of Martin Buber, Maurice Friedman. Friedman hosted Frankl in the mid 1970s at Tulane University and was somewhat put off by Frankl's arrogance, describing him as a "brilliant prima donna."[17]

Despite his persona (or maybe because of it) Frankl certainly achieved success in academia. For example, he was a professor of neurology and psychiatry at the University of Vienna, Distinguished Professor of Logotherapy at the U.S. International University, and visiting professor at Harvard, Duquesne University, and Southern Methodist University. He also received twenty-eight honorary doctorates from universities throughout the world, and the American Psychiatric Association awarded him the Oskar Pfister Award. Finally, in 1995 Frankl was nominated by the far right Freedom Party for Eherenbürgerschaft (Honorary Citizenship of Vienna), and he eventually received the high honor by unanimous vote. But arguably his most significant "achievement" was his ability to not only survive Auschwitz and Dachau, but also to retain a hopeful and positive take on life after such profound tragedy. Without a doubt, much of Frankl's intellectual and moral legitimacy stemmed from the tragic optimism exemplified by his Holocaust testimony.

In his own self-appraisal, in an article somewhat ironically entitled "Logotherapy on Its Way to Degurufication," Frankl quoted an unnamed "president of an international organization" who introduced him in these terms: "Dr. Frankl, you remind me of the Austrian emperor Charles V. Of his worldwide empire one used to say that therein, the sun never sets." Frankl concluded by adding: "And wasn't he right?"[18] Frankl's embrace of the image of himself as a reincarnation of Charles V—in a lecture on the degurufication of logotherapy—reveals a profound inconsistency in his life that deserves to be explored. Namely, while Frankl lived valuing the humbled simplicity of an ascetic, he

clearly pursued and enjoyed his worldwide fame. As we shall see, in the culturally fractured European twentieth century what could prove more alluring to a man who throughout his life strove to become someone of importance—than to be king?

Frankl's Struggles

Addressing the significance and development of his own work, Frankl claimed that "each founder of a psychotherapeutic school ... describes ... his own neurosis and ... writes his own case history." In Frankl's case this was "the hell of despair over the apparent meaninglessness of life[, the] ultimate nihilism" that he "wrestled with ... like Jacob with the angel" until he developed "immunity against nihilism."[19] According to Frankl, a fight and subsequent triumph over nihilism is the charm of logotherapy, and the grand unifying structure of his intellectual efforts.

Many commentators have noted that the prevalent existentialist world view after World War II originated in humanity's confrontation with the absurd and irrational nature of existence in the first half of the twentieth century. In this view, the response by the existentialists to horrific total war and cultural crisis was to embrace radical individualism, and the complementary claims that the recognition of human mortality/absurdity and subsequent absence of objective universal truth leads to "authentic" existence.[20] The existential posture that questions and thus undermines traditional social norms and values has led to the criticism that existentialism is beholden to relativism and ultimately nihilism. This in turn begs the question: What are we to make of Frankl's claims to have solved these profound philosophical dilemmas?

Frankl's intellectual biography is an interesting case study in how existentialism and the consequent dilemma of human meaning came to occupy intellectuals in the twentieth century. His popular existentialism and personal solution to nihilism also provide an insightful way to reflect on how and why the existential attitude became so pervasive. As he often stated, his work occupied the "border ground" between philosophy and psychology. Notably, the Holocaust impacted both Frankl's intellectual development and the reception of his ideas.

But there is also significant continuity in Frankl's development. Frankl described himself not as a "big thinker," but rather as one who thinks consequences through.[21] As we shall see, from his teenage years, Frankl continually focused on nihilism, and the analogous existential concerns with the meaning of life, the limits of rationality, and the existence of God.

Therefore, the following intellectual biography will seek to comprehend the unity of Frankl's life by examining the tensions around which it was structured. Frankl's intellectual development began with his brief immersion in Freud-

ianism in the early 1920s. According to Frankl, he initiated a correspondence with Freud that eventually led Freud to publish one of Frankl's letters in the *Internationale Zeitschrift für Psychoanalyse.*[22] But he soon found the Freudian world view disenchanting and reductionist. As his disenchantment set in he was also rejected for training analysis by the secretary of the psychoanalytic society, Paul Federn. Subsequently, Frankl joined Adler's circle in 1924. In 1925 he published an article that celebrated Adlerianism and rejected Freudian iconoclasm.[23] The next year, Frankl published an article on the psychology of intellectualism. In this article, Frankl argued that the intellectual is characterized by a "hypertrophy of the thought function."[24] The content of the article was slightly critical of Adlerianism, and revealed a young man struggling with the question of human meaning. With the breakup of Adler's circle, Frankl aligned with two of the older and more conservative departing members: Rudolf Allers and Oswald Schwarz. In addition to these influences, Frankl described how in the late 1920s Max Scheler's *Formalism in Ethics*, a phenomenological work on objectivity and values, was like "a bible" for him, and helped shake him free from "psychologism."[25]

In 1928 Frankl began working under Otto Pötzl, who had replaced Wagner Juaregg at the University of Vienna; the next year Frankl designated Pötzl as "Honorary President" of his burgeoning youth counseling movement.[26] In the late 1920s Frankl studied medicine and continued to develop the praxis of youth counseling he had begun under Adler. In the early 1930s, Frankl initially formalized logotherapy, and his prescription for youth in distress was a call for them to find a "mission."[27] Apparently Pötzl had some influence over the initial formation of logotherapy because in 1996 Frankl described Pötzl as "the true genius," ranking him above both Freud and Adler.[28] However, Pötzl was a very ambiguous figure politically, because he claimed to have paid Nazi party dues from 1930 to 1933, and he eventually joined the Nazi party in December of 1943.[29] It is quite possible that Pötzl was a "muss Nazi" and only joined, or was pressured to join, the Nazi party, because of his position at the University clinic. According to Klingberg, "Pötzl was, in Viktor's enduring estimation, 'no Nazi'—not in sympathy, not in behavior."[30] Frankl's relationships to Freud, Adler, and Pötzl are the keys to understanding his search for meaning.

After receiving his medical degree in 1930, Frankl practiced as a doctor, first under Pötzl and then under Dr. Joseph Gerstmann at the Maria Thersien-Schlössel. From 1933 until 1937 Frankl worked in the female suicide ward at the state hospital Am Steinhof.[31] In 1936–1937 he participated as a commentator in all four seminars conducted by the Austrian Landesgruppe (branch) of the International General Medical Society for Psychotherapy.[32] The International German General Medical Society was under the leadership of Carl Jung. The German General Medical Society (Göring Institute) was the largest of the national groups, and beginning in 1934 was under the leadership of the cousin of the leading Nazi Hermann Göring, Henri Mathius Göring. In 1937 Frankl

wrote an article on the "spiritual problem in psychotherapy" for the Göring Institute's journal, the *Zentralblatt für Psychotherapie*.[33] In this article Frankl reframed the notion of having a mission as one of accepting responsibility. Frankl also took a stance against the Göring Institute's political agenda with his adamant argument that the therapist was in no position to determine the content of the sense of responsibility. In January 1938, two months before the *Anschluss* (connection) with Germany, Frankl connected the logotherapeutic focus on world views to the work of some of the leading Nazi psychotherapists.[34] It is important to note that despite the affirmative statements about the focus on world views by the leading Nazi psychotherapists, he once again took a stance against the imposition of world views in therapy. He also published the article in *Der christliche Ständestaat*, which was anti-Nazi and steadfastly supported the Catholic authoritarian state. Some have suggested that Frankl's activities in the 1930s are another reason some Viennese tend to overlook his logotherapy. For instance, in June 1996 at the opening address of the World Congress of Psychotherapy, Frankl was interviewed by Professor Guttmann from the University of Vienna. Guttmann, who is also a member of Frankl's institute, cited Frankl's 1938 article in his concluding statement when trying to explain why Frankl and his logotherapy had not received the recognition they deserved.[35] Frankl's actions and writings from the 1930s are addressed in chapter 5.

In the early 1940s, Frankl conducted medical research that involved attempts to revive suicidal Jewish patients at the Rothschild hospital. For many, Frankl's medical efforts are heroic and capture the desperation of a doctor acting in unfathomable circumstances to save Jewish patients. As we shall see in chapter 6, under the circumstances some might find the extraordinary measures questionable.

In September 1942 Frankl was deported to the ghetto Theresienstadt. He spent two trying years in Theresienstadt working in the mental hospital, and three anxious days "in depot" in the unfinished "Mexico" section of Auschwitz Birkenau, before being transferred to Dachau. He then spent nearly seven horrendous months working first as a laborer, then as a doctor in two sub-camps of Dachau. After his release in April 1945, Frankl eventually returned to Vienna. In 1945, Frankl dictated both his famous Holocaust testimony and revised a work written before his imprisonment, *The Doctor and the Soul*. His continuing struggle to combat relativism and find Meaning led Frankl to publish *The Unconscious God* in 1946. This book argued not that God had been subjected to a cultural repression, but rather that individuals had a need for a personal religiousness/spirituality within their unconscious depths. This leads to compatibility between logotherapy and pastoral psychology. Also, this assertion of the existence of an unconscious god has been described by the founder of thanatology, Elisabeth Kubler-Ross, as Frankl's most "honest" book.[36]

In addition to his conviction in an unconscious desire for God, Frankl's account of his camp experience presented his survival in terms of heroic spir-

itual suffering. As we shall see, this version, which made the Holocaust seem survivable, cut against the grain of many other Holocaust testimonies. But Frankl's popular testimony affirming the existence of God after the catastrophe played well with the American religious community, and helps explain why Frankl developed a strong following among American ministers and pastoral psychologists.

At the same time, Frankl's testimony, second only to the *Diary of Anne Frank* in popularity, has raised the ire of experts on the Holocaust. For example, in the 1990s the United States Holocaust Memorial Museum in Washington purportedly refused to sell *Man's Search for Meaning* in the gift shop[37] Also, a powerful critique of Frankl's approach to the Holocaust can be found in Lawrence Langer's book *Versions of Survival*. According to Langer, Frankl presents "a very partial view," because "he excludes ... the possibility that for thousands in the deathcamps ... death may have seemed more 'worth' dying than life worth living."[38] Langer also described Frankl's interpretation as a "circumventing [of] the death encounter in favor of spiritual heroism ... to contend with the moral uncertainties of the Holocaust."[39] These issues are addressed in chapter 7.

During the late 1960s and early 1970s Frankl became very popular in America. Frankl's survival of the Holocaust, his reassurance that life is meaningful, and his personal conviction that God exists served to make him a forerunner of the self-help genre. Frankl's success was achieved despite an early 1960s critique of logotherapy by Rollo May. May, who was a founder of the American existential psychology movement, criticized logotherapy (especially its religious coloration) for being "authoritarian."[40] Perhaps this criticism moved Frankl to tone down what some saw as heavy-handed religiosity, and he promoted his work as usable by the religiously oriented as well as agnostics and atheists. However, shortly before his death, in an interview with Dan Quayle's speech writer Matthew Scully, Frankl claimed "if you call 'religious' a man who believes in what I call Supermeaning, a meaning so comprehensive that you can no longer grasp it ... then one should feel free to call me religious."[41]

Thought

In terms of the intellectual history of the twentieth century, Frankl's trajectory fits neatly into the widely prevalent existentialist critique of Freud. Like many existentialists, Frankl criticized the purported absolutism and nihilistic reductionism inherent in Freud's reliance on biology. At heart, Frankl's existential brand of analysis represented a revolt against what he saw as the nihilistic reductionism of Freud's naturalism. That is, Frankl, like most existentialists, wanted to view humans as purposeful meaning-giving subjects, rather than as biological organisms powered by drives.

In his analysis and historical reconstruction of the crisis of positivism and rationalism in European intellectual culture, Gerald Izenberg's *The Existentialist Critique of Freud* characterized Freud as a transitional figure who undermined positivism even as he attempted to shore it up. In Izenberg's view, the positivistic framework out of which the psychoanalytic theory of meaning developed had been constructed with the purpose of explaining man as a biological organism. Freud's theory of instincts was therefore an attempt to integrate the biological, physiological, and psychological perspectives. According to Izenberg, after the First World War, Freud developed the conception of the death instinct in order to provide a biological explanation for "irrational" behavior such as passivity, idealization of the object of love, etc. "But as a biological construct, the death instinct was a phantasy ... that couldn't be fitted into a theory based on survival and procreation, [and] revealed the inadequacy of a biological framework to encompass a truly human psychology."[42] Therefore, Freud's death instinct, and the endeavor to develop a non-biological explanation for self-alienation, became the take-off point for the existentialist critique of Freud.

In general terms, the existentialists insisted on the primacy of meaning in psychic life, and they wanted to develop a conception of selfhood that was free from Freud's biological determinism. Consequently, they rejected Freud's positivism, which treated the self as driven by instincts and dominated by past psychic events. Instead, the existentialists established a subjective psychology within which the self was presented as a purposeful and meaning-giving subject, capable of freedom and authenticity, as well as a surrendering of authenticity. The latter occurred when the subject conferred "an absolute determinateness on the roles and norms of one's social environment," which "gave one a sense of solidity, of sameness through time." This conception of un-authenticity allowed the existentialists to explain "the continuing power of the past in the life of the present ... and the meaning of submission to authority figures and identification with them" without reference to "the drive to inorganic stability" as Freud defined the death instinct.[43]

From Izenberg's perspective, the existentialism of Binswanger, Heidegger, and Boss appeared as a continuation of the crisis of positivism because each completely rejected a material understanding of human behavior. As Izenberg pointed out, the rejection of naturalism by the existentialists, initiated but certainly not completed by Freud's postulation of the death instinct, undermined any attempt to affirm what is healthy. Since the existentialists rejected biological norms as reductionist, they could not say what is natural, but only what is "authentic." The problem is that authenticity is "only a negative moment in which the self suddenly [becomes] aware of the irrationality of all 'necessary' beliefs and the self-constituted nature of permanent identities."[44] But beyond this epiphany of disengagement and distancing, the concept of authenticity is unable to offer anything positive. Izenberg illustrated the dilemma when he described how Freud preserved the holist concept of health by grounding it in

universal instincts, while the existentialists "had no such recourse to biological norms of health" and as a result "each took a different path out of their common dilemma."

According to this viewpoint, the open-ended concept of authenticity placed existentialists in a theoretical impasse. Sartre attempted to negotiate it by blending existentialism with Marxism. According to Izenberg, Heidegger turned to Nazism and "historical activism in the form of nationalist renewal," and after the failure of the Nazi movement to "a mystical form of idealist absolutism that betrayed his original concept of Authenticity."[45]

Although Izenberg did not deal with Frankl, his work does provide an important analytical aid. The existentialist philosophical impasse was exemplified in Frankl's struggle to overcome nihilism and find Meaning, and more specifically in his critique of the Freudians, whom he considered "the unmasking psychologists ... that negate what is authentic, the truly human, in human beings."[46] After he abandoned both Freudianism and Adlerianism, Frankl's pursuit of the genuine in human beings led him to follow an intellectual trajectory somewhat similar to that of Heidegger. Buttressed by a belief in the objectivity of values derived from Scheler, Frankl initially attempted to solve the existentialist impasse of authenticity (or in Frankl's terms, Meaning) by trying to develop a new form of psychotherapy. In Frankl's "height psychology," the focus was on will, responsibility, and having a "mission." But the actual content of these missions was an issue for the individual conscience. Relying on Scheler's conception of absolute values, Frankl was confident that the individual would find the ultimate *Meaning* of their life. Also, Frankl's therapeutic proscriptions rejected the imposition of world views in therapy; he therefore didn't address the existential concerns with submission to social norms, or identification with authority figures. Herein was the novel version of psychotherapy that Frankl promoted in the *Zentralblätt of Psychotherapie* in 1937. After the Holocaust, Frankl attempted to shore up the open-ended categories of will, responsibility, and a mission that undergirded his height psychology, with the concept of an "unconscious god." Therefore, in 1946, Frankl prescribed that "it is the task of logotherapy to remind the patient of his unconscious religiousness."[47]

Given their mutual existentialist bent, it is not so surprising that Heidegger and Frankl had a personal relationship. Frankl described their mutual visits in the 1950s and their shared philosophical conviction "that what has passed, has passed, and what has passed will come again."[48] As we shall see, Frankl's theoretical work was influenced by Heideggerianism, and his postwar intellectual position, with its mixture of existentialism and religion, may be described as a popularization of Heideggerianism.[49] These issues are addressed in chapter 8.

But there is one caveat here. As a representative figure in the existential critique of Freud, Frankl nevertheless maintained that his work was an "ontological fulfillment" of Freud and Adler. This assertion, first made in the *Zentrallblätt für Psychotherapie* in 1937 and continued as a claim on behalf of the third

school of Viennese psychotherapy after the war, might have elements of truth in it, but it was also useful as an effective promotional strategy. This latter point is especially central since the logotherapeutic focus on the tragic triad surrounding life (death, suffering, and guilt) and the claim that this triad is deeply intertwined with a spiritual dimension have much in common with Heidegger's conviction that both death and guilt are privileged forms of awareness that can lead to authenticity. As we shall see, the trajectory of Frankl's intellectual development went from Freud to an existentialism embodied in logotherapy, but there were a variety of reasons behind his desire to navigate between (and beyond) both Freud and Heidegger.

From the perspective of traditional intellectual history, Frankl's transition from Freud to logotherapy, augmented by Scheler's phenomenology and Heidegger's existentialism, may be conceived as a reactionary clinging by a bourgeois intellectual to a "mandarin" intellectual culture of spiritual values.[50] But Frankl is much more than a mere reactionary because he takes a "third path" and attempts to fulfill the revolutionary opportunities in the field of psychology offered by the collapse of the monarchy, the rise of Red Vienna, and hyper-modernization after the Great War. As we shall see, his revolutionary solution is exemplified by his "height psychology." This perspective is confirmed by Geoffrey Cocks's recent argument that the period between the wars and Nazi Germany "did not constitute the culmination of modern trends. But they did form structural, experiential and discursive continuities in Germany and the West before 1933 and in the German successor states, Europe and the West, and eventually much of the world after 1945."[51] In a way, the story of the development and worldwide success of logotherapy is a micro-history of these larger trends in modernity.

Finally, along with offering his particular solution to the crisis in values, Frankl's navigation from Freudian empiricism to the idealism of existentialism also involved a journey from a focus on eros to an affirmation of thanatos. The first orientation, exemplified by Freudianism, looked to the material, organic, and thus instinctual dimension of human existence to ground meaning. The second orientation, rooted in Kierkegaard, and initiated after the Great War by Freud's articulation of the death instinct, was fleshed out and clarified by Heidegger and other existentialists in their celebration of human finitude. As we have noted, many existentialists, with their focus on the reality of death, not life, turned toward idealist absolutism in order to locate "authentic" meaning. But as Izenberg rightfully pointed out, this position was ultimately relativistic because it could not provide normative grounds of health. How could it? As we shall see, Frankl's mature intellectual positions suggest that, like Sartre and Heidegger, he never adequately solved this impasse. Also, by remaining tethered to the claim that the "truth" and highest meaning within human existence is to be found in the tragic triad of death, suffering, and guilt, Frankl promoted spiritual values that were ultimately derived from a focus on thanatos. Aug-

mented by this theoretical position, Frankl could claim that the horrors of the Holocaust offered the possibility of a meaningful spiritual struggle, and that an ultimate "super-meaning" was to be found through a belief in God.

Frankl is therefore similar to many twentieth-century thinkers influenced by existential currents that initially were students of Freud, and in their rejection of Freud's biological reductionism looked to the reality of death in order to locate human meaning. It is not surprising that in their confrontation with human finitude, the existentialists found themselves affirming the totalizing movements of fascism, communism, or in Frankl's case, the development of a novel form of psychotherapy he labeled "height psychology." Each of these strategies attempted to close the fractured and open-ended relativism of Western modernity. But after the disappointing failure of these worldly aspirations, the existentialists took flight in either idealist absolutism—with religious or neo-religious connotations—or the nihilistic rejection of the whole of humanity. As Heidegger pessimistically stated, we must "prepare expectations" because "only a god can save us,"[52] while Sartre claimed man a "useless passion." From this perspective Frankl's quasi-religious turn toward an "unconscious god" and a "super-meaning" to solve nihilism was a similar trend.

Existentialists have justified their focus on death with the claim that it leads to a privileged form of awareness and a vitalization of life. But if viewed from a Nietzschean perspective of a life-affirming philosophy, the pervasive religious sentiment among existentialists is the most insidious form of nihilism because it denies meaning to this world. We are therefore left with the question: Does the existentialist focus on death lead to denigration or a vitalization of life? Succinctly, what is authenticity?

The reconstruction of Frankl's intellectual biography is an effective way to ponder this question, and provides fascinating insight into some of the deep tensions in the secular-humanist culture of the twentieth century. This, then, is the story of Viktor Frankl's Search for Meaning.

Notes

1. See Viktor Frankl, *Was nicht in meinen Büchern steht* (Munich: Quintessenz, 1995), 44. Frankl claimed that Wolfgang Soucek first dubbed logotherapy the "third Viennese school of psychotherapy."

2. See Viktor Frankl, "Logotherapy in a Nutshell," in *Man's Search for Meaning*, Touchstone ed. (New York: Simon & Schuster, 1984), 101–137.

3. Alfred Längle, *Viktor Frankl Ein Porträt* (München: Piper, 1998), 280.

4. Ibid., 171.

5. Haddon Klingberg, Jr., *When Life Calls Out to Us: The Love and Lifework of Viktor and Elly Frankl* (New York: Doubleday, 2001), xi.

6. The Viktor Frankl Institute's web page makes the claim that Frankl is the founder of both logotherapy and existential analysis. The Institute also maintains a current and thorough (since 1946) bibliography of Frankl's writings and a current curriculum vitae.

7. Frankl, *Was nicht in meinen*, 99.

8. Ibid., 85.

9. Frankl, quoted in Robert Leslie, "The Story of a Bestseller," *International Forum for Logotherapy* 13, no. 1 (Spring 1990): 64.

10. Frankl called the problem of meaning the "existential vacuum" and claimed it "is a widespread phenomenon of the twentieth century." See Frankl, *Man's Search for Meaning*, 111.

11. Frankl, *Was nicht in meinen*, 44.

12. For the constantly expanding list see http://logotherapy.univie.ac.at/e/bibE.html. The best introduction is *Existential Psychotherapy of Meaning: Handbook of Logotherapy and Existential Analysis*, edited by Alexander Batthyány and Jay Levisnon (Phoenix: Zeig, Tucker and Theisen, 2009). There are two other secondary works in English on Frankl. The first, Joseph Fabry, *The Pursuit of Meaning: Viktor Frankl, Logotherapy, and Life* (Boston: Beacon Press, 1968), is an attempt to popularize and simplify Frankl's work for an American audience. The second, William Blair Gould, *Viktor E. Frankl: Life with Meaning* (Belmont, California: Brooks/Cole, 1993), is a very uneven attempt to paste a philosophical background to Frankl's work. The one in German, Karl Dienelt, *Von Freud zu Frankl* (Vienna: Österreichischer Bundesverlag, 1967), is deceptively titled. Dienelt focused mainly on humanistic psychology, with Frankl's postwar formulation of logotherapy representing the most significant vision among many.

13. Frankl's autobiography, *Was nicht in meinen*, contains pictures of him with Heidegger, Binswanger, and Jaspers. Also see Viktor Frankl, Interview by Tom Corrigan (tape recording), Vienna, Austria, 1981, Graduate Theological Union, Berkeley, California. Hereafter cited as Corrigan Interview (GTU).

14. Klingberg, *When Life Calls Out to Us*, 226.

15. Ibid., 227.

16. Längle, *Viktor Frankl: Ein Porträt*, 129.

17. Interview with author, San Diego, California, 1 May 2006. Abraham Maslow had a similar response when he remarked in his journal after meeting Frankl in 1963: "3:10 a.m.—can't sleep. After Frankl evening, which wasn't unpleasant but was certainly a wasted evening...I didn't like Frankl's pushing." See Maslow, A. *The Journals of A.H. Maslow*, ed. Richard Lowry (Monterey, California: Brooks/Cole Publishing Co., 1979), 298. Finally, five years later, in 1968, Maslow wrote, "Funny thing about Frankl—he talks and writes the B-language [Maslow's terms for higher thinking; see chapter 10] and yet he doesn't *live* it. He's *still* pushing his own wagon, self-absorbed, narcissistic, just as in the past." Ibid., 888.

18. Frankl, "Opening Address to the First World Congress: Logotherapy on Its Way to Degurufication," in *Analecta Frankliana: The Proceedings of the First World Congress of Logotherapy (1980)*, ed. Sandra A. Wawrytko (Berkeley: Institute of Logotherapy Press, 1982), 7.

19. Ibid., 8.

20. For the best introduction to existentialism and its historical significance see William Barrett, *Irrational Man: A Study in Existential Philosophy* (New York: Doubleday, 1958). Also, Walter Kaufmann, *Existentialism from Dostoyevsky to Sartre* (New York: NAL Penguin, 1975).

21. Frankl, *Was nicht in meinen*, 12.

22. Frankl, "Zur Mimischen Bejahung und Verneinung," *Internationale Zeitschrift für Psychoanalyse* no. 10 (1924): 437–438.

23. Frankl, "Psychotherapie und Weltanschauung," *Internationale Zeitschrift für Individualpsychologie* no. 3 (1925): 250–252.

24. Frankl, "Zur Psychologie des Intellektualismus," *Internationale Zeitschrift für Individualpsychologie* (1926): 326.

25. Frankl, *Was nicht in meinen*, 42.

26. See Frankl, "Selbstmordprophylaxe und Jugendberatung," *Münchner Medizinische Wochenschrift* (4 October 1929): 1675.

27. Frankl, "Wirtschaftskrise und Seelenleben vom Standpunkte des Jungendberaters," *Sozialärztlich Rundschau* no. 3 (1933): 45.

28. Frankl, *Was nicht in meinen*, 48.

29. For unknown reasons, Pötzl had his application reconsidered and redated to January 1941. See Pötzl's Nazi Party file, available at the Dokumentationsarchiv des österreichischen Widerstandes.

30. Klingberg, *When Life Calls Out to Us*, 97.

31. See Index of Psychiatric Krankenhaus Baumgartnerhöhe 1934–1938, Wien Landes Stadt Archiv.

32. See *Zentralblatt für Psychotherapie* 10 (1937): 7–8.

33. Frankl, "Zur Geistigen Problematik der Psychotherapie," *Zentralblatt für Psychotherapie* 10 (1937): 33–45.

34. Frankl, "Seelenärtliche Selbstbesinnung," *Der christliche Ständestaat* (30 January 1938): 8.

35. See Viktor Frankl, interview by Giselher Guttmann, tape recording, 29 June 1996, Vienna, Austria, Opening Address World Congress of Psychotherapy. Hereafter cited as Guttmann Interview (WCP).

36. Elisabeth Kubler-Ross, author of *On Death and Dying* (New York: Macmillan, 1969), also designated Frankl as one of the three people she would like to meet before she died.

37. On this point, see Matthew Scully, "Viktor Frankl at Ninety: An Interview," *First Things* 52 (April 1995).

38. Lawrence Langer, *Versions of Survival* (Albany: State University of New York Press, 1982), 16–17.

39. Ibid., 24.

40. See Rollo May, *Existential Psychology* (New York: Random House, 1961), 42.

41. Frankl, quoted in Scully, "Viktor Frankl at Ninety," 43.

42. Gerald Izenberg, *The Existentialist Critique of Freud: The Crisis of Autonomy* (Princeton, New Jersey: Princeton University Press, 1976), 201–211.

43. Ibid., 201–211.

44. Ibid., 259.

45. Ibid., 3–12.

46. See Frankl, *Was nicht in meinen*, 104.

47. Frankl, *The Unconscious God: Psychotherapy and Theology* (New York: Simon and Schuster, 1975), 67.

48. See Frankl, *Was nicht in meinen*, 91.

49. For his part, Frankl claimed to surpass Heidegger's disciple Binswanger and his *Daseinanalyse* by suggesting it was only a form of Adlerianism. See Frankl, "Existential Analysis and Dimensional Ontology," in *Psychotherapy and Existentialism: Selected Papers on Logotherapy* (New York: Washington Square Press, 1967), 132.

50. See Fritz Ringer, *The Decline of the German Mandarins: The German Academic Community, 1890-1933* (Cambridge, Mass.: Harvard University Press, 1969).

51. Geoffrey Cocks, *The State of Health: Illness in Nazi Germany* (New York: Oxford University Press, 2013), 271.

52. Martin Heidegger, "The Spiegel Interview," in *Martin Heidegger Questions and Answers*, ed. Gunther Neske and Emil Kettering (New York: Paragon House, 1990), 57.

The First Attempt to Find Meaning

But in those days no one knew what it was moving towards. Nor could anyone quite distinguish between what was above and what below, between what was moving forwards and what backwards.
—Robert Musil, *The Man Without Qualities*

Viktor Frankl was an assimilated Viennese Jew.[1] As we shall see, he might be best described as "hyper-acculturated" because, like many Austrian Jews, he strove to be included in mainstream culture. This sentiment is captured with the quip, Austrian "Jews are just like everybody else. Only more so."[2] His father, Gabriel, was born on 28 March 1861 in the village of Porolitz in southern Moravia. Gabriel's father was a book binder and he had moved his family to Vienna when Gabriel was in high school. Gabriel originally wanted to study medicine but gave it up for financial reasons. In lieu of medicine he took a civil service job in the ministry for social administration. He worked for ten years as a stenographer in the Parliament, and for twenty-five years as a private secretary to the state minister Joseph Maria von Bärnreither. The minister, with Gabriel's help, founded and developed the central office of youth welfare and child protection. Gabriel had a religious upbringing but became an assimilated liberal Jew, a common occurrence among Jews in the civil service.[3] Frankl's mother, Elsa Lion, was born 8 February 1879 in Prague and was eighteen years younger than Gabriel. The Frankls had three children—two sons and a daughter. Viktor was the middle child, with an elder brother, Walter, and younger sister, Stella.

Notes for this section begin on page 23.

In his biography, Klingberg describes a rather idyllic family setting, describing how Viktor emerged from a "good stable."[4]

Viktor Frankl reconstructed his own life in a 1973 autobiographical sketch[5] that was updated and expanded in 1995 into the short book, *Was nicht in meinen Büchern steht.*[6] The book was published to coincide with Frankl's ninetieth birthday celebration, and contained elements appropriate to the genre of confessional literature. Stylistically his autobiography was flippant and anecdotal, and presented an impressive "Viktor Frankl."

Apparently Viktor was a rather precocious child. For example, by the time he was three, Frankl claimed he already knew he wanted to be a doctor, and he also recalled telling his mother that the cure for those who were suicidal or sick was to "give them all they wanted to eat and to drink, like shoe polish and gasoline. If they perish, then they have wanted it so. If they live, then we have discovered the medicine for those diseased."[7] It is not clear why Frankl chose to document this early memory, but the remembrance seems to reflect his lifelong desire to resolve human suffering. On the other hand, it also seems to be an example of a somewhat callous therapeutic approach.

Frankl's next significant memory, which he jokingly claimed was the founding moment of logotherapy, concerned the formation of his attitude toward death. When he was four years old, Frankl recalled "being scared awake by the revelation" that he must one day die. He then added that "at no point in his life" was he afraid of dying. Instead, he was troubled by the "question of whether or not the transitoriness of life denies its meaning." After much intellectual struggle, he came to the conclusion that "in most cases death makes life meaningful."[8] It seems the intellectual dilemma that occupied Frankl as an adult began when he was only four years old. And, after much despair and intellectual struggle, the mature Frankl felt he had triumphed over the nihilistic implications of human mortality.

On the surface Frankl's struggle with human meaning appears as not much more than the process of maturation for any sensitive soul. What made Frankl's awareness significant is that he first turned to Freud, and then Adler, before relying on existentialism and developing logotherapy for his solution. Then he elevated his answer into a universal cure for nihilism. But the key point is that the fear that he would one day die drove Frankl to come to terms with human meaning. It is this confrontation with fear that became the paradigm for Frankl's counterphobic response and solution to the problem of death: the assertion of the will to meaning.

In his autobiography Frankl appears as a bright child, already directed toward becoming a doctor, and fueled by a central intellectual preoccupation. Under normal circumstances a person of Frankl's caliber, asking important but nevertheless rather youthful questions about nihilism and meaning, probably would not have amounted to much beyond his bourgeois upbringing. But be-

ginning with the Great War, Western culture faced a radical confrontation with violence, mass death, and the meaning of human existence.[9] Frankl's questions therefore took on a profound resonance, and by persistently asking them he was able to fashion himself into a figure of worldwide repute and popular influence. In order to fully understand Frankl we must first diverge to reconstruct the social context within which the young Frankl's consciousness was formed.

The Viennese Modern

A large body of work exists on Viennese modernism, but the most significant remains Carl Schorske's *Fin-de-siècle Vienna: Politics and Culture.*[10] Schorske tied the vitality of Viennese modernism to the crisis and ultimate failure of liberalism in Austria. According to Schorske's synthetic view of culture and politics, there were three generations of Viennese politicians, cultural theorists, and artists between 1848 and 1914, and each generation represented a unique, more radical, and more alienated form of cultural experience. Since Schorske equated rationalism with liberalism, and claimed this tradition was in a contest with the aristocratic Catholic culture of grace, the failure of liberalism in Austria subsequently became the advent of the irrational.

Schorske recounted how the liberals were defeated in 1848, but nevertheless managed to establish a constitutional government in 1867 after Bismarck's defeat of Austria destroyed a "Grossdeutsch" solution to the German problem. But liberal failure in the areas of "national unity, social justice, economic prosperity and public morality … converged … to produce a deep crisis in liberalism before it had the chance to stabilize its new power."[11] According to Schorske, the crisis of liberalism led to an outpouring of irrationality. In the political sphere the irrational was manifested in numerous ways. There was the pan-German student movement led by the anti-Semitic and conceivably proto-fascist Georg von Schönerer; there was also the Christian socialism of Vienna's Mayor Karl Lüger, who was anti-Semitic but nevertheless successful from a municipal point of view; finally, there was the father of Zionism, Theodor Herzl.[12] Thus, "as Schönerer's first task was to break the German liberals, and Lüger's to break the Catholic liberals, so Herzl fought the Jewish ones."[13]

In the second generation, the emblematic figure of the irrational was Freud, who undermined the illusions of liberal rationalism through the charting of the instinctual mind.

The third and most radical generation of the Viennese modern comprised the Expressionists and their celebration of individual and subsequently psychological alienation. This generation was exemplified for Schorske by the painter Oskar Kokoschka, the architect Adolf Loos, and the composer Arnold Schönberg. Accordingly, the Expressionists were:

too free of specific loyalties to define themselves in relation to history, to cultural structure and function in a temporal sequence. Not even 'modern' had much utility as a concept for them, for the modern must derive its meaning in negative relation to that which, as history, precedes it. The Expressionists had taken up the task of overcoming history where the fin-de-siècle explorers had left it, and pressed forward on the 'voyage interieur' to the realm of raw, existential anxiety or anger, where all previous structures seemed phenomenological sham. Not the past, not modern life was the object of their apocalyptic vision, but human existence as such.[14]

In the Expressionists' flight from political and social reality, and the subsequent rejection of all that the nineteenth century represented, Schorske saw the culmination of the crisis and failure of Austrian liberalism. Schorske's penetrating description of the crisis of liberalism provides an important cultural context to our intellectual biography. Since Frankl's first intellectual production concerned the psychology of Freud, and he eventually rejected Freudianism, Schorske's positioning and interpretation of Freud takes on prime interest for our story.

Schorske placed Freud in the second generation that was loosely equated with the discovery of the irrational. But for Schorske, Freud's eternal oedipal conflict stopped short of the excessive cultural rebellion of the Expressionists for "unlike the others, he kept the face of his father—its self-conscious Judaism, its principled liberalism, and its rationalism." Although Freud shared the cultural crisis with the Expressionists, he "subsumed the uniqueness of that experience under the eternal verity of father-son relations."[15]

Freud therefore represented a transitional figure "who kept the face of his father" without becoming overrun by the irrational, but "where the fin-de-siècle recovered the sexual instinct, eros, the Expressionists recovered Thanatos."[16] Schorske's historical description of Viennese modernism and his cultural configuration of Freud illuminates the context of Frankl's initial intellectual quest and connection to Freudianism.

The Young Frankl

As the Great War ended, Frankl was only fourteen years old, but nevertheless was already reading the German physical chemist Wilhelm Ostwald and one of the founders of experimental psychology, Gustav Theodor Fechner. These studies suggest Frankl was struggling with life questions and, according to Klingberg, was already experiencing an "agnostic period."[17] In his struggles, he came to the conclusion that there must be a universal balancing principle both in the microcosm and macrocosm. Frankl describes experiencing this balancing principle while lying on the deck of a Danube steamer with the starry sky above him. This "aha" experience was portrayed as "nirvana" or "a warm death seen from within."[18]

Frankl's memories suggest that he had begun to intellectualize death as both part of a cosmic balance and as nirvana, or nothingness. This ambivalent and slightly contradictory attitude toward death reveals that Frankl had not yet come to his more "mature" existentialist attitude. That is, he had not taken the existential turn that "internalized" death as the source of authentic existence. Instead, based on his readings of Ostwald and Fechner he articulated an organic vision, where death remained "external" to life as part of a natural balance. Apparently, at this youthful stage Frankl was coming to terms with the naturalistic philosophy of the Enlightenment, while his reflection on death and nirvana was probably attributable to the violence and cultural upheaval of the war.

At this point, still a teenager, Frankl became interested in experimental and applied psychology and also attended lectures from two of Freud's disciples, Paul Schilder and Eduard Hitschmann.[19] Around this time Frankl discovered the works of both Freud and Max Scheler. He also gave his first public lecture at an adult education school, and the subject was the meaning of life. Frankl described his lecture as "pioneering existentialism" because he argued that the question is not what the meaning of life is, but rather how "we have to answer the questions life poses to us."[20] From the subject of the lecture, and the conclusion, it seems the spiritual struggles that beset Frankl at fourteen were continuing into his later teens. As he stated, he was "passing through an atheistic period."[21] We can also conclude that he recognized that traditional cultural forms, such as religion, were not providing satisfactory answers. The self-assertive Frankl therefore began to search for solutions or answers to the questions life posed.

Freud and Frankl

Within the context of the fractured world of Viennese modernism and the collapsing Habsburg Empire, Freud's world view began to resonate with Frankl. A superior high school student, Frankl wrote his required graduation paper on the psychology of philosophical thinking.[22] In the paper Frankl interpreted philosophical thought from a Freudian perspective. Apparently he was so taken with Freudianism that he started a correspondence with Freud.[23] Thus began Frankl's first attempt "to become a man of some importance."

Although their correspondence was destroyed by the Nazis, one remnant survived. Freud, without Frankl's prior knowledge, sent one of Frankl's letters to the *Internationale Zeitschrift für Psychoanalyse* for publication. This short but fascinating document, written in Frankl's favorite spiritual workplace, the Prater-Hauptalle, was published in 1924. The fact that Freud thought the letter-turned-article worthy of publication is impressive. From Frankl's description of their "chance encounter" on the street, it was clear that Freud was quite taken with him. It seems that a few months after the publication, Frankl, thinking he

recognized Freud, followed him to Bergasse to be sure, and introduced himself. Freud responded by citing from memory Frankl's address. Frankl, surprised, questioned whether Freud knew of a recently published book by La Grange on the death instinct. Freud claimed he didn't but suggested Frankl write a review for the psychoanalytic periodical, *Imago*. Frankl declined because he had already joined the Adlerians.[24]

Frankl was a self-proclaimed "thinker through," and this first article revealed this quality by logically developing the premises of the Freudian world view. Given what we know about Freud's dogmatism and expectations of deference from his followers, Frankl's publication of an article with his support can be attributed to his intellectual consistency and initiative.

Immersing himself in the naturalistic materialism of the Freudian perspective (pre–death instinct), Frankl's article was radically biological and anthropological in orientation. The central argument was that the primary character of the head movements of approval and denial (i.e., nodding yes and no) was "emotional."[25] The article began by suggesting that the nodding of the head to assert approval stemmed from the chewing movement. Nodding was conceived as an exaggerated form of chewing that became the universal symbol for approval. "The chewing movements … transformed themselves into the more conspicuous movements of the whole head. Later on, these movements—the nodding of the head—were used as the typical symbol of approval, therefore also as a symbol of thought."[26]

Since the head movement signifying approval was conceived basically as an extension of ingesting food, Frankl could then argue that approval obviously originated in the hunger instinct. Also, because the orthodox Freudian vision was (at this point) dependent on the opposition between the hunger instinct and the sexual instinct, Frankl connected the head movement to the sexual instinct. He thus argued that the "humping movement" of coitus became displaced, or "shifted" to the head because it also symbolized approval. "The coitus movement was a symbol for the sexual act, sexual drive and sexual excitation. It was, therefore, also used as a symbol for the desire to consummate the sexual act…. By using the coitus movement as a symbol, the head was considered to be the origin of the execution of movements, so the humping movement was 'shifted' to the head."[27]

Head nodding was conceptualized as both an extension of the chewing movement, and a displacement of the humping movement to the head. Frankl then connected the character of mimic denial to the emotion of disgust. Following through with the logic of his argument, he suggested that the extension of disgust to head and hand movements corresponded to the process of displacement that occurred in the extension of affirmation. "Denial through head shaking originated through symbolic use of shaking movements in disgust. The gradual expansion of the use follows as it was described in the origin of mimic approval … now it is likely that they are of secondary origin, in-so-far-as the

corresponding head movements are directly carried forward to the hand. Following this assumption, it should be possible to prove that it (the hand movement) emerged later than mimic denial."[28]

Thus, both the shaking of the body in disgust and the humping movement were displaced to the head. In this process of "refinement" denial was eventually extended to the hand.

Finally, Frankl used Freudian instinct theory to argue that the ultimate instinctual origins of denial and approval were unified. In order to make this connection Frankl turned to Freud's concept of the libido. "The cause of disgust could originate in the nutritional drive as well as the sexual drive. As for the explanation for mimic approval, the differences (that are presupposed by referring to the two basic elementary life drives…) cancel each other out, as soon as we define the two elementary life drives as a conceptual unity in the sense of the 'libido.'"[29]

What was most impressive (and perhaps disturbing) about this article was that Frankl, at only eighteen years of age, had fully mastered the basic tenets of Freudian theory. He had focused in on a simplified view of Freudian anthropology that had intellectual roots in Darwin's analogy of man as an animal.[30] Through his understanding of Freudian instinct theory, Frankl connected somatic expression to the psychic realm. This allowed Frankl to make claims for a relationship between the body and psychic experience. Moreover, he substantiated this claim by showing how the physical realm was transformed through the processes of evolution to further promote the expansion of the psychic. Ultimately, Frankl was making an argument for the instinctual basis of language formation, which in true Freudian fashion left no room for conceiving symbolic thought as an independent mental or meaningful process. Although in some respects crude and one-sided, this dogmatic Freudianism makes Freud's support in publishing the article easy to understand.[31]

Frankl's article also revealed that his answer to the question of human meaning (insofar as it related to understanding the origins of conceiving right and wrong) was being filtered through Freudian materialism to become a problem of instinct and energy cathexis. Discovering the irrational organic substructure to human behavior must have been a double-edged sword for Frankl. On the one hand, guided by Freud's theories, Frankl had the intellectual ground to probe the question of meaning. On the other hand, the organicism also had disturbing elements that could lead to pessimism and despair. That is, humping as the source of approval is premised on recognizing the "beastliness" of human origins. Perhaps because Frankl so thoroughly understood the uncomfortable intellectual implications of Freud's biological materialism, he began to move away from orthodox Freudianism.

Frankl's journey away from Freudianism began around the same time the article was published. Frankl continually described his own intellectual work not as a rejection of Freudianism but rather as a complement. But in his more

honest moments it became clear that Frankl was deeply disturbed by Freud's biological reductionism. In 1982 Frankl framed his "break"[32] with Freudianism, and subsequent move toward the Adlerians, within the context of his visit to the secretary of the Freudian Psychoanalytic Society, Paul Federn.

In 1924 Frankl acted on Freud's suggestion in their ongoing exchange that he should visit Federn to discuss when he should begin training analysis. Federn seems to have rejected him, which must have surprised Frankl given his burgeoning relationship with Freud. But he was still quite young, and they ended the meeting by agreeing Frankl should pursue his medical studies before beginning training analysis.[33]

This meeting apparently had a very significant impact on Frankl's intellectual development. It seems Frankl was irritated when Federn initiated their discussion by staring intensely at him for two minutes, and then asking: "And so what about your neurosis?" Frankl responded that he was "an anal character with proneness towards obsession." Despite this apparently apt self-insight, Frankl recalled leaving the office disturbed and disgusted. He thought psychoanalysts always wanted to unmask everything, leaving no room for genuine behavior or authenticity. At this point Frankl "felt he had looked into the abyss of the nihilism of reductionism."[34]

Apparently the first attempt to overcome nihilism, or as Frankl was then formulating it, "to find the meaning of life," had only led Frankl to experience what he considered a more profound and unsettling form of nihilism. Also, his rather original insight that nodding the head in both affirmation and denial originated in the instinctual realm is a rather cold answer when questioning life's ultimate meaning. Therefore it appears that Freud's stoic rationalism—which kept the face of his father—failed to provide satisfactory answers for the young "pioneer of existentialism."

But to what degree Frankl's so-called break stemmed from a rejection of what he had discovered when "thinking-through" Freud's anthropological conception, or from Federn's subtle rejection, or even from his burgeoning existentialism, is not exactly clear. Throughout his life Frankl claimed he rejected Freudian reductionism because it interpreted human behavior in terms of a psychic mechanism and thus denigrated the spirit.

Interestingly, Frankl's publication on head movements was not his first published article. In January of 1923, "Freude, Schöner Götterfunken…" (Joy, Beauty, and Divinity) was published by Frankl in the youth section of *Der Tag*. The short article begins with the stark statement "I hate nothing more than common sense." He also rejects "blind optimism." These statements make it clear that Frankl is intensely and honestly probing life's meaning, especially when he adds "we need to face the truth with the courage of Oedipus if one is not to be blinded." After few brief, poetic comments on how Schopenhauer and Nietzsche displayed the courage of Oedipus, he argues that both thinkers fell short of experiencing of what he envisions as a redemptive joyfulness. For

Frankl, only a rare few (Schiller and Beethoven are his examples) are capable of "spiritual joy" which is the "unity of aestheticism and the ethical ideal." To capture this "highest consciousness" he describes how Beethoven's Pastoral Symphony represents the "pleasure of the evening sun and rainbow after a thunderstorm."[35]

From this short piece it is clear that Frankl is coming to some initial resolutions to his youthful struggle for meaning. Indeed, although he is rejecting "common sense" and easy solutions, he is also beginning to take comfort in "higher" more spiritual pursuits. Arguably, the connection between aesthetics and the ethical ideal suggests his initial reading of the phenomenologist Max Scheler is providing some avenues to escape from what he is beginning to conceive as the nihilism behind scientific reductionism.

In conclusion, there were apparently a number of intellectual and personal factors that moved him away from Freud and that set him adrift in the sea of the Viennese modern, but as we shall see he was already within sight of the safe harbor of the Adlerians.

Notes

1. According to Klingberg, Frankl was a lifelong privately practicing Jew. See Klingberg, *When Life Calls Out to Us*, 30. According to Längle, Frankl "held to the Jewish faith staunchly" but "did not go to synagogue often, perhaps twice a year." Längle also claims that although Frankl was critical of Christianity's mandate to accept Christ, he nevertheless felt an affinity for Christianity because of the "positive value placed on suffering." See Längle, *Ein Porträt*, 194. According to Rabbi Reuven Bulka,

> Frankl was 'courted' by the Christian community, to the extent that rumors were afloat for a while that he had converted. He vehemently denied this. I actually saw the tefflin that he wore. They were worn out. I also vividly remember a call I received from him around 1982, from San Diego, in the middle of Passover, when he informed me, with pride, that he had done a Passover Seder for the first time since the end of the war. That is a long hiatus, of close to 40 years. And the Passover Seder is one of the main staples, so his not doing it reflected some disaffection with Judaism at least. It is clear from his writings that he was not enamored with the Jewish community, certainly not the psychological group, whom he felt were more loyal to Freud than to Moses. So, if you add it up, he felt that Jews shunned him, but he was not about to embrace another religion, leaving him with no link to established religion. But beginning with the Seder, that changed, and the Jewish connected was, to put it in an odd way, resurrected.

Personal communication, 27 Februrary 2007.

2. Lisa Silverman, *Becoming Austrians: Jews and Culture between the World Wars* (New York: Oxford University Press, 2012), 18. The quip is attributed to Dorothy Parker. Silverman's introduction also has an excellent discussion of the issue of Jewish assimilation.

3. On the elder Frankl, see *Was nicht in meinen*, 4–5. On Jewish experience and assimilation in the late Habsburg era, see Robert Wistrich, *Socialism and the Jews: The Dilemmas of Assimilation in Germany and Austro-Hungary* (Rutherford, New Jersey: Farleigh Dickinson University Press, 1982), 162–224.

4. Klingberg, *When Life Calls Out to Us*, 41.

5. See Frankl, "Viktor Frankl," in *Psychotherapie in Selbstdarstellung*, ed. Ludwig J. Pongratz (Vienna: Verlag Hans Huber, 1973), 177–204.

6. *Was nicht in meinen* was translated as Frankl, *Viktor Frankl—Recollections: An Autobiography*, trans. Joseph Fabry and Judith Fabry (New York: Insight Books, Plenum Press, 1997).

7. Frankl, *Was nicht in meinen*, 7.

8. Ibid., 9

9. For the cultural impact of the Great War, see Modris Eksteins, *Rites of Spring: The Great War and the Birth of the Modern Age* (New York: Doubleday, 1989). For a more philosophic look at the issue of man-made mass death in the twentieth century, see Edith Wyschogrod, *Spirit in the Ashes: Hegel, Heidegger, and Man-Made Mass Death* (New Haven: Yale University Press, 1985).

10. Alongside Carl Schorske, *Fin-de-siècle Vienna: Politics and Culture*, Vintage ed. (New York: Knopf, 1981), stands the collaborate effort of Allan Janik and Stephen Toulmin, *Wittgenstein's Vienna* (New York: Simon & Schuster, 1973). In addition, see Jacques Le Rider, *Modernity and Crisis of Identity: Culture and Society in Fin-de-siècle Vienna* (New York: Continuum, 1993).

11. Carl Schorske, "Generational Tension and Cultural Change: Reflections on the Case of Vienna," *Daedalus* 107, no. 4 (1978): 112.

12. On the formation of the political right in Austria, see Andrew Whiteside, "Austria," *The European Right*, ed. Hans Rogger and Eugen Weber (Berkeley: University of California Press, 1965).

13. Schorske, *Fin-de-siècle Vienna*, 169–170.

14. Schorske, "Generational Tension," 119–120.

15. Ibid., 121.

16. Ibid., 120.

17. Klingberg, *When Life Calls Out to Us*, 44.

18. Frankl, "Viktor Frankl," 179.

19. Frankl took a university extension course with Hitschmann and attended lectures of Schilder, who "spoke every Saturday evening for two hours in the university hospital." See David Cohen, "The Frankl Meaning," *Human Behavior* 6, no. 7 (July 1977).

20. Frankl, "Viktor Frankl," 180.

21. Frankl, *Was nicht in meinen*, 37.

22. Frankl, "Viktor Frankl," 183.

23. Frankl, *Was nicht in meinen*, 30. Also see Cohen, "The Frankl Meaning," 57.

24. See Frankl, *Was nicht in meinen*, 30–31.

25. See Frankl, "Zur Mimischen Bejahung und Verneinung," 437–438.

26. Ibid., 437.

27. Ibid.

28. Ibid.

29. Ibid., 438.

30. For a discussion of Darwin's impact on Freud, see Frank Sulloway, *Freud, Biologist of the Mind: Beyond the Psychoanalytic Legend* (New York: Basic Books, 1983), 238–277.

31. Freud's support might have also stemmed from the fact that at eighteen Frankl was a prime candidate to become a disciple.

32. To claim a "break" with Freud seems an overstatement by Frankl. Although perhaps effective to build his reputation, Frankl's brief adolescent letter exchange and short paper do not amount to a discipleship.

33. Thus the exact circumstances remain unclear. But Ernst Federn claimed that his father told him Frankl didn't want to go through training analysis, which at the time would have amounted to about a six-month period (Ernst Federn, interview by author, Vienna, 12 June 1996). Lydia Marinelli of the Freud archive suggested Frankl may have been too young for consideration (Lydia Marinelli, interview by author, Vienna, 8 June 1996). Klingberg hints that Frankl was already "flirting with Adler's psychology." *When Life Calls Out to Us*, 53.

34. Corrigan Interview (GTU). On Frankl's view of nihilism and psychoanalysis, see Frankl, "Collective Neuroses of the Present Day," *Psychotherapy and Existentialism*, 118–121.

35. Frankl, Viktor. "Freude, Schöner Götterfunken…," in *Frühe Schriften: 1923-1942* (Wien: Verlag Wilhelm Maudrich, 2005), 23.

The Second Attempt to Find Meaning

After all, each thing exists only by the virtue of its limitations, in other words, by virtue of a more or less hostile act against its environment: without the Pope there would be no Luther, and without the heathens, no Pope, and so it cannot be denied that man's most deeply felt association with his fellow men consists in dissociation from them.
—Musil, *The Man Without Qualities*

Frankl found his next intellectual anchor in the individual psychology of Alfred Adler. Adler was a member of Freud's original circle but broke with him in 1911. Therefore, Frankl's attachment to Adler was intellectually consistent because they both had rejected psychoanalysis. Frankl's decision was also fitting because Adler was second only to Freud in terms of fame and power within the psychoanalytic movement. In order to continue our reconstruction of Frankl's intellectual development, it is important to first grasp the substance of Adler's break with Freud and the main tenets of his thought.

Freud and Adler

Adler was Freud's most important disciple from 1902 until their break in 1911. The story of Freud's and Adler's rift varies, and the differing interpretations can usually be traced to the allegiances of the commentator.[1] Blame is subsequently placed either on Freud's authoritarianism or on Adler's inability to play second

Notes for this section begin on page 42.

fiddle. Whatever the merit of these interpretations, clearly there were signifi-
cant intellectual differences that led to their separation. In the meetings of the
Vienna Psychoanalytic Society that preceded the break, Freud referred to these
differences when attempts were made to patch things over. To those members
who found no difference of substance between Adler's ideas and Freud's, Freud
responded, "I want to point to the fact that two participants do find a contra-
diction, namely Adler and Freud."[2]

What then were these differences? Most commentators speak of Adler's
work as a more humanistic, subjective psychology versus Freud's so-called mech-
anistic, objective psychology. The work Frankl produced under the influence
of Freud and Adler certainly exemplified these differences. But at the core of
Freud's and Adler's intellectual dissension were diverging theories of human
nature. This difference led them to ultimately posit different models for expli-
cating human behavior.

Both Freud and Adler were deeply dependent on the Darwinian revo-
lution, and both were influenced by Nietzsche. But they varied in how they
incorporated the insights of these thinkers and how they solved the problems
they raised. Adler was arguably more indebted to Nietzsche than Freud, and
subsequently "shared" much of Nietzsche's iconoclastic take on evolution.[3]
This is not to suggest that Adler and Nietzsche, beginning from similar concep-
tions of human nature, came to similar conclusions regarding philosophy and
politics. On the contrary, on these issues Freud was much closer to Nietzsche.
Nevertheless, Adler shared many Nietzschean premises about evolution. For
instance, Nietzsche claimed the "strong must be protected from the weak,"
because the outcome of the struggle for existence is "the defeat of the stronger,
the more privileged...."[4] Therefore, for Nietzsche survival of the fittest meant
that the stronger were weeded out and the weakest survived. Nietzsche also
argued that Darwin overestimated "external circumstances ... to a ridiculous
extent: the essential thing in the life process is precisely the tremendous shaping,
form creating force working from within...."[5] According to Nietzsche, Darwin
had failed to factor the "will" into his theory of evolution. Finally, Nietzsche
recognized that evolutionary theory is not necessarily teleological and progres-
sive, because "the whole animal kingdom does not evolve from the lower to the
higher—but at the same time in utter disorder."[6]

In Adler's conception of nature, humans were considered inferior creatures
that had to constantly compensate for their weaknesses. Although this under-
standing of human nature may not be directly attributed to Nietzsche, it was
similar to two aspects of Nietzsche's reading of Darwin. First, Adler not only
recognized with Nietzsche that humans have no grounds to claim species supe-
riority, but even went one step further by claiming human inferiority. Second,
Adler provided the organic grounds to Nietzsche's will to power, thus support-
ing Nietzsche's claim that Darwin's theory missed the "will." In his theory of
organ inferiority and compensation, Adler extended the concept of the will to

power to include psychic experience. "From the point of view of nature, man is an inferior being. But this inferiority with which he is afflicted, and of which he becomes aware through a feeling of deprivation and insecurity, acts as a continuous stimulus to find a way of adjusting, of providing, of creating situations in which the disadvantage of position seems compensated."[7]

Adler's conception of psychology from an evolutionary perspective led to his postulation of an inferiority complex as the basis of neurosis, and, as the quote hints, the subsequent "law of overcoming" as inherent to human nature. Adler therefore used Nietzsche's will to power and shared his iconoclastic reading of evolution.

Freud also placed consciousness within a Darwinian framework,[8] but without much of the Nietzschean iconoclasm. In the simplest of terms, Freud suggested that consciousness, or ego, is produced by a conflict between the instincts and the reality principle. The point is that, although both Adler's and Freud's different conceptions of consciousness stemmed from the Darwinian incorporation of humanity into nature, "nature"—ultimately conceived as the "unconscious"—was interpreted in ways that were simply irreconcilable. Ultimately, Freud's biologism, which perceived human behavior in terms of instincts, and traced neurosis to childhood libidinal development, was too narrow of a vision for Adler.

While studying in Freud's circle, Adler had become deeply immersed in Freud's organicism, but he broadened the organic vision by assimilating elements of Nietzsche's conception of consciousness as driven by a will to power. Against Freud, Adler argued that an individual's instincts (or eros) are just one aspect in the person's total pattern of existence—or what Adler called the "style of life." Adler, unlike Freud, granted limited independence to consciousness by determining existence not in terms of libido, but rather in terms of feelings of inferiority and esteem—or more aptly, power. Freud responded to Adler's new conception by calling it ego psychology, and a reaction against recognizing the predominant role sexuality plays in human experience. In 1911 he claimed that Adler "has created for himself a world system without love, and I am in the midst of carrying out the revenge of the insulted goddess Libido on him."[9]

Despite Freud's attack, Adler maintained his belief that human nature was driven by the feeling of inferiority and the consequent need to "overcome." Then Adler took his clearest stand against Freud when he claimed the individual was best understood in relation to each individual's "unconscious" life goals, rather than as a consequence of instincts, drives, or past traumatic psychic events. Individual psychology therefore insisted "on the indispensability of finalism for understanding of all psychological phenomena." According to Adler, causes, powers, instincts, and impulses could not serve "as explanatory principles," only, "the final goal alone can." This led to Adler's "arrangement" theory of neurosis, where "every individual acts and suffers in accordance with his particular teleology."[10] According to Adler, neurosis was an emotional disturbance

that was ultimately a "compensation" for a feeling of inferiority. At the heart of Adler's (and eventually Frankl's) rejection of Freud's biological reductionism was a desire to view human experience as autonomous and meaningful. The individualistic components of a focus on the future and the striving to realize goals were the key elements of both Adler's individual psychology and Frankl's Logotherapy (existential analysis). But how then did the individual relate to social life for Adler?

Against the stoic individualism of Freud (and Nietzsche), Adler argued that the individual's unique teleology was inherently social, because individuals could only express themselves in relation to the community. By viewing the social as a realm of fulfillment, rather than a limit to human possibility, Adler could then claim that a fundamental characteristic of human experience was *Gemeinschaftsgefühl* (community feeling). This community feeling was also based in an extended view of evolution. Adler claimed that humans survived as a species only by compensating for physical weakness, which required learning to live in societies. Therefore, society played an essential part in the process of adaptation, and "the psychological organ had from the beginning to reckon with the conditions of society. All its abilities were developed on a basis which embodied the component of a social life." Thus "human thought" was structured in order to do "justice to a community."[11] In this way Adler's understanding of evolution deeply integrated the individual into the community. Accordingly, the natural psychological process is for the personality to establish a meaningful "style of life" by integrating the dual urges of overcoming inferiority feelings and expressing social feelings. From this explication, it is easily understood why Adler's individual psychology was often used by the Socialists in Red Vienna to support and justify their policies.[12]

Red Vienna

The Austromarxist cultural project of Red Vienna was born in the midst of political crisis and disintegration. By the beginning of the Great War, the crisis of liberalism in the Habsburg Empire had led to political paralysis, and the monarchy was crumbling under the pressure of Czech and Slav separatism. By 1913, the Austrian Parliament ceased to function as an institution, and the empire became a victim of government by decree.[13] The political crisis was initially quelled by the outbreak of war, but by the summer of 1918 the monarchy was disintegrating. Social and national revolutions threatened, and in October of 1918 the monarchy finally collapsed. Unlike France in 1789, the first republic in Austria was a child of dissolution, not revolution. Despite the absence of revolution, the political landscape was irrevocably different. Gone was the monarchy and the multi-state empire, and Wilson's Fourteen Points guaranteed that the "China of Europe" would be dismembered at Versailles. Statehood led all

political parties to question the national and economic feasibility of Austria.[14] Subsequently, all parties (except for a few members of the Christian Socials) leaned toward an *Anschluss* (connection) with Germany. In this uneasy situation it was left to the Socialists to become "the caretakers of the new Republic because of their unique ability to deal with the returning soldiers, unemployed workers, and radical crowds...."[15] However, after the signing of the Treaty of St. Germain, which outlawed an *Anschluss* with Germany and amputated the South Tyrol, Austrian national politics began to drift to the right. In June 1920, the Socialists resigned the chancellorship. In 1923, in response to the right-wing paramilitary groups of the Heimwher and Heimat, the Socialists began to organize their own defense corps—the Schutzbund.

The Socialists' retreat from the national government was offset by their successful municipal election in Vienna. Instead of forging political power in the republic, the Socialists turned defensive and put their energies into constructing a model city. Anson Rabinbach describes that "with the fall of the second coalition the Austrian Socialists retreated to 'fortress Vienna,' a 'spiritual state within a state,' which buttressed its vision of the 'new human being who can build a new, better world with intelligence, energy, and idealism' with an array of institutions encompassing all ages and occupations."[16] Red Vienna was therefore a social experiment unto itself, and represented Austria's first attempt to fully digest the logics of modernity, mass politics, the concurrent problem of the individual's relation to the community, and the construction of a secular workers' culture. Subsequently, Adler's psychology of overcoming inferiority complexes and discovering fulfillment in social life dovetailed nicely with the Austromarxist revolutionary cultural programs. For many intellectuals in Red Vienna, Adler's views were "infused with socialism," and even Adler claimed "socialism is deeply rooted in community feeling. It is the original sound of humanity."[17]

However, Adler's commitment to socialism was not steadfast because in the early 1930s he, like so many intellectuals, distanced himself from Socialist politics. This distancing was probably due to the rise of Austrofascism, but, arguably, Adlerian psychology had a strong individualistic component that made Adler's Socialist political commitment a matter of choice. Nevertheless, Adler's circle supported the Socialist cultural politics of *Bildung* and the creation of *neue Menschen* through youth organizations, adult education programs, lending libraries, and a variety of cultural events.[18] Adler was also involved in the novel educational reforms established by Otto Glöckel, the councilor for schools and education. As early as 1919, Adler was providing advice to teachers on how to handle students. But after the fall of the second coalition and the Socialists' departure from national government in 1920, school reforms became limited to the Socialist experiment in Vienna. In Vienna, Adler and his colleagues provided lectures on child guidance for Vienna's new parent associations. They also continued their work through the initiation of child guidance clinics in the schools.[19]

Frankl and Adler

According to Klingberg, as Frankl's "confidence in psychoanalysis waned" he drifted toward Adler's individual psychology. Apparently Frankl first met Adler when he was a senior in high school while visiting an Adlerian guidance clinic. Frankl was introduced to Adler by Dr. Hugo Lukacs, and Lukacs subsequently became a "principal mentor in individual psychology" for Frankl.[20] Along with this burgeoning connection, Frankl's move away from Freud made sense due to the influential and expanding role of Adlerian psychology in Red Vienna. Because Frankl began his medical studies in 1924 at the University of Vienna, his move toward the popular Adler also seems logical on intellectual and professional grounds. Finally, in the atmosphere of Red Vienna his connection with Adler made political sense. Over 80 percent of Jews in Red Vienna voted for the Socialists, and the official stance of the party was to remain more or less neutral on anti-Semitism (although Socialist anti-capitalism often took on anti-Semitic undertones).

In terms of personal political commitments, we know that for a short time Frankl was president of the Social Democratic student movement in Austria.[21] Also, he remarked that his father named him after the founder of the Socialist party in Austria, Viktor Adler.[22] It is clear that Frankl, like his father, was committed to assimilation and in addition the Socialist "party made it quite clear that to enter its ranks meant to abandon all aspects of Jewish identity."[23]

Frankl's drift toward Adler almost seems destined. Both Frankl and Adler moved philosophically from the stoic individualism of Freudianism to the communal socialism of Red Vienna. They were both from Leopoldstadt, the Jewish quarter in Vienna. They were both assimilated Jews (Adler converted to Protestantism) with Socialist political leanings, and on a deeper intellectual substratum, they both shared a childhood confrontation with their own mortality and the commitment to study medicine.[24] Given the similarities, their connection seemed logical, almost inevitable, within the small intellectual circle of Vienna.

As he embarked on his medical studies at the University of Vienna Frankl initially contemplated becoming a dermatologist or a gynecologist, but eventually settled on becoming a psychiatrist.[25] In 1925, Frankl was one of the founding student members of the Academic Union for Medical Psychology.[26] He was vice-president, and the goal of the union was to integrate the basic ideas of the differing psychological schools into the medical studies of the students. There was also the proclaimed need to understand the "psychological component of sickness" through developing the study of medical psychology.[27] The list of professors who were members is quite impressive, but it is noteworthy that the leading Adlerians, Rudolf Allers and Oswald Schwarz, belonged. In 1925–1926 Frankl assisted Allers at his lab in "testing the reaction time of caffeine." Schwarz was an urologist and a founder of psychosomatic medicine. Since "both Allers

and Schwarz met regularly with the Society of Individual Psychology," they were central for helping Frankl grapple with Adlerian psychology.[28]

Healing World Views

In 1925 Frankl published an article in Adler's journal the *Internationale Zeitschrift für Individualpsychologie*. This short piece captures Frankl's movement away from Freudianism, and subsequent immersion in the Adlerian perspective. In the article, entitled "Psychotherapy and World View: On the Fundamental Critique of Their Connection," Frankl examined his principal intellectual concerns: the meaning of life and the role of psychotherapy. The biological and anthropological point of view, which marked his article published under Freud, was abandoned. By turning to concentrate on "world views," Frankl made the transition to what he described as his lifelong principal intellectual occupation: the border between psychotherapy and philosophy.[29] Frankl described himself as a "pioneer of existentialism,"[30] and he recalled that his reading of Kierkegaard in the early 1920s led him to study psychiatry.[31] His turn toward the issues of world views and meaning certainly contained an emergent existentialism. But the article was also marked by a rather stringent Adlerian perspective. Thus, for the second time in his life Frankl mastered the main tenets of an elder's thinking in an attempt to come to terms with human meaning.

The article began by affirming the standard Adlerian line on the defensive "arrangement character" of neuroses and how these neuroses originated ultimately in the unconscious "life goals" of the neurotic. Thus Frankl described how "often a neurotic seeks to justify his attitude toward life with a fixed world view," such as a "philosophical system, or a metaphysical religious philosophy." But according to Frankl, "every modern psychologist knows that these highest abstractions, emotions, … and philosophic views are ultimately established, conditioned and determined by the unconscious life of the neurotic."[32]

He then discussed the cure for neurosis, which was "to abolish the logical superstructure of the world-view with the emotional understructure," thus making it easy to remove the "fictional hold" of the neurosis.[33] According to Frankl, this methodology, and subsequent focus on the psychology of world views, is especially important "for certain individuals who are inclined toward intellectual argumentation to explain their failures in life."[34] Frankl was referring to "intellectual neurotics," whose self-esteem first needed to be increased before they could criticize their own world view. In order for the "philosophic neurotic" to carry out this critique it was necessary to first establish "the value of health, and of life in the widest sense, as the highest recognizable value."[35]

Frankl therefore connected the pessimism and critical stance of the "intellectual neurotic"—referencing Schopenhauer as an example—to the theoretical grounds of psychotherapy. He wanted to develop a "critical foundation

for the treatment of the intellectual neurotic and psychotherapy in general" that was essentially "ethical and moral." Thus "every treatment presupposed the final aim of health and assertion of life's worth." But Frankl argued "there are no absolute values … independent from a valued will. Therefore the value of life cannot be proven, only accepted … because in the end there is no other worth, and no other 'higher' worth is possible." When treating the intellectual neurotic, Frankl claimed, "because values are not revealed apriori … what we can prove—and what the philosophical neurotic must prove—is that his whole disdain for life, world, and community is uncritical and moreover 'unfit.'"[36] Essentially, the "unfitness" of the intellectual neurotic's world view was in Frankl's opinion "uncritical," because it viewed life only negatively. According to Frankl, upon truly critical reflection (Adlerianism), this negative attitude toward life would be recognized as no more than a neurotic arrangement.

When Frankl described how values cannot be proven but only accepted, he seemed uneasy with the organic grounds of Adler's epistemology. This uneasiness was exemplified when he tried to affirm meaning through communalism from the perspective of two old men dying.

> For me, at this stage, it is only a picture. Two old men are dying. One has lived embracing the principle of egoism. For him, everything was purposeful only in relation to his individual life. Thus … everything is purposeless for him, meaningless. It is different for another whose meaning in life, and his worth, he has found in the community. Even dying, his life appears to him full of meaning, because he is situated in the supra-individual and stays untouched from the destruction of the separate parts. One old man has always lived with the thought, "what can I buy with this?" From this perspective his whole life must seem pointless, because for his whole life he can buy nothing. The other is liberated, because these thoughts don't even present themselves: he didn't do anything, he didn't live, to be able to 'buy something with this'![37]

Frankl seemed to recognize he was approaching the problem from a new perspective when he stated, "at this stage it is only a picture." This is a significant turn in Frankl's thinking because it underscored Frankl's burgeoning existentialism and the crisis of values in two ways. First, the recognition of *mortality*, rather than some organic urge, was the source of why an individual would pursue meaning through the community. Second, Frankl recognized that the individual had to *choose* to live for the community rather than for oneself, thus undermining the notion of an organic tendency toward community feeling.

The tension between individualistic egoism versus connected communalism that Adler had solved by positing an organic urge toward community feeling was now being viewed by Frankl from the perspective of a good and meaningful death, or anxiety over dying. But Frankl stopped short of a full-blown existential posture, because he remained tethered to Adler's community feeling to locate meaning. Therefore, Frankl's turn toward a psychology of world views, which focused on intellectuals and the philosophic problem of meaning, led him to an affirmation of community feeling from the perspective

of old men dying. Frankl was certainly beginning to pioneer existentialism. But the tension here is that from the perspective of old men dying, there is nothing that would lead one to the conviction, or belief, that community feeling originated in an organic urge or tendency. Therefore, to stay within the Adlerian project of community feeling required Frankl to debunk the radical individualism of the existential perspective where one would only live "to be able to buy something with this." He therefore conceptualized a quasi-spiritual justification of community where for a person "dying, life appears full of meaning," not because of his individual life, but "because he is situated in the supra-individual and stays untouched from the destruction of the separate parts."[38]

Frankl concluded his discussion of intellectuals and values with the Adlerian vision that "our essential and most important task is to be affirmative about our community."[39] With the complementary claims that life's meaning was located in the life goal of the individual, and that meaning would be discovered ultimately in the community, Frankl was clearly promoting the Adlerian vision. Finally, this intellectual tension between valuing the individual or community led Frankl to position the role of the therapist as the key figure in "the love of life and the desire to give back wholly to the community." The therapist could do this by providing "a critical explanation" which will make "the value of life and society clear, but not provable, given, but not demanded."[40] Frankl's concluding remarks, where meaning was ultimately achieved through the absorption of the individual into the community, fit the social milieu of Red Vienna. Also, the quasi-priestly role of the therapist fit quite well with the Austromarxist cultural project of *Bildung*.

Authoritarian?

This tension between valuing the individual or community raises the question of the political culture of Red Vienna. A variety of historians have explained why the liberal tradition failed in Austria and Germany until after 1945.[41] In Red Vienna there was certainly no strong conviction in favor of liberal democratic values. The Austrian polis in the twenties was divided between the Christian Socials, Pan-Germans, and Socialists. Even among the Socialists, there was debate surrounding the question of how committed they should be to parliamentary democracy, or whether they should only conceive parliamentarism as a temporary stage in a static class war.[42]

Helmut Gruber attempted to revise the standard interpretation of the social and political reality of Red Vienna. According to Gruber, most historians take at face value the myth of Red Vienna that was originally perpetrated by the makers themselves.[43] In his revision, Gruber claimed there was an authoritarian element implicit in the humanitarian ideals of the Austromarxism. For Gruber, the Austromarxist commitment to creating *neue Menschen* who would be so-

cially and intellectually prepared when the conditions for revolution appeared ripe presupposed two interrelated problems. First, Austromarxism "assumed an individual malleability in the process of socialization and raised the specter of workers as objects." Second, the cultural project "embodied the conflict between leaders and masses, authoritarianism and passivity."[44]

Significantly, Gruber argued against the interpretation that Adlerian psychology played a positive ideological role in Red Vienna. Instead, he held that Adlerian psychology had only limited practical influence. In his discussion of the party's approach to worker culture and sexual counseling he stated "there is little evidence of the frequently claimed close relationship to Adlerian individual psychology." Yet, Gruber also believed that Adlerian psychology was appealing to the Socialists because it would buttress their authoritarian, objectifying practices. Therefore, Gruber argued that the Adlerian "idea of human malleability subject to intervention and improvement was attractive to socialist leaders and experts embarked on creating 'neue Menschen.'"[45] Gruber's arguments, although perhaps one-sided,[46] have provided a critical reading that effectively undermined the putative humanism of the Socialists and Adlerian psychology. From Gruber's perspective, Frankl's Adlerianism, which expected the therapist to play a central role in integrating the individual into the community, arguably had authoritarian elements. Was Frankl then absorbing authoritarianism from Adler? This seems possible, but as a medical student and aspiring psychotherapist, Frankl was apparently motivated by a deep humanitarianism.[47] And Frankl eventually rejected what he considered to be the reductionist and dehumanizing tendencies of Adlerianism. Therefore, was Frankl's emerging existentialist stance developed by his recognition of the underlying authoritarian implications of Adlerianism? Or, did Frankl begin to conceive of Adlerianism as objectifying and dehumanizing *after* he was rejected by Adler?

The Breakup of Adler's Circle

We know Frankl didn't break[48] with Adler, but rather was dismissed by him. According to Frankl and his followers, intellectual tensions were at the heart of this parting of ways.[49] Klingberg describes how Allers and Schwarz "pointed out Adler's reductionism" and that as they became more "disenchanted with individual psychology" Frankl "was inspired by both their insight and courage."[50] Apparently, Frankl, following Schwarz and Allers, had become dissatisfied with Adler's description of neuroses. Neurosis, Frankl maintained "did not always have this 'arrangement' character but could also be a genuine expression of the person."[51] On this point Frankl was following Schwarz and Allers's criticism of Adler's idea of community feeling on the grounds that it was "too

rigidly structured" and disregarded "the individual's unique ability to use his or her will to change."[52] In 1927 this disagreement led to a confrontation between Frankl and Adler immediately after Allers and Schwarz had presented their divergent views and left the society. In the lecture hall Adler turned to Frankl and another young Adlerian and demanded "Ihr Helden bekennt Euch! What sort of heroes are you? Show that you are courageous enough to speak up! Do you take their side or mine?" Frankl replied that he was of the same opinion as Schwarz and Allers but believed that what they had said was in essential agreement with Adler.[53] Apparently Adler was demanding that Frankl choose between his allegiance to Schwarz and Allers, or him. Frankl seemed to hedge and remained intent on initiating reconciliation, but "made a strategic mistake by referring to Schwarz as his teacher."[54] Frankl's allegiance was obviously torn. Klingberg adds that in the exchange Adler also "ridiculed" what Frankl had said "about the spiritual dimension in humans and its significance."[55]

As it turned out, Schwarz had just recently praised Frankl's outline of a book "as doing for psychology what Kant's *Critique of Pure Reason* did for philosophy."[56] Nevertheless, Frankl attempted to remain inside the circle because he wanted to use Adlerian journals to promote the youth counseling services he was then initiating.[57] But eventually Adler insisted he leave the society, and Frankl was expelled. Frankl described how: "[F]rom that moment on, Adler never spoke to me. When I approached the tables where the Adlerians sat at the Cafe Siller ... Adler left. He never greeted me. I felt very hurt. I loved and admired him. I knew his weaknesses but I liked him.... Finally, Adler decreed I was no longer a member. He excommunicated me. It was embarrassing for me. But, in another way, it was beneficial perhaps because I no longer had to consider problems of loyalty."[58]

Frankl claimed that Adler failed to fully understand the criticisms of Allers and Schwarz because he was not philosophical enough. And the philosophical tension between individualism versus community feeling did seem to be the heart of the matter—at least for Schwarz and Allers. Evidently, Frankl followed because Adler forced his hand. But from our analysis of Frankl's article "Psychotherapy and World-View" it seems his philosophic interests were moving him away from the standard Adlerian position that community feeling originated in an organic urge and toward an individualistic existentialist posture. Frankl's intellectual development suggests that breakup of Adler's circle was at least partially attributable to the conflict between individualism and community feeling. From this perspective the breakup is perhaps best understood as a disassembly of the two key components of Adlerian psychology. That is, Frankl's emergent existentialism was beginning to focus on the individualistic aspects of "individual" psychology. Therefore, Frankl was in solidarity with Schwarz and Allers's claim that community feeling was too rigidly structured and thus undermined individualism.

Anti-intellectualism?

We can gain further insight into the intellectual tensions that led to Frankl's ex-
clusion by analyzing a lecture he gave on the eve of his departure. In 1926, just
before his complete rupture with Adler, Frankl gave two public lectures: one
in Dusseldorf at the Third International Congress for Individual Psychology,
and another at the Vienna Section of the International Union for Individual
Psychology. The latter was published in the *Internationale Zeitschrift für Individu-
alpsychologie* in 1926. Since the lecture was published in this prestigious journal,
it is somewhat surprising that Frankl referenced his "Psychotherapy and World-
View" often and with pride, but only mentioned the second article obliquely
as "another one which followed" in 1926.[59] However, late in life Frankl stated
"I would not authorize those papers" (from the 1920s), which may be the
central reason that there is little mention of the paper.[60] The subject of this
lecture-turned-article was the psychology of intellectualism. Frankl basically
developed the line of argument in his article "Psychotherapy and World-View"
that world views are a factor in therapeutic situations. He begins by defining
an "intellectual as a psychological type of man whose attitude towards life is
in general characterized by a certain hypertrophy, or overdevelopment of the
thought function."[61] Frankl supported this rather critical view of some intellec-
tualism by claiming that although "you can't claim in general that what we call
sick is wrong ... we in individual psychology consider the intellectual perspec-
tive toward life wrong."[62]

Frankl's relativistic claim that "what is sick is not necessarily wrong" was
justified as an effective psychological tool that allowed for an impartial and ob-
jective evaluation of neurotics. Frankl therefore claimed that "we cannot make
the mistake of psychologism, and try to infer the validity of the content from
the reality of the psychological act." In order to exemplify this attitude of psy-
chologism, Frankl described a doctor who treated a case of syphilis phobia
without inquiring whether or not the patient actually had syphilis. According
to Frankl, such an attitude "overlooked a certain autonomy, and possible legiti-
mate justification of pathological acts."[63] This point both revealed his emerging
critique of Adlerianism and affirmed the point that Frankl wanted to look at
neurosis as something more than an arrangement. That is, for Frankl a neurosis
could be both an arrangement and a genuine (legitimate) expression, grounded
in reality.

Frankl then turned to delineate the origins of intellectualism. He began
by claiming that the overdevelopment of the thought function "is caused by a
biological urge, for the preservation of life, which becomes an end in itself."[64]
By asserting the biological grounds of intellectualism, Frankl connected the
act of thinking to Adler's conception of the will to power. Thus, "thought," as
essentially a reflection of will to power, became the cornerstone of defining in-
tellectualism. But it also followed that the will to power had to be the source for

both negative and positive thought. This point was exemplified when Frankl claimed Adlerianism offered an adequate explanation for the origins of negative thought: "Years ago I believed that it was a mere expression of universal 'balancing principle' … which was exhibited as a psychological as well as a physical asthenia. As an individual psychologist I learned for the better that feelings of inferiority or weakness were unreal, and were to be viewed as arrangements to unmask. This was based on the conviction that there are no negative tendencies—for example the 'death instinct' in psychoanalysis—but that positive ones often used seemingly negative means."[65]

Frankl therefore used Adler's "will to power" to refine his understanding of a "universal balancing principle," and Freud's conception of the death instinct as a possible explanation for negative valuations of life.

Frankl then turned to develop a typology of negative hypertrophic thought. He claimed there were four types of "hypertrophic" intellectuals: "eager for knowledge," "mystical," "skeptical," and "onesided." Those "eager for knowledge" were conceived as "striving for power." Frankl argued that these intellectuals' will to power was an expression of the need for a "securing of life."[66] Frankl concluded his brief reflection on those eager for knowledge by claiming that the hypertrophy of thought could be connected to compulsive neurosis, because "the connections between the compulsion to ponder and the compulsively sick are striking."

In the second category, "mystical," Frankl noted the similarities with those "eager for knowledge." But he claimed, in contrast, "it is not the thought act which is overgrown, but the content that shows something exaggerated or grandly superlative."[67] Citing the work of the Adlerian Dr. Erwin Wexberg and the philosopher Karl Jaspers, Frankl claimed that "mysticism," such as "theosophy, occultism … or exaggerated forms of metaphysical system building, is nothing more than an expression of the will to power." According to Frankl, "the clinical prototype" was "paranoia with an over-developed sense of megalomania."[68] By defining mysticism in terms of megalomania and paranoia, Frankl closed the door on the paranormal. Since we know that Frankl turned to the concept of an "unconscious god" as a source of "Super-meaning" in his postwar writings, this critique of metaphysics is perhaps another reason he didn't authorize this article.

After debunking the mystic, Frankl then turned to tackle the psychology of skepticism. The relativistic implications of skepticism, perhaps best exemplified by the eighteenth-century Scottish philosopher David Hume, and then developed by Nietzsche, are well known. Frankl was not unaware of the power of skepticism and thus stated "the majority of skeptics are related to relativists.…"[69] To muster a critique of skepticism, he relied on "the individual psychological fact which says: doubt is the negation of responsibility—with the aetiology of despair." In his explication, Frankl described how the skeptic "moves between discontent and sickness" and represented "a tendency to escape … life's tasks."

Frankl then dismissed the skeptic as a case of "hypertrophic 'negative' thought" and as "an obstructive discusser of life."[70]

The final intellectual type that Frankl described was the "onesided" (*Einseitigkeit*). Onesided was defined as a set of "diverse symptoms of the intellectual" that are widely prevalent, and exemplified by "the tendency to schematize and pattern." This was a slightly ironic claim given the nature of the article. In this rather jumbled category Frankl placed "fanatic apostles of 'direction,' members of schools, and party members," along with "a form of scientific intolerance like a 'caste spirit' of intellectuals, with their specific and arrogant talents. Moreover, their typical ways of teaching, and their unnecessary mania for using foreign words, … [and] excessive, raging desire to discuss. Finally in their appearance, which I once named 'spiritual sportiness.'"[71]

After this somewhat comical—but perhaps pointed—diatribe against intellectual types, Frankl delineated the origins of the onesided. He claimed that the tendency for an intellectual's onesidedness may be due to an anxiousness over the "tragically gigantic mass of problems in consideration of his modest power" and therefore a need to "grasp stifled abstractions." Frankl then hedged his criticism further, and claimed the problem was that "the original valuable onesidedness becomes hypostatized and an end in itself."[72] Since Frankl eventually criticized Freud as a reductionist, it is possible that Frankl's rejection of Freud was the background to this criticism of reductive thinking.

Genesis of the Third Path

If these four categories provided a typology of neurotic thought, what was good thought for Frankl? In order to provide the philosophic grounds for healthy thought, Frankl called for a pragmatic philosophy, which he coined "Biologik." Biologik was Frankl's original conception, which attempted to combine the organic realm with social experience. In short, Biologik was a positive valuation of practical arguments, achieved by grounding logic in an organic tendency. This idea, occupying in Frankl's words, the "border between philosophy and psychology,"[73] was to be the intellectual supplement to Adler's community feeling. Thus, Frankl claimed that Biologik could be "brought into conformity" with individual psychology and provide the grounds for overcoming intellectualism. This pragmatic philosophy was conceptualized as the "connecting viewpoints of a (logical-psychological and biological-cultural) … called 'Biologik'—a concept which can easily be brought into agreement with the individual psychological opinion for the utility of the community. As soon as we are fully aware of such a fundamental basis, we can consider the possibility of overcoming intellectualism."[74]

Thus Frankl, at only twenty-one years of age, was beginning to conceptualize fundamental ideas that may (or may not) be easily brought into agreement

with the Adlerian world view. Clearly it was slightly pretentious of the young Frankl to make the theoretical claim of overcoming intellectualism. According to Frankl, practical philosophy is the "full unconditional recognition of the value of life and—meaning ... in Kant's language it sets out 'the primacy of practical reason' and immediately points to action."[75] While Frankl concluded his rejection of intellectualism with a call to action, he also took aim at his own position as an intellectual and aspiring psychologist. He thus claimed "we should not be surprised that if approached from a psychological, humanistic point of view ... the call to life and action remains lip service."[76]

For Frankl, the debilitation of action, created by the intellectualizing that is characteristic of intellectuals, is a "circulus vitiosus." He thus argued that "we have to demand that this serpent [read intellectual] which is biting its tail will finally someday eat itself. However, more often it will choke on itself."[77] Frankl then extended this criticism to incorporate individual psychology, because "almost all of us encounter individual psychology based on intellectual interests. Therefore it is only expected that many still carry a piece of the intellectual with them. If more or less 'already eaten into' there is a necessity for a practical point of view and for self-educational work."[78]

In Frankl's prescription, individual psychology needed to purge its ranks of intellectualism and engage in self-educational work. Frankl's argument clearly reflected the intellectual tensions within Adler's circle when he turned to describe how individual psychology must "sail through a Scylla and Charybdis" where "on the one side is the false opinion of those, which have preserved their naive belief in the ideal.... On the other hand we see those who doubt its realization. Both are at fault. Both make the same mistake. That is to say they take the ideal literally. They don't know that ideals don't exist in order to realize them, but rather to idealize reality!"[79]

Apparently Frankl hoped his call to action would be viewed as the best way to continue the program of individual psychology. Between the Socialist "idealists" and conservative "skeptics," Frankl attempted to mark out a third path—a path that wanted to idealize reality through action. What are we to make of this call to action?

The call to action, especially for the realization of ideals, fit nicely with the Austromarxist commitment to *Bildung* and what Anson Rabinbach has called the "politics of pedagogy."[80] Although it could be argued that Frankl's "third path" was leading him toward the political matrix of Austrofascism, at this point he clearly remained under the rubric of Austromarxism. The youthful, energetic Frankl was simply attempting to resolve the tensions within individual psychology.

Frankl concluded by remaining "true to the individual psychology motto. What one believes is not of interest to us, only what one does! In this aspect individual psychology appears as the art of life, as a technique for actualizing people, based on the resolution of their problems.[81] The notion of

individual psychology as a technique for actualizing people certainly fulfilled Helmut Gruber's argument that the appeal of Adlerianism was the "idea of human malleability subject to intervention and improvement."[82] But Frankl's position did not necessarily appear authoritarian. His third path was simply an attempt to sustain (by redirecting) the revolutionary energies of Austromarxism. This led to Frankl's call for action and a rejection of hyper-intellectualism as too problematic. In his anti-intellectualism that differentiated between positive and negative thought, and the corollary focus on practical action, we also see the beginning of Frankl's lifelong therapeutic strategy of setting limits to self-reflection and introspection.

On His Own

Frankl's 1926 piece also sheds light on why he was rejected by Adler. On the one hand, Frankl was beginning to consider neurosis as a "genuine expression of a person" and therefore as something that couldn't be viewed simply as just an arrangement. On the other hand, Frankl was apparently disturbed that Adler had failed to understand the issues raised by Allers and Schwarz. (They claimed community feeling overlooked the individual's unique ability to change.) In "The Psychology of Intellectualism," Frankl suggested that he was revising Adler's notion of neurosis as an "arrangement" by claiming that pathological acts may have a worthwhile justification. We can assume that despite Frankl's claims for originality, it is likely that Adler would also recognize that pathological acts may have a worthwhile justification. Also Frankl's claim for autonomy did prefigure the existential therapeutic approach of viewing neurosis as part of a person's "being in the world." But again, Adler's notion of a unique teleology incorporated in the term a "style of life" also prefigured this existential trend. The clearest example of Frankl's revisionism occurred when he claimed "Biologik" could be amended to Adler's idea of a predetermined community feeling. Along with this claim, Frankl was trying to sail between the Scylla and Charybdis of individual psychology. Now, it may be that Adler not only rejected Frankl's solution, but also found his claims pretentious and, along with his revisionism, objectionable. Most likely, it was a combination of these factors that led to Frankl's departure.

In his biography of Adler, entitled *The Drive for the Self*, Edward Hoffman suggested that political differences were at the heart of the breakup of Adler's circle. He drew this conclusion based on the remembrances presented in Phyllis Bottome's 1936 biography of Adler, entitled *Alfred Adler: A Portrait from Life*. According to Hoffman:

> As recalled nearly fifteen years later by the participants, the catalyst for the rupture was the recently published book on psychopathology by Oswald Schwarz, ...

Armed with a hidden agenda, several of the younger figures in the society politely asked Schwarz to present his new work at the next meeting. When he cordially did so, he found himself suddenly attacked as a reactionary by the younger, more politically minded Adlerians. Schwarz defended himself and then criticized severely this younger faction, led by Manes Sperber and Viktor Frankl. Joining Schwarz in his criticism was psychiatrist Rudolf Allers…[83]

Since Frankl claimed he sided with Schwarz and Allers, Hoffman's presentation of the breakup is most likely wrong. Hoffman's misinterpretation can be attributed to the fact that Bottome's 1936 biography was very crude, and made no reference to specific names due to the interwar political circumstances. In fact, Bottome's chapter on the breakup is tastelessly entitled "The Nigger in the Woodpile." In this chapter, an unnamed person, who is obviously the leftist Manes Sperber, is held responsible for forcing Adler to reject the older members of his circle. Bottome also claimed Adler wanted to keep his psychology "simple," and he therefore sided with Sperber.[84] From all this confusion we can conclude there was at least a subtle political element to the breakup.

The politics were probably due to Manes Sperber, who was Adler's youngest and most esteemed disciple. (Frankl made no mention of Sperber.) Sperber was a Communist, and in his autobiographical *All of our Yesterdays* he described the breakup in these terms:

> the non-marxist Adlerians, even the most conservative among them, felt neither alarmed nor compromised by the fact that a large number, perhaps the majority, of Alfred Adler's associates and active adherents belonged to the social democratic party or allied organizations. Yes, there were defections; for example, some right-wing physicians had broken with Adler. There were other reasons for this defection, however, and it was largely due to differences of opinion that had almost nothing to do with politics and little with ideological questions.[85]

Thus politics played a role but probably was of secondary concern. At the forefront were intellectual and personal differences that led to Frankl's departure from Adler.

Apparently, the "thinker-through" had once again tested the logical limits of a mentor's thinking. His philosophic questions led him to construct a therapy that took world views seriously. The focus on intellectuals led Frankl toward an existentialist posture, and he attempted to make a differentiation between positive (socially useful) and negative (excessive) thought. Although he originally tried to maintain an Adlerian perspective, it seems his focus on the individual and world views was beginning to push Adler's premises about the individual and social life further than Adler was apparently comfortable with. Thus, ironically, and apparently against Frankl's will, these ideas actually became the initial stage of his slide to the political right—at least in terms of how politics played out in the field of psychology. Thus, after losing his connection to Freud and being dismissed by Adler, Frankl had little choice but to follow the more conservative medical members as they departed Adler's circle.

Since Frankl did not leave the circle by his own choosing, his options for career paths suddenly became quite limited. In 1928, he apparently had two options available. He could continue his association with Schwarz and Allers and their experimental sensory-physiological center or develop his own burgeoning work in youth counseling. Perhaps because he was subconsciously (or consciously) fulfilling his father's concern with promoting the welfare of Austrian youth, Frankl turned toward counseling. But, obviously, this concern with youth and their "psychic hygiene" dovetailed with his own intellectual struggles with life's meaning and his prescription to take action. We should also remember that Frankl was still in medical school. At this point, only twenty-one years old, Frankl turned to youth counseling—his first practical attempt to overcome nihilism.

Notes

1. For a concise description of the rift, see Peter Gay, *Freud: A Life for Our Time* (New York: Doubleday, 1988), 220–224.

2. Sigmund Freud, quoted in Alfred Adler, *The Individual Psychology of Alfred Adler*, ed. Heinz Ansbacher and Rowena Ansbacher (New York: Harper and Row, 1964), 73.

3. In using the term "shared" I am trying to suggest that Adler came to similar conclusions as Nietzsche about the significance of evolution. Whether Nietzsche, Adler, or Darwin was the source of the idea is a secondary point. Unlike Adler, Freud never acknowledged studying Nietzsche, nor did he claim to be influenced by Nietzsche. For a discussion of the relationship between Nietzsche's ideas and Freudianism, see Ronald Lehrer, *Nietzsche's Presence in Freud's Life and Thought: On the Origins of a Psychology of Dynamic Unconscious Mental Functioning* (Albany: State University of New York Press, 1995).

4. Friedrich Nietzsche, *The Will to Power*, trans. Walter Kaufman and R.J. Hollingdale (New York: Vintage Books, 1957), 362.

5. Ibid., 344.

6. Ibid., 364.

7. Adler, *Individual Psychology*, 129.

8. See Sulloway, *Freud, Biologist of the Mind*, especially "Darwinism and Psychoanalysis: An Overview," 257–258.

9. Freud, quoted in Gay, *Freud*, 221.

10. Adler, *Individual Psychology*, 129.

11. Ibid., 129.

12. See Edward Hoffman, *The Drive for the Self: Alfred Adler and the Founding of Individual Psychology* (New York: Addison-Wesely, 1994), 124–138. Also, Ernst Glaser, *Im Umfeld des Austromarxismus: Ein Beitrag zur Geistesgeschichte des österreichischen Sozialismus* (Vienna: Europaverlag, 1981), 273–287. To support his claim for the influential role of Adlerianism in Red Vienna, Glaser cited Frankl's description of his youthful debates over "Lenin and Marx, Freud and Adler" in the early 1920s. Ibid., 287. For a critical view of Adlerianism in Red Vienna, see Helmut Gruber, *Red Vienna: Experiment in Working Class Culture 1919-1934* (New York: Oxford University Press, 1991), 112–113, 175.

13. On the collapse of the monarchy and Austrian politics, see Anson Rabinbach, *The Crisis of Austrian Socialism: From Red Vienna to Civil War, 1927-1934* (Chicago: University of Chicago Press, 1983), 7–31. Also, John Boyer, *Culture and Political Crisis in Vienna: Christian Socialism in Power, 1897-1918* (Chicago: University of Chicago Press, 1995).

14. For an excellent summary of these issues, see Bruce Pauley, "The Social and Economic Background of Austria's *Lebensunfähigkeit*," in *The Austrian Socialist Experiment*, ed. Anson Rabinbach (Boulder, Co.: Westview, 1985).

15. Rabinbach, *Crisis of Austrian Socialism*, 20.

16. Ibid., 28.

17. Adler, quoted in Hoffman, *Drive for the Self*, 125.

18. There is a vast literature on the politics of *Bildung*. For a positive view, see Glaser, *Im Umfeld des Austromarxismus*, along with Josef Weidenholzer, *Auf dem Weg zum "Neuen Menschen": Bildungs- und Kulturarbeit der österreichischen Sozialdemokratie in der Ersten Republik* (Vienna and Munich: Europa Verlag, 1981). For a critical reading, see Gruber, *Red Vienna*. A balanced assessment is to be found in Alfred Pfoser, *Literatur und Austromarxismus* (Vienna: n.p., 1980), and Rabinbach, *Crisis of Austrian Socialism*.

19. Hoffman, *Drive for the Self*, 128–130. For an opposing view of the success of educational reforms in Red Vienna, see Gruber, *Red Vienna*, 76.

20. Klingberg, *When Life Calls Out to Us*, 57.

21. Frankl, "Viktor Frankl," 183.

22. Viktor Frankl, Interview by Franz Ferdinand Wolf (video tape) Politische Akademie der Freiheitlichen Partei Österreichs, Vienna, 1 November 1994. Hereafter, Wolf Interview (FPÖ).

23. Helmut Gruber, "Red Vienna and the Jewish Question," *Leo Baeck Yearbook* (1993): 106. Gruber also described how the Socialists failed to deal with the "Jewish Question" in a positive way.

24. On Adler's sickly childhood, see Hoffman, *Drive for the Self*, 1–15.

25. Frankl, *Was nicht in meinen*, 32.

26. In his writings Frankl mentioned the union only in passing. In his first autobiographical piece he noted that he first spoke of logotherapy there in 1926. See Frankl, "Viktor Frankl," 187. We also know that the union promoted Freud's eightieth birthday celebration with lectures by Thomas Mann and Ludwig Binswanger. See *Neue Frei Presse* (9 May 1936): 6. Finally, Otto Pötzl, who played a significant role in Frankl's life, became "Obmann des Wissenschaftlichen Beirats in 1938" until it was disbanded in 1942. See Elke Mühlleitner, *Medizinische Psychologie und Psychotherapie in Oesterreich: 1900-1950* (unpublished), 122.

27. See Frankl, "Viktor Frankl," 187. Also, Wolfgang Huber, *Psychoanalyse in Österreich seit 1933* (Vienna: Geyer-edition, 1977), 29. The union's declaration with a list of initial members is available at the Freud Archive at the Library of Congress. Also see Mühlleitner, *Medizinische Psychologie und Psychotherapie*.

28. Klingberg, *When Life Calls Out to Us*, 60.

29. See Frankl, "Viktor Frankl," 184.

30. Corrigan Interview, (GTU). Frankl made this remark in reference to his early concern with human meaning. Also, Karl Krauss, Frankl's high school French teacher, recalled that Frankl was philosophically interested and "wrote about reading Nietzsche." See Karl Krauss (with Joseph Fabry), "My Most Famous Student," *NRTA Journal* no. 29 (November–December 1978): 23.

31. Frankl, *Was nicht in meinen*, 32.

32. Frankl, "Psychotherapie und Weltanschauung," 250–252.

33. Ibid., 250.

34. Ibid.

35. Ibid.

36. Ibid.

37. Ibid., 251.

38. Ibid.

39. Ibid.

40. Ibid.

41. For Austria these issues were discussed in a comparative perspective by John Boyer, *Culture and Political Crisis in Vienna*, and Gerhard Botz, *Kontroversen um Österreichs Zeitgeschichte: verdrängte Vergangeheit, Österreich-Identität, Waldheim und die Historiker* (New York: Campus Verlag,

1994). In the latter, see Karl Dietrich Bracher, "'Austrofaschismus' und die Krise der Demokratien." For Germany, see David Blackbourn and Geoff Eley, *The Peculiarities of German History: Bourgeois Society and Politics in Nineteenth-Century Germany* (New York: Oxford University Press, 1984).

42. See Rabinbach, *Austrian Socialist Experiment*, especially Melanie A. Sully, "Social Democracy and the Political Culture of the First Republic."

43. Gruber blamed the distortion on the Socialist historians themselves "for shaping a heroic past to serve as a tradition usable by the post-war socialist party." See Gruber, *Red Vienna*, vii.

44. Gruber, *Red Vienna*, 34.

45. Ibid., 175.

46. Gruber is intent on debunking the myth of Red Vienna, but in his commitment to his argument he portrayed the Austromarxists as having a powerful influence—albeit a demonic rather than benevolent influence, i.e., as "authoritarian and objectifying."

47. However, he claimed, "My father did more than encourage me to become a doctor; he wanted me to fulfill his dream." See Frankl, quoted in Cohen, "The Frankl Meaning," 56.

48. As with the case of Frankl and Freud, it is an overstatement to claim Frankl broke with Adler since he was only associated with the circle for two years.

49. See Gould, *Viktor E. Frankl*. Also, Stephen Kalmar, "A Brief History of Logotherapy," in *Analecta Frankliana* (Berkeley: Logotherapy Press, 1982).

50. Klingberg, *When Life Calls Out to Us*, 61; also see Frankl, *Was nicht in meinen*, 41.

51. Kalmar, "A Brief History of Logotherapy," xviii.

52. Gould, *Viktor E. Frankl*, 4.

53. Ibid.

54. Corrigan Interview (GTU). Also, Kalmar, "A Brief History of Logotherapy," xix.

55. Klingberg, *When Life Calls Out to Us*, 62.

56. Corrigan Interview (GTU). Also see Frankl, *Was nicht in meinen*, 39–40.

57. See Frankl, *Was nicht in meinen*, 43.

58. Frankl, quoted in Cohen, "The Frankl Meaning," 57.

59. Frankl, *Was nicht in meinen*, 40. Also, Eugenio Fizzotti seemed unaware of the publication in his otherwise very thorough article on the writings of the young Frankl. See Eugenio Fizzotti, "Prolegomena zu einer Psychotherapie mit menschlichen Antlitz in den Schriften des jungen Viktor E. Frankl 1923-1942," *Journal Des Viktor-Frankl-Instsituts* 3, no. 1 (Spring 1995): 29–39.

60. Klingberg, *When Life Calls Out to Us*, 58.

61. Frankl, "Zur Psychologie des Intellektualismus," 326.

62. Ibid., 327.

63. Ibid.

64. Ibid.

65. Ibid., 327–328.

66. Interestingly, Frankl claimed that this was a "case of a biological securing, not the arrangement of individual psychology." After this subtle "revisionism," Frankl differentiated between the individual psychological conception of the intellect and a Freudian one. Thus, the psychoanalytic "attempts to master the instinctive, ... we emphasize in essence the prospective tendency, to deal through knowledge of the environment with endeavors that lie in the future." Frankl, "Zur Psychologie des Intellektualismus," 329.

67. Ibid., 329.

68. Ibid., 329–330.

69. Ibid., 330.

70. Ibid.

71. Ibid., 331.

72. Ibid., 330.

73. Ibid., 327.

74. Ibid., 331.

75. Ibid.

76. Ibid., 332.

77. Ibid., 330.

78. Ibid., 332.

79. Ibid.

80. See Anson Rabinbach, "Politics and Pedagogy: The Austrian Social Democratic Youth Movement 1931-1933," *Journal of Contemporary History* 13, no. 2 (April 1978): 337–356.

81. Frankl, "Zur Psychologie des Intellektualismus," 333.

82. Gruber, *Red Vienna*, 34.

83. Hoffman, *Drive for the Self*, 143.

84. See Phyllis Bottome, *Alfred Adler: A Portrait from Life* (New York: GP Putnam's Sons, 1936), 162–171.

85. Manes Sperber, *The Unheeded Warning: 1918-1933*, trans. Harry Zohn (New York: Holmes and Meyer, 1992), 88.

Frankl's Ordination

From Theory to Praxis

The sensitive minds of the time, endowed with the finest capacity of the scent of things to come, spread the tidings that ... united these two poles, usually separate in the world, and they encouraged the rumor that here a modern force was on the way, ordained ... to guide the destinies of the Reich and ... perhaps the world, too towards better days.
— Musil, *The Man Without Qualities*

In the first republic, youth counseling was a prevalent concern of both Adlerians and Socialists. Consequently, numerous counseling centers were set up throughout the city of Vienna. The majority of the centers were Adlerian in orientation, but in 1926 there were at least "forty agencies dealing with the problems of child-rearing." These educational counseling centers were located within the city limits, and were often quite informal.[1] Sometimes civic groups donated space, or volunteers staffed meetings held at schools or assembly halls. Adler used the centers in a didactic manner, and they became a forum to promote his theories on child psychology among teachers, parents, and mental health workers. In addition, the famous child psychologist Charlotte Bühler, supported by a grant from the Rockefeller Foundation, established a very successful research center on child development at the University of Vienna.[2]

Notes for this section begin on page 58.

Frankl's Praxis

In the late 1920s and early 1930s Frankl developed his own counseling centers. Frankl's initiative probably stemmed from his experience working within the Adlerian counseling centers and his commitment to "take action," as well as his father's influence. From 1926 to 1937, Frankl produced no theoretical papers. But, in 1933, and again in 1935, he wrote summary articles on the praxis of youth counseling. These summations were preceded by over twenty short articles describing, promoting, and summarizing the problems confronted in youth counseling.[3] For example, in 1926, just before his rupture with Adler, Frankl wrote numerous short articles in different journals calling for the establishment of youth counseling. These journals, *Der Abend, Die Mutter,* and *Zeitschrift für Kinderschutz, Familien—und Berufsfürsorge, Gemeinschaft, Mitteilungsblatt der Sektionen des Internationalen Vereins für Individual-Psychologie, Die Praxis, Mitteilungen für die Organisationarbeit der Sozallistischen Arbeiterjungend Deutschösterreichs, Der Mensch im Alltag,* were all used to promote a Socialist agenda. Since Frankl was still a medical student, these initial articles were often edited by a member of the university medical faculty. To buttress his credentials Frankl also referred to his experience in the counseling centers, which was undoubtedly done in the Adlerian branch of the educational counseling movement for children.

Frankl justified his proposal for a "quick and energetic" establishment of youth centers on the grounds that counseling was occurring in other countries and Austrian society was "short on initiative for confronting youth suicide." According to Frankl, "physical neglect and spiritual troubles led many youths, perhaps the best youths, to suicide." His solution was "counseling on life's questions by parents." But often, due to "family conflict," children could not turn to their parents; therefore, "competently trained specialists" were necessary.[4]

In a systematic early article on the necessity of youth counseling, Frankl reiterated his claim that children were in need of guidance in confronting life's questions. To substantiate his call, Frankl mentioned that in the "first three months of 1926, 20 suicides had already occurred." Frankl was frustrated and dissatisfied with the "pitiful" psychological explanations for the suicides, especially the claim that they had "unknown motives."[5]

Frankl also supported his call for the establishment of youth counseling by giving short summary sketches of two case studies taken from his personal experience. The first case was a young man of eighteen, who initially appeared to be suffering from schizophrenia. But after counseling and "a lifting of his courage and self-esteem," he reintegrated with his family and took a job.[6] The second was the case of a young man who came to discuss "eccentric and banal thoughts in connection with a future ideal social order." After attempting to reveal the fallacy of his ideas, (perhaps he was a Communist) the counselors discovered that "the young man was a manifest homosexual, onanist, and stood isolated from society."[7]

In 1926, Frankl had not developed a very sophisticated response to these problems. He claimed that "the fundamental psychological idea" of a "good upbringing by the parents" was of central importance. However, the absence of good parental guidance necessitated counseling to "overcome the helplessness and insecurity" of the young.[8] This simplistic, Adlerian solution was the fundamental position from which Frankl began to tackle the struggles of the often suicidal, troubled youth. Apparently, Frankl had found his role in the youth counseling movement, and this preoccupation with the suicidal would occupy him for the next twenty years.

Criticism of Frankl's call for counseling centers came as he was removed from Adler's circle. Von Heinrich Soffner, taking a dogmatic Socialist position, argued that Frankl's article proposing youth counseling centers in the *Der Abend* "sidetracked the entire question." Soffner claimed that the focus on counseling to confront "the spiritual/mental needs of the young" overlooked the social and economic troubles that were at the heart of youth distress. According to Soffner, reform should focus on "family life, school, and cultural projects" along with "a little counseling."[9] Soffner's critique relied on the Austromarxist commitment to the politics of *Bildung* that aimed to create a Socialist *neue Menschen* through educational and cultural programs. But as Soffner pointed out, these politics of social reform seemed absent from Frankl's prescriptions for the troubled youth.

In 1927 Frankl responded to Soffner's criticisms writing under the pseudonym Lola Elberger. Frankl' response was conciliatory. He began by stating "we do not overlook the importance" of economic crisis for the youth, but we also "are far from regarding" social reform "as a panacea." Rather than focus solely on social reform, Frankl argued for "individual initiative" using the analogy that a "cowardly man would remain a coward, even under socialism." Then he asks, in the struggle for a better society why should we not have a "courageous fighter?" He concludes by addressing Soffner's downplaying of the significance of youth counseling by claiming "easing emotional distress" through counseling "in addition to the political efforts for social transformation" is the "best way to achieve our goals."[10]

After Soffner's criticism, in penning his response Frankl dropped his deference to the medical faculty and began signing his articles "Leader Viktor Frankl." This was updated to "Leader of the Office for Youth Counseling" in 1928. Due to his energetic efforts centers were established in Prague, Zurich, Dresden, and Berlin, and were spreading to Poland, Yugoslavia, and Lithuania by 1930.[11]

However, Soffner's "more Socialist than thou" criticism coincided with both Frankl's exit from Adler's circle and a period of profound social and political turmoil within Red Vienna. On 15 July 1927, the fortunes of Viennese socialism were radically altered. On this date, a spontaneous worker riot occurred in response to a jury's acquittal of three right-wing activists accused of murdering two Socialists. Unfortunately, the party apparatus failed to support

the workers in their uprising, and subsequently the government was not forced to recognize, much less concede to, the workers' demands for justice. The Socialist failure of political will in 1927 was the key turning point in the demise and capitulation of the Socialist movement in Austria to right-wing forces. As Anson Rabinbach argued in *The Crisis of Austrian Socialism*, "the paralysis of interwar Social Democracy … is a key aspect of the victory of the authoritarian dictatorships of the 1930's, not simply a consequence of it."[12]

Frankl's relationship to this demise of Red Vienna is difficult to decipher. In his autobiographical work he never referenced the cultural crisis and collapse of Red Vienna. We do know that when he left Adler's circle he also lost his forum, especially *Der Abend*, to promote his youth counseling centers.[13] This loss, combined with Soffner's attack, left Frankl without any "leftist" institutional support. A few months later Frankl found a harbor in the University of Vienna's clinic, under the supervision of Otto Pötzl. As mentioned Frankl described how "apart from Freud and Adler, Pötzl was … 'the' true genius."[14] Like it or not, Frankl, Pötzl, and the rest of Austria were sliding into the matrix of Austrofascism.

Pötzl and the Third Path

Frankl's attachment to Pötzl began in 1928 and represented his most enduring intellectual and professional relationship.[15] We know from his Nazi Party file that Pötzl claimed to become a committed Nazi between in 1930 and paid party dues until 1933, when Nazi Party membership was outlawed.[16] While Pötzl's involvement with Nazism is not surprising given the pan-Germanism of Austrian political trends, it is somewhat surprising that Pötzl was also a member of the psychoanalytic union from 1917 until 1933. Freud described Pötzl as a *zweideutigen Charakter* (ambiguous character),[17] but probably thought he would be useful to the union because he was a medical practitioner and, we can surmise, not Jewish.[18] Clearly both Freud and Adler significantly influenced the direction of Frankl's thinking. But by claiming Pötzl's genius surpassed Freud and Adler, Frankl seems to suggest Pötzl had a significant influence on him. Notably, in 1987 Frankl dedicated his collected essays to the memory of Otto Pötzl.[19] The connection with Pötzl also coincides with the beginning of Frankl's journey to the *third* Viennese school of psychotherapy. As we shall see, Frankl's third path attempted to surpass both Freud and Adler. Essentially, Frankl tried to unify the stoic individualism of Freud with the communal socialism of Adler in order to help patients find meaning in their lives.

Frankl's connection to Pötzl was illustrated by an article on youth counseling he published on 4 October 1929 in the prestigious *Münchner Medizinische Wochenschrift*. In the article, Frankl claimed that the "Vienna Youth Counsel" was founded in February 1928. Recall that in 1927 Frankl claimed that he

was the Leader of the Office for Youth Counseling. The change is perhaps explained by Frankl's attachment to Pötzl, because in the conclusion of the article, Frankl stated that "Dr. Otto Pötzl is honorary president of the Union of Youth Counseling." After losing the support of Adler, it appears Frankl turned to Pötzl for founding and developing new counseling centers. The relationship between Pötzl and Frankl was mutually convenient. Frankl gained the recognition of Pötzl, the head of the university clinic, and Pötzl, recently relocated from Prague, gained leadership of a youth counseling movement. Indeed, Klingberg suggests Pötzl took the initiative in cultivating the relationship with Frankl. Apparently, at the inauguration ceremony for Pötzl's appointment as chief of the university clinic, Frankl was spotted in the crowd by Pötzl and summoned Frankl to a "choice seat" next to him.[20]

Nevertheless, Pötzl's influence on Frankl's intellectual development is difficult to document. Frankl worked under Pötzl in 1930 at the University clinic.[21] From his relations with Freud and Adler, we know Frankl was adaptable and capable of aping the world view of more mature thinkers. Frankl also acknowledged that Pötzl gave him support in organizing his youth centers. Pötzl also "made an exception" and allowed Frankl to practice psychotherapy before he acquired his medical license.[22] (Frankl acquired his M.D. in 1930.)

Frankl also described how the volunteer counselors at the youth centers included the Adlerians Erwin Wexburg and Rudolf Dreikurs; the Freudian August Aichhorn; and the leader of the child research center, Charlotte Bühler.[23] Bühler, who was pictured on the page opposite Pötzl in Frankl's *Was nicht in meinen Büchern steht*,[24] also had rather questionable politics. In the late 1920s the "radical students were antagonistic toward [her] conservative (some say fascistic) political ideals and her conformity to social standards; she has been said to have been 'mildly anti-Semitic.'"[25] The anti-Semitism is somewhat surprising because Bühler was a Jewish convert to Protestantism.

To this picture of the demise of Red Vienna and Frankl's transition in the late 1920s we can add other intellectual influences. In 1931, Frankl's former teacher, Rudolf Allers, contributed to the *Essays in Order* series that attempted "to examine the possibilities of co-operation and of conflict that exist between the Catholic order and the new world."[26] From his autobiographical statements we know that Frankl had begun to read Martin Heidegger[27] and had continued interest in Max Scheler.[28] We know Heidegger became a committed Nazi in 1933, and there is a great deal of debate about the relationship between his ideas and political commitments.[29] Frankl stated that in the late 1920s, "Scheler's *Formalism in Ethics* became a bible for me." Scheler's work, although fluctuating immensely, contained a consistent reactionary quality that rejected Western rationalism and defended spiritual values. It seems clear that after losing his connection first to first Freud and then to Adler Frankl was surrounded with conservative political trends and figures.[30] Young, energetic, and professionalizing, Frankl was headed toward the "third path." Nevertheless, Frankl's politics

are not explicit. He made no specific comments on the politics of the time and in 1929 even claimed that youth counseling and counselors in particular should be "unpolitical."[31] Arguably the call to be unpolitical under the circumstances represented a particular type of politics.[32]

The period 1927–1934 in Austria may be described as a latent civil war. After 1927, the Socialist movement was under attack from right-wing forces, while the party's youth movement stagnated. The Socialist party, under Otto Bauer's conservative leadership, tried to control and pacify the radical youth and appease the right.[33] Also, the combination of Frankl's unpolitical position and the criticism of his prescriptions by Soffner (and his response) suggest he doubted if not outright rejected the Socialist politics of *Bildung*. For example, in 1929 he declared that the majority of youth came for counseling (he claims 1,500) on sexual and familial problems, and that "economic need was rare," and "in no way the direct cause of mental need."[34] As we shall see, his promotion of the palliative of "individual courage" in face of crisis and adversity is an embryonic form of logotherapy—a form of therapy that will focus on the human spirit to create a new, higher form of therapy.

The Genesis of Logotherapy

Frankl stated that he first spoke of logotherapy at the Academic Union for Medical Psychology in the 1920s, and by 1933 he had "systematized" his therapy.[35] However it is highly possible that he might have derived the "logo" in logotherapy from the famous speech therapist Emil Froeschels, who held a professorship in logopedics at the University of Vienna from 1924 to 1938. Froeschels is credited with coining the term logopedics, and in 1927 Frankl wrote a review of Froeschels book *Freihet trotz der Naturgesetzlichkeit*.[36]

Frankl conceived logotherapy in order to overcome what he viewed as the depersonalization and dehumanization of Freudian and Adlerian therapies. In the early 1930s he had enough confidence and conviction in his newly forming ideas to give classes on mental hygiene at the Wiener Volkhochschule. Already by 1930, he discovered what many considered his most important technique: paradoxical intention. In jocular fashion he described how the "discovery" of the technique actually originated with his patient. It seems Frankl flippantly told a patient to make fun of his obsessions without really reflecting on his idea as therapy. When the patient returned the next session cured, he reported that he took Frankl's advice to laugh at his obsessions seriously. To both Frankl's and the patient's surprise, it worked.[37]

Frankl also stated that by 1929 he had been exposed to the three possibilities from which the meaning of life can be derived. "A deed we do, or a work that we produce, an experience, such as love, and finally the attitude we take toward an unalterable fate."[38] Although one could argue that Frankl was only

projecting backward some of his more mature ideas, he had apparently resolved with some conviction his most deeply troubling problems. This sense of resolution was reflected in his description of a "peak experience" that came at this point in his life.

> In 1930, when confronted with the daughter of a world famous zoologist at the University of Vienna, ... I was treating her for obsessive compulsive neurosis ... with something like paradoxical intention, and she confessed it worked ... and she had a close encounter. I had compassion and pity for her ... I felt I really had helped her ... I had a feeling like she is mud in my hands ... and I was creating a new person ... molding her into a new and happy human being with meaning in life ... I had a feeling of mastership but a humble feeling ... the power to help and to rescue ... there is only one power, the power to help, and only one honor, the honor to rescue ... this rewarding feeling is the same feeling that comes when I receive letters from all over the world saying how I have helped them.[39]

On the basis of this recollection, it appears that Frankl had begun to resolve his youthful struggle with meaning. The quote might appear a bit self-aggrandizing, but the subtle arrogance was combined with a "humbled" power to help the psychologically ailing. It seems this humbled power, combined with paradoxical intention, or laughing at one's fears, were the key elements in Frankl's first solution to his own struggle with meaning. That is, Frankl had found his own "mission" of helping others find meaning, and his therapeutic techniques supported this project by providing effective means for alleviating anxiety.[40]

After he received his medical degree in 1930, Frankl worked initially for Pötzl at the university clinic, and then for two years at Am Rosenhugel, under Joseph Gerstmann.[41] In 1930 he also started a "special action" against youth suicides, and initiated a program for counseling high school students before the dreaded final exam. In this period, he also developed his test for measuring the retention of suicidal impulses. The test consisted of asking a patient if he was still having suicidal thoughts. If he said "no" the therapist was directed to immediately ask, "why not?" If he could not answer immediately, it meant the patient was bluffing, and was not over his suicidal urge. Although the test seems playful, it was an idea that Frankl would assert as effective throughout his career.

Pacification and Austrofascism

Frankl's confidence in his newly emergent logotherapy was evident in the two articles, published in 1933 and 1935, that summarized the goals and praxis of youth counseling. The first article was published in the medically oriented *Sozialärtzliche Rundschau*. In this article, entitled "Economic Crisis and Mental Health," Frankl reversed the claim he made in 1929 that economics was an insignificant concern. Now, in the midst of the depression that left 50 percent of the young people between the ages of sixteen and twenty-five unemployed,[42] Frankl discussed the "influence of the economic crisis on the entire life of

young people." Frankl claimed the economic crisis impacted the relationships between young women and men. "Boys often voluntarily renounced the love for a girl when they became unemployed … and on the other side is the girl, whose parents intervene to forbid relations with an unemployed boy because he has no future."[43]

Frankl also pointed out that unemployment "intensified the old generational struggle" between parents and children that was rooted in "the ideological and psychological" tensions that appeared at "the end of the world war." For fathers, the significant issue surrounding unemployment was a feeling of "powerlessness." For the sons, the issue concerned the inability "to contribute to the domestic economy." This led to "a concerned family dominated by nervous tension and unrest; for the youth, a danger in mental-hygiene is depicted."[44]

Although Frankl recognized the negative impact of the economic crisis on the youth, his therapy continued to focus on the role of the individual to confront economic hardship instead of calling for social reform. Frankl thus directed the patients to find their own resolutions to the crisis. According to Frankl, "the economic situation is in interplay with the psyche." That is, the economic situation of an individual is "partially the cause, and partially the outcome of the psychic disturbance." In Frankl's view, the task of the therapist was to untangle "the overlapping of economic need and psychological states."[45] Thus "the economic crisis does not directly affect a neurotic person, but passes through an intermediary zone, a realm in which those well trained in caring for neurosis can interfere."[46] The "interference," or care, consisted in an attitude adjustment. For example, the therapist could point out from an Adlerian perspective that "economic need gives the patient a scapegoat on which to place the responsibility for a botched existence." By illuminating the "defensive arrangement character" of this attitude, the patient could begin to accept responsibility. In most cases, the therapist was limited to instilling a certain stoic attitude toward economic fate. This was because "the therapist, unfortunately, is hardly capable of changing the economic position of the youth, so he must influence his attitude towards it." According to Frankl, the therapist should bring about "a conversion of concerns" and help the patient achieve the capability to "bear his economic need when necessary" and when "possible to remove it."[47]

Frankl's therapeutic strategy of attitude adjustment seemed intent on mobilizing the youth in a socially productive manner. This approach was exemplified by his description of unemployment neurosis. According to Frankl, "a specific form of neurosis stemmed from unemployment." He called it "apathy" where "the young men remained in bed until midday … and then after midday went to the coffee house and spent their last pennies on coffee." This apathy was easily spreadable to other young men and in some cases led to suicide. Frankl's solution was to call for "true heros … that with grumbling stomachs work in some organization, or as volunteers." According to Frankl, the problem of unemployment "eased, when the youth were fulfilled from their devotion to

a thing, to an idea, perhaps a struggle for better times, or a new world."[48] Frankl summed this idea up by enthusiastically claiming that "subjective troubles and objective struggles" can be overcome when one "has a task—a mission!" Obviously energized, Frankl connected his prescription to a rejection of the idea that employment is the only means for achieving a meaningful life. Frankl argued, "vocational work is not the only chance to shape a meaningful life ... one must look for, and find the next concrete task given." He then gave the example of a young man who began learning English as representative of one who has "that feeling of something achieved."[49]

Frankl's response to the economic crisis and latent civil war was to instill a sense of a mission into the youth. Whether these prescriptions represented a realistic palliative to someone in dire material, and thus spiritual, circumstances is debatable. Frankl's call for a mission, and fulfilling the next concrete task given, attempted to mobilize the youth in a socially positive direction. In this way logotherapy revised Austromarxism by focusing on the individual, rather than the community, as the best way to counteract the crisis. Notably, Adler's response to the economic crisis was somewhat similar because he "directed his appeals for ethical consciousness and responsibility towards those who experienced involuntary social decline." Also, "early in the thirties Adler ... distanced himself from the leftist individual psychologists..."[50]

In Frankl's case, the absence of a clear political commitment led him to make the open-ended and vitalized call for "a mission!" in 1933—on the eve of the collapse and death of the Austrian republic. The problem was that youth could find a mission from "a devotion to a thing," or a "struggle for better times, or a new world," in either the Heimwehr, which was the home-grown Austrian fascist movement inspired by Mussolini, or in the expanding National Socialist movement, which was quite successful in the 1932 and 1933 Austrian national elections.[51] There was also the possibility of a mission in the Communist movement that was spreading among the youth because the Socialists were failing to take forceful measures against the rise of the right.[52] By 1933, Engelbert Dolfuss had begun to implement the Austrian variant of fascism when he started governing without parliament.

From historical hindsight it is clear that the Socialists failed to take proper action against the rightist trends. Nevertheless, some figures in the party did recognize the political volatility and subsequent desperation of the Austrian youth in 1931. Party leader Julius Deutsch described the "terrible ... spiritual and emotional distress of the youth," and how "one can comprehend why they now and then succumb to phrases that bombard them from the left and right."[53] In these circumstances Frankl's prescription of a mission may seem naïve, or perhaps opportunistic, but to be fair, there were no easy solutions to the cultural crisis.

These political and social tensions culminated in the "civil war" of February 1934, and the establishment of the corporate state on 1 May. The creation

of the Austrofascist state led to the abolition of all Social Democratic institutions and when Kurt Schuschnigg assumed power after Dollfuss's murder in July of 1934, "the Adlerian clinics were summarily dissolved."[54]

Frankl and Youth Sexuality

Apparently Frankl's counseling was unaffected by these political changes,[55] because he published his second summary article "On the Practice of Youth Counseling" in 1935. Frankl began the article by crediting the banker Hugo Sauers of Berlin for first promoting youth counseling in 1914 (Frankl first credited Sauers in 1929 in the *Münchner Medizinische Wochenschrift*). Frankl repeated his discussion of the relationship between economic crisis and mental health and once again prescribed discovering a social task.

In this article, Frankl centered his comments on sexual issues. Questions about sexuality concerned masturbation, pregnancy, venereal disease, and frigidity. Absent from Frankl's discussion were the issues of abortion and birth control. It is likely that Frankl's omission of these key issues stemmed from the unease these matters raised in Viennese society. For example, although part of the Socialist program, abortion and contraception were not taken up on a practical level because of a fear of the political responses by the Christian Socials and the Catholic population.[56]

Frankl's interest in sexual issues was initially exemplified by his contribution to the Congress for Sexual Reform IV held in Vienna in mid September, 1930. Frankl commented that at the Vienna youth counseling centers, "one third of the cases concerned sexual problems." He discussed onanism and the relationship between hypochondria and suicide. He concluded by calling for educational measures and counseling because "responsibility is the mainstay of sexual ethics; while the great enemy of sexual hygiene is ignorance."[57]

The Freudian Wilhelm Reich was also concerned with the sexual problems of Austrian youth. Frankl described meeting Reich in the early 1930s when Reich gave Frankl a ride in his car and they discussed the sexual problems of the young.[58] But Frankl's views on sexuality, along with his apparent absence of political commitment in response to the civil war, stand in stark contrast to Reich. For example, in order to counteract the Socialist Party's tacit acceptance of the conservative Catholic attitude, Reich opened "six sexual consultation clinics … in 1929 … dealing with coitus and contraception in a clear and supportive manner."[59] Significantly, Reich's actions were conducted without Socialist Party help.

Politically, after the Socialist leadership failed to act in support of the workers in 1927 (an event Reich personally experienced), Reich moved steadily further to the left. Incensed with the leadership of the Socialists and their concessions to the right, he created the "Social Democratic Revolutionary Committee" in

1929. This committee consisted of dissatisfied workers and youth-movement members. For these political actions Reich was eventually banned from the party in 1930.[60] Reich's practical actions, and his desperate attempt to politicize the youth to stave off the impending crisis, contrast with Frankl's aversion to key sexual issues and "unpolitical" position.

In his work on youth sexuality, Frankl focused his discussion on a phenomenon he labeled *Onaniehypochondrie* (masturbation hypochondria). He briefly reviewed two cases that related to suicide. In the first case, the patient became suicidal after masturbation because "his friend had masturbated and a short time later died." Another was suicidal, because he feared contracting an illness following masturbation. Frankl, who described masturbation as "truly unnecessary, but unharmful," did not describe the therapy pursued in these cases, only footnoting that once sexual activity began, masturbation stopped. But he did argue against prostitution, claiming "it is risky in physical and mental hygiene" because it "trains the young men in the experience of sexuality solely as a means to pleasure." Frankl finished by suggesting that "the prescription for a positive indication for sexual relations comes however in the patient's religious, ethical, and social dependence."[61] This last point reflected Austrian social norms because there was a great deal of tension surrounding the question of the proper age for beginning sexual relations. Frankl prescribed no specific age, and instead focused on traditional structures to provide guidelines. But this point made it apparent that the nature of the counseling and the problems confronted were problematic for the counselor. Frankl described the counselor as caught "between their positive responsibility for the contents of consultation, and their negative responsibility for the complete integrity of their decisions." Frankl concluded "the counselor must be free to make a responsible choice."[62]

Finally, in 1937 Frankl took these issues up in his first English language article, "Erotic Problems of Modern Youth" in the international journal *Marriage Hygiene*. In this article Frankl developed a typology of youths that fail to develop "an ideal mature personality" through a "psych-intellectual companionship" that fulfills the monogamous sexual experience.[63] Based on his experiences counseling youth, Frankl claims there are three types of "disturbance" evident in "the process of sexual pubescence." The first is the "resentful type" that "renounces the psycho-spiritual adequateness of his partners and is satisfied with their readiness for sexual intercourse." The second is the "resigning type" who "do not believe in the possibility of experiencing the happiness of a synthesis of sexual and psychospiritual intimacy" and thus "expect mere sexual relations right from the beginning." The third type is the "inactive type" that includes "young people who are not only too discouraged to look for more than sexual intercourse, but who are even too discouraged for sexual intercourse itself."[64] These latter individuals express their sexuality through masturbation. Frankl's proscription is for these young people experiencing "sexual distress" is to advise

them to find a "beloved partner" in "a youth organization" that has "members of both sexes that suit them ideologically."[65]

Frankl and the Rise of Austrofascism

We can better appreciate Frankl's choices and difficulties by reflecting on a few general themes. Frankl was a very youthful member of a generation that came to maturity within the first Austrian attempt to construct a democratic republic. Frankl therefore became one of a multitude of "social engineers" in Red Vienna. These engineers attempted to implement a secular and rational culture, to replace the tradition-bound Catholic culture. Frankl, young, precocious, and ambitious, was a willing contributor. He certainly expected youth counseling to be his contribution. The experiment in socialism began to fall apart for Frankl when he was dismissed from the Adlerians. Frankl's departure also coincided with the cultural demise of Red Vienna. Politically isolated and experiencing economic crisis, Austria began slowly succumbing to the reactionary/revolutionary configuration of fascism. With the crumbling of Red Vienna, and subsequent advent of Austrofascism, Frankl struggled to develop a workable world view for himself and the troubled youth of Vienna.

Frankl's work in this period also represented the furtive beginnings of the "third school of Viennese psychotherapy." From the beginning this third path was something beyond the stoic individualism of the Freudians and the communalism of the Adlerians. In Frankl's synthesis the individual was held accountable for finding a socially responsible mission. Certainly this prescription made sense to the young Frankl. Within these volatile circumstances Frankl developed the idea of paradoxical intention, or the strategy of laughing at your fears. As much as paradoxical intention reflected Frankl's counterphobia and capacity to adapt to changing situations, it also closed the door on the irrationality and absurdism that his own "intellectualism" had uncovered. Apparently, it was also an effective therapy for the crisis-ridden, troubled youth of Vienna. Therefore, the beginnings of Frankl's third school reflected both the vitalization that stemmed from his emerging existential individualism and deference to social norms. In 1926 Frankl had made a call to idealize reality through action. But when crisis struck, Frankl apparently thought a lack of political program, and a subsequent deference to the social norms, was the "ideal" choice. Faced with the rise of fascism, many intellectuals made similar accommodations.

But what about the politics of Frankl's logotherapy in light of the rise of Austrofascism? In the mid 1920s Frankl embarked on a revision of Adlerianism, when he began to view neurosis as something more than an arrangement. Following Schwarz and Allers, he also agreed that community feeling was too rigidly structured and disregarded and individual's unique ability to change. Zeev Sternhell has argued that the origins of fascist thought can be traced to a

"revision of Marxism" and a "revolt against materialism."[66] Frankl's intellectual development that rejected Freud's biological reductionism and revised Adler's individual psychology seemed to be following this intellectual trajectory.

One thing is for certain. The publication of an article in 1935 on youth counseling suggested that, unlike the Freudians and Adlerians, Frankl was at least tolerated by the Catholic authoritarian state. And the conclusion of Frankl's 1935 article, as well as his proscriptions for erotically distressed youth, suggested that he was willing to work within the confines of the new Catholic political ideology and emerging fascist public sphere. This point was best exemplified by Frankl's description of a counseling session with a suicidal youth. After counseling the youth abandoned his suicidal intention, and he described the counselor as having "the same effect that the sound of bells and chorus had on Faust as he offered the cup with poison as the last greeting of the coming Easter morning."[67] Frankl was citing the famous passage of Goethe's *Faust*, where the suicidal Faust was "called back into life" by a chorus of angels announcing Christ's resurrection on Easter morning. The new Catholic political order certainly found nothing disagreeable with Frankl's description of the quasi-religious impact of the youth counselor. Frankl had survived the political crisis and advent of Austrofascism intact.

Notes

1. Sheldon Gardner and Gwendolyn Stevens, *Red Vienna and the Golden Age of Psychology* (New York: Praeger, 1992), 134–135.

2. Ibid., 195–205.

3. See Frankl, *Frühe Schriften 1923-1942*.

4. Frankl, "Schafft Jungendberatungsstellen," *Die Mutter* no. 39 (1926): 8.

5. Frankl, "Über die Notwendigkeit der Schaffung von Jungendberatungsstellen," *Zeitschrift für Kinderschutz, Familien- und Berufsfürsorge* 18, no. 7 (1926): 131.

6. Ibid., 131.

7. Ibid.

8. Ibid.

9. Von Heinrich Soffner, "Die Seelische Not unserer Jugend und ihre Bekampfung," *Die Bereitschaft* 7, no. 2 (1927): 17–18.

10. Frankl, *Frühe Schriften 1923-1942*, 67–68.

11. See Fizzotti, "Prolegomena zu einer Psychotherapie," 31.

12. Rabinbach, *Crisis of Austrian Socialism*, 30.

13. Frankl, *Was nicht in meinen*, 43.

14. Ibid., 48.

15. For example, in 1947 Frankl contributed an article to Pötzl's festschrift, and after returning from the concentration camps in 1946, Pötzl consoled Frankl over the loss of his wife. Frankl also had an urge to "protect" Pötzl from the reprisals against Nazis and contributed to his de-Nazification proceedings.

16. Pötzl's file is available at the Dokumentationsarchiv des Österreichischen Widerstandes. His file revealed he did not join the party until 31 December 1943, but then had his membership redated to 1 January 1941. He also claimed he paid dues from 1930 to 1933 but never received his

party card. We should add that both Paul Federn and Else Pappenheim, who knew Pötzl in the 1930s, claimed he was no committed Nazi. But Pötzl's 16 May 1945 "personalblatt," available at the Archiv der Universität Wien, revealed he was an "Anwärter" of the NDSAP from September 1938 until July 1943.

17. S. Freud, quoted in Karl Fallend, *Sonderlinge Träumer Senstitive: Psychoanalyse auf dem Weg zur Institution und Profession,* Veröffentlichungen des Ludwig-Boltman-Institutes für Geschichte und Gesellschaft (Vienna: n.p., 1995), Band 26, ftn. no. 6, 364.

18. Also, Paul Federn remarked that Pötzl remained helpful and friendly to the Freudians throughout the 1930s. Federn Interview, Vienna.

19. See Frankl, *Logotherapie und Existenzanalyse* (Munich: Piper, 1987).

20. Klingberg, *When Life Calls Out to Us,* 66.

21. Frankl, *Was nicht in meinen,* 52.

22. Ibid.

23. Ibid., 47.

24. See ibid., 48.

25. Gardner, *Red Vienna and the Golden Age,* 150.

26. See Rudolf Allers, *Essays in Order* (London: Sheed and Ward, 1932), v. Allers's essay was on psychology and the Catholic faith. Also in 1940 Allers wrote *What's Wrong With Freud: A Critical Study of Freudian Psychoanalysis* (Fort Collins, Co.: Roman Catholic Books, 1941).

27. Frankl recalled using Heidegger in the adult education classes he taught. Corrigan Interview (GTU).

28. Frankl, *Was nicht in meinen,* 42.

29. The literature on the Heidegger controversy is immense. The best introduction is Richard Wolin, *The Heidegger Controversy* (New York: Columbia University Press, 1991). Also see Richard Wolin, *The Politics of Being: The Political Thought of Martin Heidegger* (New York: Columbia University Press, 1990). The controversy rages on with the recent publication of Emmanuel Faye, *Heidegger: The Introduction of Nazism into Philosophy in Light of the Unpublished Seminars of 1933-1935* (New Haven: Yale University Press, 2011).

30. Although, as Jeffrey Herf, *Reactionary Modernism* (Cambridge, Mass.: Harvard University Press, 1984), and Zeev Sternhell, *Neither Left nor Right: Fascist Ideology in France,* trans., David Maisel (Berkeley: University of California Press, 1986) have shown, the political configuration of fascism is beyond the traditional categorization of left and right.

31. Frankl, "Selbstmordprophylaxe und Jugendberatung," *Münchner Medizinische Wochenschrift* (4 October 1929): 1675.

32. Rudy Koshar argues that "[r]ejecting mass parties as the sole or dominant instruments of national political representation, many volunteer organizations used apoliticism ... to build an antisocialist movement, an effort which Nazi agitators eventually exploited by mobilizing diverse social networks." *Social Life, Local Politics and Nazism: Marburg, 1880-1935* (Chapel Hill: University of North Carolina Press, 1986), xiv.

33. For a compelling description of this situation, see Rabinbach, *Crisis of Austrian Socialism,* especially 59–79.

34. Frankl, "Selbstmordprophylaxe und Jugendberatung," 1675.

35. Frankl, *Was nicht in meinen,* 44.

36. See Frankl, "Wille und Vernunft," *Wiener Medizinische Wochenschrift* no. 13 (1927), in which Frankl reviews Froeschels's book and discusses how Froeschels's therapy, which took psychological factors into account in treating speech maladies, is a useful corrective for Freudian and Adlerian forms of therapy.

37. Frankl, *Was nicht in meinen,* 52.

38. Ibid., 44.

39. Corrigan Interview (GTU). Frankl also repeated this story in Frankl, *Was nicht in meinen,* 36.

40. Frankl claimed that he responded to *Who's Who in America* with the statement "the meaning of [my] life is to help others find the meaning of theirs." Frankl, *Was nicht in meinen,* 106.

41. Frankl, *Was nicht in meinen*, 52. Gerstmann was Jewish and emigrated to the United States in 1938.

42. Gruber, *Red Vienna*, 173.

43. Frankl, "Wirtschaftskrise und Seelenleben vom Standpunkte des Jungendberaters," *Sozialärtliche Rundschau* no. 3 (1933): 44.

44. Frankl, "Wirtschaftskrise und Seelenleben," 43–44.

45. Ibid.

46. Ibid.

47. Ibid., 46.

48. Ibid., 45.

49. Ibid., 46.

50. Bernhard Handlbauer, "The Emigration of the Viennese Individual Psychologists," *The Cultural Exodus from Austria*, ed. Peter Weibel and Friedrich Stadler (Vienna: Loecker Verlag, 1993), 129.

51. On the Heimwehr, see C.E. Edmondson, *The Heimwehr and Austrian Politics, 1918-1936* (Athens, Ga.: University of Georgia Press, 1978). On the Austrian Nazi movement, see Bruce Pauley, *Hitler and the Forgotten Nazis: A History of Austrian National Socialism* (Chapel Hill: University of North Carolina Press, 1981).

52. On the failure of Otto Bauer and the Socialists to adequately respond to the rise of the right and the subsequent spread of communism, see Rabinbach, *Crisis of Austrian Socialism*.

53. Julius Deutsch, Protokoll des sozialdemokratischen Parteitages 1931, abgehalten vom 13. bis 15. Nov. 1931 im Kammersaal in Graz (Vienna: 1931), 13, quoted in Rabinbach, *Crisis of Austrian Socialism*, 73.

54. Gardner, *Red Vienna and the Golden Age*, 136. Also, Handlbauer, "The Emigration of the Viennese Individual Psychologists," 128.

55. The change did affect Frankl's recreational mountain climbing. When the regime dissolved the Socialist-oriented Naturfreunde, Frankl joined the non-Aryan section of the rightwing alpine club, Donauland, under Rudolf Reif. See Frankl, "Der Alpinismus und die Pathologie des Zeitgeistes," *OEAV-Mitteilungen* (June 1987). Also, R. Amstädter, *Der Alpinismus* (Vienna: WUV-Universitätsverlag, 1996), 284, 554–555. On the makeup of Donauland, see *Alpenvereinsjahrbuch Berg 1992* (Herausgegeben vom Deutschen und Österreichishen Alpenverein, Munich und Innsbruck), 280.

56. See Gruber, *Red Vienna*, 161–162.

57. Frankl, commentary in *Sexualnot und Sexualreform: : Verhandlungen der Weltliga für Sexualreform. IV Congress. Abgehalten zu Wien vom 16. bis 23. September 1930*, ed. Herbert Steiner (Vienna: Elbemuehl-Verlag, 1931), 114–115.

58. Frankl, *Was nicht in meinen*, 48.

59. Gruber, *Red Vienna*, 161–162.

60. On the significance of February 1927 for Reich, see his autobiographical sketch, Wilhelm Reich, *People in Trouble* (New York: McGraw-Hill, 1976). For Reich's relationship to the Socialists and the youth movement, see Rabinbach, *Crisis of Austrian Socialism*, 66–70.

61. Frankl, "Aus der Praxis Jungendberatung," *Psychotherapeutic Praxis* no. 7 (1935): 155–156.

62. Ibid., 159.

63. Frankl, "Erotic Problems of Modern Youth," in *Viktor E. Frankl: Frühe Schriften 1923-1942*, 139.

64. Ibid., 140–141.

65. Ibid., 141.

66. Zeev Sternhell, *The Birth of Fascist Ideology*, trans. David Maisel (Princeton, N.J.: Princeton University Press, 1994), 5.

67. Frankl, "Aus der Praxis der Jugendberatung," 159.

The Third Viennese
School of Psychotherapy

It might have made a difference had psychotherapists ... said "nein"
or at least "ohne mich" ("without me"). And even had such actions
not stopped or slowed Hitler, this would have been the right thing to
do. Hardly any psychotherapists did this right thing ...
—Geoffrey Cocks, *Psychotherapy in the Third Reich*

Frankl's articles in 1935 and 1937 were his last significant writings on youth counseling. Although the volunteer counselors handled over two thousand cases a year, the venture apparently dissolved since it was never connected with a formal institution. There may have been a connection between the Austrian political crisis and the project's dissolution, but Frankl never made such a claim.

Nevertheless, the political difficulties surely affected Frankl. From 1933, until the *Anschluss* with Germany in 1938, Austria was governed by a Christian authoritarian regime. After Engelbert Dollfuss was murdered by the Nazis on the 25 July 1934, the Austrian minister of education, Kurt Schuschnigg, became the leader of the Patriotic Front. Schuschnigg essentially continued Dollfuss's policies of creating an "authoritarian, Christian and German" corporate state, and tried to maintain, with the support of Italy, Austrian independence. In 1936, the July agreement with Germany supposedly achieved this goal. This pact guaranteed Germany's recognition of Austrian independence, promised non-intervention in Austria's internal affairs, and acknowledged that Austria would conduct a foreign policy parallel to Germany's. As the last point suggested, in the long run the agreement only furthered German penetration into

Austria, especially since the agreement suppressed all anti-Nazi propaganda. Finally, Italian support was lost with the formation of the Rome/Berlin Axis in 1937, and the fate of an independent Austria was sealed.[1]

During these tumultuous times Frankl had an institutional base because after completing his residency he worked at the psychiatric hospital Am Steinhof from 1933 until 18 November 1937.[2] On a personal level, Klingberg describes how Frankl's experience at Am Steinhof made him profoundly homesick and lonely since the hospital was on the outskirts of Vienna and he rarely was able to visit his parents.[3] Perhaps it was this loneliness that led Frankl to engage in a bit of promiscuous behavior with the nurses at Am Steinhof that he later regretted.[4] His behavior was also at odds with the values he affirmed in his articles on youth counseling. Frankl's sullen mood was also likely colored by rise of both fascism and anti-Semitism as dominant features of Austria in the 1930s.

Since the civil war in 1934 led to Austrofascism, and the Socialist Party was outlawed, the political options for Viennese Jews became extremely limited. The most obvious alignment for Jews was to support the authoritarian, Christian government. The choice was clear, because the most likely successor to the Austrian corporate state was not social democracy, but National Socialism. Thus, "Jews of nearly all political shades" dissociated from the Socialists and declared "their loyalty to the new Austrian state and the Fatherland Front. One might term such behavior opportunistic ... but it was merely pragmatic."[5]

Frankl's political allegiances are not explicit. We know he became a member of the Fatherland Front on 23 February 1934, and was described as "politically perfect" on 8 February 1937 in a survey of Fatherland Front party membership. However, it is likely that Frankl's membership in the Front was mandated by his position at the state hospital Am Steinhof. Significantly, the Front's membership survey is the only document in his Gauachten file (these files were created by the Nazi party and described individuals' ideological orientation) in the State Archive in Vienna.[6] It also appears the full documentation is missing because many files were cleansed after the war.

Clearly life was extremely difficult for all Jews in Vienna under Austrofascism. The long tradition of Austrian anti-Semitism reached a new height. For example, Frankl describes numerous anti-Semitic verbal assaults against him while he worked at Am Steinhof. He also claimed that as he became accustomed to these anti-Semitic outbursts from psychotics, he subsequently developed "immunity" when he experienced the rabid anti-Semitism after the *Anschluss*.[7] In interwar Austria anti-Semitism was also institutionalized because the clerical government attempted to remove Jews from social life by segregating schools, excluding Jews from government positions, banks, and insurance companies, and scaling back the educational possibilities of Jewish doctors and attorneys.[8] On the other hand, Schuschnigg also limited overt anti-Semitism in order to differentiate clerical fascism from the underlying secularism and racial anti-Semitism of Nazism. Arguably, this policy may have allowed many

Viennese Jews to repress the peril that from historical hindsight was so close at hand. In addition, Hitler moderated anti-Semitism in the mid 1930s because his policies had not been well received by the majority of Germans. Finally, "the fact that many heads of families in Austria were war veterans, and Hitler had ... treated Jewish veterans less severely ... provided further grounds for encouragement."[9] Many Austrian Jews therefore thought that a Nazi takeover would not present any great new problems. The emigration figures tell the story: "On March 13, 1938, there were 185,246 Jews in Austria, as against 191,458 in 1934"; in the same period, "Viennese Jewry declined from 177,869 to 169,978."[10] However, once the Nazis arrived Jews quickly realized the peril Nazism posed. For instance, when Frankl's lecture was interrupted by an SS man after the *Anschluss*, a stunned Frankl thought to himself, "Could this have happened under Schuschnigg?" He also recalled consoling his mother, who was crying after Schuschnigg bade farewell to the Austrian people in 1938.[11]

One historian remarked "that the Austrian Jews with all the signs of the coming catastrophe around them behaved like ostriches."[12] Even Freud seemed slightly indifferent when he claimed, "the future is uncertain: either a type of Austrian fascism or the swastika. In the latter case we must leave: we are prepared to take a fair amount from local fascism, since it will hardly treat us as bad as its German cousin."[13] Subsequently, the psychoanalysts (the majority of whom were Jewish) "reacted by adopting as an official policy an attitude of political abstinence, accompanied by self-censorship, or they went into exile."[14]

In contrast to the Freudians, Frankl didn't take the path of an "inner exile," and instead made a third attempt at becoming someone of importance. Professionalization and the desire to develop his novel form of psychotherapy led Frankl to become involved with the Nazi psychotherapy movement.

Catching the Wave

At Steinhof, Frankl was in charge of the pavilion for suicidal women.[15] He also compiled a short book (that apparently was never published), entitled *... und Narren reden die Wahrheit* (... and Fools Speak the Truth). The book consisted mostly of comical phrases that his patients relayed to him in response to his questions. Frankl claimed that this experience taught him that "2+2=4 even when a paralytic states it."[16]

During this period Frankl also participated in the seminar of the Union for Applied Psychopathology and Psychology in Vienna. This seminar was team taught by Dr. Otto Pötzl and Dr. Karl Bühler in the summer and winter semesters of 1935.[17] Frankl's comments from the seminar reveal that he had an interest in the typology of schizophrenia. He reflected on the relationship between "sleepy-thought and dream-thought." The former, Frankl connected to

schizophrenia "as the insufficiency of thought" or "half-fabricated thought."[18] In a sense this echoed his claim in 1926 that intellectuals were guilty of a hypertrophy of thought; now he suggested that schizophrenics were victims of an insufficiency of thought.

Frankl also contributed to the typology of schizophrenia in an article published in 1935. The article was entitled "A Frequent Phenomenon of Schizophrenia," and the frequent phenomenon was something Frankl labeled the "corrugator phenomenon." These were the facial twitchings, or "sheet-lighting," that appeared uncontrollably on the countenances of schizophrenics. Frankl's article consisted of a brief description, and six photographic plates that documented the phenomenon, but to the untrained eye it is difficult to see the effect.[19]

The article also reveals that one of Frankl's superiors at Steinhof was "Dr. Alfred Mauczka, Director: Landes-Sanitätsrat."[20] We know that Mauczka became an "Anwärter" (candidate) of the National Socialist Party on 15 April 1940 and was a "Kriegsteilnehmer" (war participant).[21] The fact that Mauczka became a Nazi is not surprising because there were over eighty "illegal" Nazis working at Steinhof from 1933 to 1938.[22] But Mauczka was apparently not a rabid anti-Semite because he allowed Frankl to conduct a Kol Nidre on the eve of Yom Kippur in 1935 for Jewish patients at Am Steinhof. Frankl published a description of the event in the Newsletter of the Association of Jewish Physicians.[23] The ceremony was led by Rabbi Bela Fischer and according to Frankl's description the celebration was quite moving for all participants. Even some of the catatonic patients were impacted, and Frankl suggests that the ceremony doubled as a form of therapy to reconnect the psychotic with the world. For example, Frankl quotes one patient's description that "it was so dignified and beautiful, a real blessing ... for us at Steinhof."[24]

Since Steinhof was a harbor for many illegal Nazis and anti-Semitism was pervasive, Frankl's ability to persuade Mauczka to allow the ceremony is admirable and surprising. It is also emblematic of Frankl's willingness to push boundaries, in this case using religion as a form of therapy, as well as holding a Jewish ceremony in a state institution under Austrofascism.

Frankl was apparently open to all forms of religious expression. Klingberg describes how he had a "broad appreciation of religion" and "moved confidently among people of different religions."[25] Based on his religious openness, Klingberg also describes how Frankl hosted Cardinal Innitzer when he made a visit to Steinhof. That Frankl was willing to entertain Cardinal Innitzer might appear somewhat surprising since Innitzer was a fervent supporter of both Austrofascism and the *Anschluss* with Germany. As a Jewish doctor working at a state institution within the rubric of the Austrofascist public sphere, Frankl was undoubtedly confronting personal and professional challenges.

Along with being Frankl's superior at Steinhof, Mauczka was also "Stellvertreter" (second in command) of the Austrian General Doctors Society for

Psychotherapy and Mental Hygiene founded in 1936. This was the Austrian "Landesgruppe" (branch) of the German psychotherapy movement in Austria.[26]

For some readers the very conception of psychotherapy and Nazism seems antithetical, but Geoffrey Cocks's pioneering work on psychotherapy in the Third Reich demonstrated the reality of Nazi psychotherapy. And, as we shall see, the German psychotherapy movement was both crude and ideologically driven, and yet also aspired for revolutionary innovation.[27]

After the Nazi seizure of power, the German General Medical Society for Psychotherapy was formed in September of 1933. The international organization was headed by Carl Jung, and the German contingent was led by the cousin of Reich Marshall Hermann Göring, Matthias Heinrich Göring. The purpose of the society was "to assemble in the spirit of the National Socialist German government all physicians who are motivated by the belief that the doctor in every treatment must consider the whole personality of the patient so that he does not ignore the person's soul; above all, those who are willing to acquire and practice a psychotherapeutic medicine in the spirit of a National Socialist world-view."[28]

Under Göring, an institutional structure was developed with the proclaimed goals of unifying the different schools of psychotherapy, developing a form of therapy that considers the whole personality of patients, and ridding the science of Jewish influence. In 1936, the German Institute for Psychological Research and Psychotherapy (also known as the Göring Institute) was established. The Institute survived and gained quasi-governmental status by 1945.[29]

The Vienna branch of the Göring Institute (I use the term Göring Institute as shorthand for the German dominance over the affairs of the *International General Medical Society for Psychotherapy*) was established in March 1936, and was disbanded in March 1938 after the *Anschluss*. Although Jews could be members, they could not hold office or present papers.[30] Frankl's involvement in the Austrian branch was certainly curtailed because he was Jewish, but nevertheless he was a commentator on all four seminars conducted by the Austrian branch from 1936 to 1937.[31]

Anti-Semitism was problematic for the Göring Institute because most of the best minds in psychology were Jewish. The anti-Semitic tension was exemplified by the fact that Frankl's teacher, Rudolf Allers, who was a Jewish convert to Catholicism,[32] was the editor of the book review section of the institute's official journal, *Zentralblatt für Psychotherapie*, from 1933 to 1936. When Carl Jung was questioned about his involvement with the German psychology movement,[33] he defended himself by claiming he had allowed Allers, a Jew, to stay on as editor of the review section of the *Zentralblatt*. Jung also inserted a circular letter in the December 1934 *Zentralblatt*, declaring that the "international society is neutral as to politics and creed."[34] Perhaps Aller's actions, and Jung's circular, led Frankl to overlook the Göring Institute's blatant anti-Semitism and

political agenda. But after 1936, just as Frankl began his participation in the Austrian branch, Allers no longer reviewed books for the *Zentralblatt*.

Significantly, both Oswald Schwarz and Rudolf Allers participated in the seminars, along with a number of other distinguished Viennese psychiatrists.[35] The seminar members and the subsequent content of the discussions contained no blatant Nazi agenda. However, Erwin Stransky did present the transparently anti-Semitic "Race and Psychotherapy" in 1936. Stransky, Jewish by birth, converted to Christianity in adulthood. Cocks summarized the paper and had these reasoned comments about it:

> whatever Stransky's unconscious motives, his paper attempted to deal with the questions of the therapeutic alliance between Aryan and Jew and the "Aryanization" of psychoanalytic theory. He concluded that the documented successes of such racially mixed doctor patient relationships were due to the "deghettoized" or "ariotropic" nature of the Jewish physician, or to the natural social subordination of the Jewish patient, both of which derived their experiences in the predominant Aryan racial culture. As for the utility of Freudian and Adlerian doctrine, Stransky cited the work of Jung, Göring, Künkel, and others as proof that in the proper racial hands even Jewish thought could be beneficial to non-Jewish practitioners and patients.[36]

The crudity of Stransky's acrobatic denial of the importance of Jews and their denigration reflects the Nazi conundrum: being outwardly anti-Semitic yet relying on "Jewish," i.e., Freudian and Adlerian, psychology. Also, since Stransky's paper was published by the in the *Zentralblatt* in 1937, his work is one confirmation of Cocks's assessment that intellectual production in the field of psychotherapy during the Third Reich was of poor quality. There is no record of Frankl's comments.[37]

Riding the Wave

Frankl published one article in the *Zentralblatt für Psychotherapie*, entitled "On the Spiritual Problem in Psychotherapy."[38] In 1995, two of Frankl's main disciples, Joseph Fabry and Elisabeth Lukas, described the article in these terms: "1938: The first fundamental scientific publication by Viktor E. Frankl is printed in the most important professional journal in the German Language, the *Zentralblatt für Psychotherapie...*"[39] The *Zentralblatt* was certainly the central journal in the German language at the time, but the date cited was wrong. The article is often referenced as being published in 1938, not 1937.[40] However, it appears that this misdating occurs because only six issues of the journal appeared in 1937–1938, and the articles were all bound together.

"On the Spiritual Problem in Psychotherapy" presented Frankl's novel vision of therapy that he had developed while counseling youth. On a theoretical level, Frankl's goal was to fully articulate the vision of psychology that originated with his critique of Freud and Adler. Coincidentally, his theoretical vision

shared the proclaimed goal of the Göring Institute: unification of the differing branches of psychology.[41] Frankl argued that Freud and Adler were the "great historical representatives" of the "observable trends in the history of the human mind." According to Frankl, Adler evolved from Freud "out of ontological necessity." Based on his ontological reading of the Freudian and Adlerian conception of consciousness, Frankl concluded that the "deepest foundations of existence" were "to be I, (I-being) which means 'being conscious' and 'being responsible.'"[42] He also discussed the theoretical differences between Freud and Adler over the genesis of neurotic symptoms. (As mentioned, neuroses for Freud stemmed from trauma and repression, while Adler emphasized the arrangement character of neurotic symptoms as attempts to avoid responsibility.) According to Frankl, in psychoanalysis, "the 'I' as a conscious being is somehow constrained (eingeschränkt) in the unfolding of neurosis, while, in an approach informed by individual psychology, a reduction in 'being responsible' occurs."[43] Frankl therefore used the Freudian and Adlerian conceptions of neuroses to establish what he considered to be the deepest foundations of existence. Then Frankl dismissed Freud's and Adler's "so-called" differences and claimed that their conceptions were complementary "anthropological formulas."

Frankl also criticized Freud and Adler by claiming that their anthropological perspective united them on an even deeper, structural level. He thus accused both visions of being "guilty" of reductionism and a limitation of phenomenological reality. Thus, "psychoanalysis, in the final analysis, only acknowledges libidinal things." In contrast, "individual psychology reduces the mental world, since ... neurotic forms are represented as unreal, as a means to an end, in the sense ... of an arrangement."[44] According to Frankl, Freudianism was shortsighted because there was more to the content of neuroses than just libido. His criticism of Adlerianism was a restatement of his claim in 1926 that neurotic symptoms were not only means to an end (arrangements), but were primarily "immediate expressions." Thus when Frankl stated "2+2=4 even if a paralytic says it," he was arguing against the reductionism in the Freudian and Adlerian perspectives that did not recognize the "authentic," or justifiable grounds of neurotic behavior. With this conception Frankl asserted the genuineness of the neurotics "being in the world."

In Frankl's ontology, the Adlerian view of subjectivity represented a stage beyond the Freudian notion of the ego. If the goal of Freudianism was to adapt the instincts to the reality principle, Adlerian therapy "arrived at a courageous arrangement of reality by the individual 'I,' which went beyond individual adaptation."[45] Adlerianism was therefore reconfigured not only as an ontological necessity of Freudianism, but "valued" as an assertion of a "courageous individual."

By framing Freudianism and Adlerianism as stages in an unfolding of both psychological theory and subjectivity, Frankl could then position his own work as the revolutionary next stage in the development of psychotherapy. "If we

now ask whether, besides adaptation and arrangement, there is not to say a further dimension into which man has to advance, if we want him to become healthy again. Or, we ask ourselves what last category we have to include into our image of man in order to do justice to his mental reality—that is where we arrive at the point of view that it might be the category of fulfillment, of finding meaning."[46]

But immediately a problem arose. Since one could argue that contained under the rubric of "arrangement" was the struggle to give meaning and ultimately value to life, it was not readily apparent exactly how this new dimension of meaning represented a category that was different from individual psychology. Apparently, Frankl was dissatisfied with the "courageous I" that struggled to give meaning and value to life. In order to overcome the lingering relativism of the individualistic "courageous I," Frankl argued the third dimension that psychology must enter was the realm of responsibility. "... while psychoanalysis is focused on the past ... individual psychology essentially has recourse to the timelessness -something beyond time- that is absolute ... [or] an objectiveness of values. Or, if individual psychology sets the will ... against mere necessity, so we will still have to ask: What about the third category of 'Sollens' (should, obligation, responsibility)."[47]

For Frankl, individual psychology opened the way to an absolute objectiveness of values, but failed to cover the full distance. In attempting to cover that distance, and give a final resolution to his struggle with meaning, Frankl called for a third category of responsibility. Therefore, the crystallization of Frankl's new therapy aspired to solve the crisis of meaning by fulfilling "man's highest possible values."

To support his call for focusing on the fulfillment of values, Frankl referenced the philosopher of phenomenology Max Scheler. Then he tied his claims directly to the work of the Göring Institute. He cited two of the more politically moderate members, the Adlerian Fritz Künkel, who focused on issues of community, and the psychiatrist and neuropathologist I.H. Schultz, who was a founding member.[48] Frankl quoted Schultz's description of a realm of "higher existential values," stating that "[he or she] who is at home there is able to suffer without becoming ill or neurotic." Frankl attempted to give voice to Schultz's vision by stating there was a need for a psychotherapist to "incorporate these 'higher' strata of human existence ... and in contrast to a 'depth psychologist' would "merit the name 'height psychologist'..." This was to be an "existential analysis" that went "beyond the realm of the psychic," and acknowledged "the whole of human existence in all its depth and height."[49] Frankl apparently aspired to be both a "height psychologist" and to provide the theoretical underpinnings for this new form of psychology.

But this animated passage calling for a new form of therapy that focused on the whole of human existence was immediately followed by a distancing from the Göring Institute's pronounced mission of building National Socialism.

Thus, he stated: "Of course, there are those psychotherapists who find it easy ... being [both] a physician and ideological leader to consciously devote their psychological practice to the service of their Catholic convictions or political value system. But it is exactly here where there is danger ... of transgressing purely medical practice ... [by] the 'octroi' of the physician's personal world-view onto the sick person."[50]

Even at this point of resistance, however, there was an underlying element of ambiguity. That is, Frankl's act of resistance also contained a component of accommodation because he referenced Göring Institute members to support his argument. Thus, he used the "leading thinkers" of the Göring Institute to support his claim for a psychotherapy that avoided imposing world views on patients. "... for quite some time voices of cautions have been raised. One of the leading 'thinkers' of German psychotherapy Hans Prinzhorn ... asked the question 'in the name of what kind of authority' ... Weizsäcker reminds us that psychotherapists should 'not create human beings, but make them possible.' Finally nobody less than Kretschmer warns that the physician might turn into a priest."[51]

Frankl, as well as everyone else, was apparently very aware that psychotherapy could be used to indoctrinate people. And, by citing Prinzhorn, Weizäcker, and Kretschmer[52] against those psychotherapists who found it easy to implement their world view, Frankl was honorably, and one might claim courageously, arguing against the misuse of psychotherapy. For Frankl, the focus on world views, objective values, and responsibility offered the possibility for psychological health, not indoctrination. But attempting to construct a new form of psychotherapy, focused on world views and absolutes, without indoctrination was a difficult task. His problem was also treacherous because under the rubric of the Göring Institute this new therapy obviously could not represent overt opposition to National Socialism. Trapped in a dilemma, Frankl turned to offer a solution, or a way out for the newly emerging psychotherapy.

In attempting to provide direction, Frankl turned to discuss the "the other side" who "demand ... a conscious incorporation of world views and values into psychotherapeutic praxis." He cited I.H. Schultz, Carl Jung, and Kurt Gauger, who directly discussed "the question about the meaning of human existence" as the "question of psychotherapy." They also designated "mental health" as "nothing else but the right answer to the question about the meaning of life."[53] Why Frankl placed Schultz and Jung in the same category as Gauger is not clear. Schultz was clearly a moderate and remained a "candidate" of the NDSAP, while Jung ambiguously claimed his "purpose was a clarification of various teachings, theories, and practices within a political context even though psychotherapy itself had nothing to do with politics."[54] But certainly Kurt Gauger represented "the other side." He was a Nazi ideologue, so intellectually crude that Jung refused to name him managing director of the society. Gauger eventually moderated his positions, but Jung was rightfully "aghast" at Gauger's

book *Politische Medizin*.[55] In response to these demands "from the other side" (Schultz, Jung, and Gauger), Frankl attempted to ground a psychotherapy that was capable of promoting values, and yet did not fall victim to an "octroi of world-views." In order to achieve this, Frankl returned to his fundamental anthropology that placed a sense of responsibility at the heart of human existence. But Frankl's promotion of responsibility as the highest feature of human nature had to avoid the imposition of world views. Frankl therefore turned to discuss the problem of the therapist's authority. He asked: On what grounds could a therapist induce a sense of responsibility in the patient? Frankl was adamant that it was up to the patient, "on his own initiative" to discover to whom, or to what, one should feel responsible. Thus, the therapist should create an attitude of responsibility, not the content. Frankl then provided the solution to the concern that he, along with others—on his side—felt about ideology and psychotherapy. Thus, "… when we allow a person to understand fundamentally that his existence is a matter of responsibility … the implications for him are truly enough, and an unconditional binding force/obligation (Verbindlichkeit) to come to a value laden point of view. In other words, a human being who has become conscious of his responsibility is somehow forced in any case to evaluate things from the vantage point of this very responsibility; but how he values, what kind of value hierarchy he might endorse that is already beyond the influence of the physician."[56]

The focus on imbuing responsibility that would "somehow force" an individual to endorse a value hierarchy seems a somewhat questionable prescription to offer those experiencing mental suffering during the latter 1930s. Nevertheless, Frankl's focus on individual choice was far from what Nazi ideologues would have desired. On the other hand, Frankl's brand of therapy had no way to stand in the path of those therapists who wanted to make Nazi values central. Thus, "binding force" that is "truly enough" to lead the patient to values allowed Frankl's therapy to accommodate the Nazi psychotherapy movement. Perhaps most significant is that the focus on "Sollens," (responsibility/obligation) combined with the conception of a "courageous I," mirrored the National Socialist ideology that called for confronting neuroses with the same intellectual armament: will and responsibility.[57]

In the end, Frankl hedged even further because he provided the "direction" to the sense of responsibility. According to Frankl, the patient was to decide, "to whom" and "for what" one would feel responsible. The patient was also to decide what values he turned to "with devotion," from which "direction" he found "meaning in life," and which "tasks constitute fulfillment."[58] Overlooking the political implications of deriving value from "devotion" and "direction," this formula avoided consideration of the relationship between mental health and issues of guilt, repression, deference, and identification with authority figures, etc.

Techniques

Frankl continued by reconfirming the solution to life's meaning that he developed when "pioneering existentialism" in his first public lecture at the age of eighteen. When the patient pondered "the question of the meaning of life," Frankl claimed, "we have primarily to bring to his consciousness, that, ultimately, he is not the person posing the question but the person this question is directed at ..."[59] This existential solution placed full responsibility for life's meaning on the shoulders of the individual. At its core, height psychology was really a heightening of responsibility by directing the individual to assume responsibility for "answering to" life.

Frankl cited numerous examples of how one could "bring the realization of responsibility as a foundational feature of human existence closer to a common person's comprehension." One strategy was: "... to point out ... that human beings are alone with their destiny and nobody is able to take this burden away from them. The task to fulfill is unique and exclusive. From this consciousness of the specific task ... follows automatically the consciousness of responsibility vis-a-vis this task, indeed, almost the feeling of a special mission."[60]

Another was to heighten the consciousness of mortality: "... when we ask him to imagine that he has arrived at the end of his life and was about to write his own biography and he would just this very moment stop at that chapter which deals with the present and it would now ... be totally in his hands to make corrections ... the parable would force him, to act and live according to the complete feeling derived from his responsibility."[61]

When Frankl succeeded in making the patient realize his essential responsibility in "being there," there were "still many apparent counter-arguments and routes of escaping from freedom." These attempted escapes were philosophical. One example is the argument that death or the limits of individual possibility made life meaningless. Frankl countered these arguments with the existential notion that only through realization of temporal finality was life given any possibility of meaning. "Hence it is death which gives meaning to life and our 'being there' as something unique."[62] The problem of individual imperfection and the subsequent fragmentary character of life were solved by the absorption of the individual into a "higher whole." "As in a mosaic where each little part is indispensable only by means of, and in so far as, no other has an equivalent form and color, the individual in the community becomes an absolute valuable member in a higher whole. (In this way community, beyond the bond of belonging can be justified as something to be achieved, as an essential task of the human being.)"[63]

In Frankl's view the fulfillment of meaning was ultimately achieved by the individual's absorption in the community "beyond the bond of belonging." Accepting responsibility and subsuming oneself in the community was Frankl's solution to the philosophical problem of individual alienation, and the absence

of "Meaning." Frankl exemplified his point by claiming "in an organism built to the principle of a division of labor, the loss of omnipotence is the important price paid for the highly differentiated cell within the whole."[64] Although Frankl was recognizing individual differences, the claim for a "loss of omnipotence" would sit rather well with the Nazi insistence that the interests of the individual be subordinated to the community.

In Frankl's existential therapy, the patient was vitalized by being made conscious of his unique individuality. This was a "heightened responsibility" that was ultimately anchored in the individual's confrontation with death. Frankl also attempted to impute this sense of responsibility into the "ill" person. Once the person acknowledged responsibility, he could then achieve mental grounding and stability and be "fulfilled" in the community. Frankl was now articulating a purely existential perspective on the origins of a meaningful life.

Frankl also outlined three situations when existential analysis appeared to be indicated: (1) intellectual types, who were mentally unstable and wrestling with the meaning of life; (2) neurotics who were strong enough and could live up to discussions of their world view in order to unburden themselves of less severe symptoms; and (3) those cases in which suffering stemmed from an unsurpassable fact, such as a disability or unchangeable economic misery.[65] In these cases the issue of values became central to the cure. Frankl also articulated what he considered the three possibilities within the human condition for realizing values. Frankl claimed that "these people" had to be reminded that a "responsible life" is not always about "the creative realization of values" or "fulfillment through experience." Instead there is "a last category of values … designated as attitudinal values" which depend on how a person reacts "to lasting and unavoidable circumstances" or "matters of destiny."[66]

The focus on attitudinal values is the foundation stone of logotherapy. The stoic individualism of this perspective came across when Frankl claimed successful therapy often occurred when doctors appealed "to the morality of the sick person who … no longer wanted to let the doctor depict him as a tyrant or a coward afraid of life." Instead, the patient with "the last quantity of energy left, transcends the symptom."[67] Significantly, Frankl's appeal to heroic individualism to combat neurosis was very close to the view of the Freudian Carl Müller-Braunschweig. In 1933 Müller-Braunschweig tried to show the compatibility between psychoanalysis and the ideals of Nazism by defending therapy "as a technique which in proper hands transformed weaklings and asocials into heroic and productive members of society."[68] In both of these visions a patient was transformed by the therapeutic process into a heroic individual.

To summarize, the intellectual approach of Frankl's article was to make a tactical accommodation of Nazi psychotherapy. Frankl positioned himself as representing "one side" of the movement and then offered a solution to the intellectual division he perceived within the movement. Frankl's height psy-

chology, which criticized the reductionism of both Freud and Adler and also proclaimed to synthesize the schools, fit neatly within the central goals of the Göring Institute.[69] On the other hand the Göring Institute (and Nazism in general) was in a phase of political moderation at this point, and wanted to create a more pragmatic and less ideological science. Frankl's call for no "octroi of world-views" seemed to fit the bill. But Frankl's "height psychology" certainly did not contest the heart of Nazi ideology. Instead, his central focus on will and responsibility to confront neurosis mirrored the central components of the Nazi psychotherapy movement.

Frankl was surely not interested in promoting National Socialism, but surprisingly, he was not overtly in opposition and instead felt his brand of therapy offered a possible direction for the Göring Institute. As a Jew, Frankl was in an obvious personal contradiction (and perhaps eventual danger) promoting these ideas within the movement. It is therefore hard, perhaps impossible, to fully understand his decisions and activity. Apparently, he wanted to develop his vision of "height psychology" and viewed the Göring Institute as an opportunity to do so. It is also likely that Frankl turned to the Göring Institute to promote his brand of analysis because it was literally the only game in town. Since he had only one year left on his contract with Am Steinhof, and was beginning to develop a private practice, even a loose affiliation with the Göring Institute probably represented both support and professional opportunity. There was also complicity between Frankl's ideas and the Göring Institute's goals. Frankl's claims about Freud, Adler, and height psychology revealed he took the project to "consider the whole personality of the patient" earnestly. This raises the question: since neither Frankl nor society was forced into publishing his work, what exactly was the "intellectual" substance of the relationship between Frankl and the Göring Institute?

Cocks has argued that the society's goals as written in the statutes, "were essentially a protective device composed of rhetoric" and "there transpired no battle, much less a victory, for ideas in Nazi Germany ..."[70] In general this may be true, but the case of Frankl seems to illustrate that the statutes of the Institute had significance and that there were realistic goals. At least for Frankl, there were issues of intellectual substance to be debated. Since Frankl was Jewish, that he was able to promote his ideas in the *Zentralblatt* can be attributed to the umbrella of the Göring name, the Institute's "concern of appealing to foreign scientific opinion," and the need to "show that 'real international science' was still alive in Germany."[71] Apparently, for both the Göring Institute and Frankl there was a commitment to, and a perceived substance in, the ideas. They both took the *risk* of having his work published. What the Institute saw in Frankl's article is difficult to fathom.[72] But apparently Frankl saw a forum for promoting his own novel brand of therapy. It also appears that Frankl viewed the thinkers of the Institute as having a similar focus and goals. He therefore thought he

could mobilize the Institute toward his own peculiar view that focused on world views without imposing them.

Obviously the intellectual project of providing a "psychotherapy of world views" based on "responsibility" within a fascist state, which was mobilizing (in Germany) in a totalitarian direction, was problematic. Some would argue that Frankl's decision to confront and mediate the Nazi attempt to politicize psychotherapy was profoundly courageous. Others might argue he appeared profoundly naïve at best, deluded and opportunistic at worst. Whatever one thinks about Frankl's actions it appears Frankl desired to resolve the ideological tensions between the science of psychotherapy and Nazism/fascism. His solution was to claim that a world view could serve as a therapy, but psychotherapy had to avoid imposing world views. Overall his actions appear as a *tactical accommodation* of Nazi psychotherapy.

On the Crest

On 30 January 1938 Frankl published "Appraising Psychiatry" in *Der christliche Ständestaat*. The date and choice of journal were significant. *Der christliche Ständestaat* was founded by the Catholic philosopher Dietrich von Hildebrand. The journal promoted the Austrian authoritarian state but was against any form of collectivism, especially National Socialism and Bolshevism.[73] In January of 1938, with the *Anschluss* at hand,[74] Frankl turned to this journal to promote his "height psychology" in Austria.

The article reflected the same intertwining of resistance and tactical accommodation that marked Frankl's contribution to the *Zentralblatt*. Frankl began by reiterating the claim that psychoanalysis has for a long time become "outmoded" by other forms of therapy. He then argued that there was a need for a reorientation of psychotherapy that took "spiritual suffering" seriously, and that therefore included discussion of world views in psychotherapeutic work. To support this redirection Frankl cited Jung's statement that "neurosis is 'the suffering of a soul that has not found meaning.'" Frankl also referenced another influential and leading member of the Göring Institute, Leonard Seif. Seif was an Adlerian, and he held that the task of psychotherapy centered on "forming a vital community (Lebensgemeinschaft), a 'we' relationship."[75] Seif, although never a Nazi Party member, was a founding member of the German General Medical Society, a member of the NDSAP Physicians League, and, like Jung, internationally recognized. Frankl cited Seif's claim that "'the starting point and aim of the community work (Arbeitsgemeinschaft) between the doctor and patient to cure a neurosis is the question of the meaning of life.'"[76] Frankl also connected his aspiration to focus on world views in psychotherapy with the work of other leading thinkers of the Göring Institute. In his call for a focus on world views, he claimed:

We can see for ourselves, by randomly sampling a few relevant writings: Just like among the modern authors, who promote within psychotherapeutic work an expansion in world-view, as we described it above, there are those who represent a certain tendency—and in the realm of caring for the sick—also advocate it. I confine myself to short examples and quotations. Karl Häberlin for instance, ("The importance of Ludwig Klages and Hans Prinzhorn for Psychotherapy") writes: "Thus Psychotherapy comes to the service of the powers of life ... that life and our value of leadership remains, so that the spirit is maintained in life's decline." Also one of the leading Reichdeutschen psychotherapists Gauger, is of a similar interpretation. The meaning of life is not different from life itself. (Gauger, "Political Medicine".) Another, Prof. M.H. Göring, finally spoke openly there of ... "the 'German General Universal Doctor's Society for Psychotherapy' ... had the task ... to bring together ... above all ... those doctors, that are willing to acquire and practice psychotherapy in spirit of the National Socialist world-view.[77]

As with his article in 1937, Frankl immediately followed this passage with the claim that psychotherapy had to avoid imposing world views on patients. Nevertheless, Frankl cited these figures in a neutral fashion, as representing a new trend that is advocated. Essentially then, he was publically promoting some of the central ideas and figures of the German Psychotherapy movement in Austria. Given the editorial position of the journal and Frankl's continuing criticism of imposing world views in therapy, his actions could be viewed as courageous resistance. On the other hand, as the article was written on the eve of the *Anschluss*, it could be argued that Frankl was positioning himself to promote his particular vision of "height psychology." That is, by calling for a focus on world views in psychotherapy, and supported by his conviction that this tendency was represented by the Göring Institute, Frankl apparently thought he could lead this new trend of "height psychology" in Austria.

In the article, Frankl cited three central figures of the Göring Institute: Häberlin, Gauger, and Göring. For clarity, it is worth taking a closer look at the passages from which Frankl quoted. Carl Häberlin was a charter member of the German General Medical Society, while Matthias Heinrich Göring was the director. As mentioned, Kurt Gauger was the greatest ideologue of Nazi psychotherapy, but his political fanaticism kept him estranged from the center of power. A cursory summation of the ideas presented in the works Frankl cited uncovers the unsavory aspects of the German Psychotherapy movement.

Häberlin was a doctor at a sanitarium in Bad Nauheim and he joined the Nazi party along with the Nazi physician's league in 1933. The article by Häberlin that Frankl quoted from was summarized by Cocks in these terms: "Häberlin saw the thought of Prinzhorn and that of the philosopher/graphologist Ludwig Klages as the foundation on which a Germanic psychology and psychotherapy could be built. He used both to support that the Germanic triad—of life, blood, and people—was superior to the Western ideal of freedom, equality and brotherhood."[78]

The tone and style of Häberlin's piece was nationalistic and anti-modern, but Frankl quoted from a seemingly innocuous passage. Closer analysis reveals

that Frankl also quoted rather selectively. The first statement, "Thus Psychotherapy comes to the service of the powers of life," was taken from page fifty, after a long paragraph celebrating a "biocentric" ideal that overturned the supposed social leveling of Freudian psychology. The second half of the quote, (presented as a continuation of the first) was taken from page forty-two and was in reference to Ludwig Klages's cultural vision.[79]

Frankl also quoted a rather innocuous passage from Kurt Gauger's *Politische Medizin*. Gauger's work was a theoretically simplistic but rabidly National Socialist call for a "German psychotherapy." In May of 1934, Gauger presented the work to the General Medical Society to promote a National Socialist revolution in medical psychology. The substance of his vision was a radical condemnation of Freud and the materialism of Western civilization.[80] Last, Frankl cited M.H. Göring, who was the head of the German General Medical Society. The passage from Göring was excerpted from the first paragraph of the society's statutes. As mentioned, after citing Göring Frankl immediately began qualifying his affirmation of the Göring Institute's focus on world views. Along with referencing his own article in the *Zentralblatt*, Frankl cited Wladimir Eliasberg. Eliasberg was Jewish and had fled to Vienna in 1933 after he had resigned from the General Medical Society when Jews were forbidden to be executives. Frankl cited Eliasberg's claim that it was not the therapist's task to choose values for the patient, much less to "push meanings down the throat of the patient."[81] Eliasberg's argument echoes Frankl's admonition to avoid an "octroi of world-views." Also, in a debate over the role of the psychotherapy and state policy, Eliasberg, "who left Germany in 1933, soon warned from Vienna that a profession had a responsibility to impose standards on state policy, and not vice versa."[82] But Frankl's "tactical accommodation" of Nazi ideology was subtly different from Eliasberg's affirmation of a policy of imposing standards on the state. In Frankl's therapy of imbuing responsibility, the choice of whether to embrace a political or religious ideology was left to the patient. In Eliasberg's view, the essential issue was to maintain the autonomy of therapeutic practice from state intervention. On this issue Frankl remained neutral, and apparently he thought he could get along with the movement. But it is also very clear that Frankl was not enthusiastic about Nazism, and likely his accommodation was a matter of professional opportunism. His critical tactics and qualifications reveal that although he apparently saw professional and intellectual possibilities in the Nazi psychotherapy movement, he was by no means taken in or deluded by Nazism.

The tendency that led Frankl toward the German psychology movement is also reminiscent of his relationship to both Freud and Adler. Once again, he was attempting to position himself within a psychological school. This time, Frankl had matured and was therefore promoting his own vision of psychotherapy. The difficulty was that he was attempting to promote his new therapy in a movement that was ultimately ideologically buttressed in anti-Semitism. Frankl

was therefore necessarily limited in his affirmation of the Göring Institute's agenda. Nevertheless, he was clearly positioning himself to be a major player. His focus on will and responsibility mirrored the main ideas of the movement in much the same fashion that his earlier articles reflected the central ideas of Freud and then Adler.

When reflecting on the goals and vision of the Göring Institute, and Frankl's statements and activities, the questions arise: Was Frankl promotion of "height psychology" courageous and heroic resistance to Nazism as his followers argue?[83] Or was he being just opportunistic and thus fulfilling Cocks's conclusion that "... the history of psychotherapy in the Third Reich is not an inspirational tale of advances in sophisticated theory and the alleviation of mental suffering, but rather of a morally and intellectually ambiguous accommodation to the established powers of Nazi Germany, on both an individual and collective level, in pursuit of professional and institutional status"?[84]

Frankl's case seems to fit Cocks's description of a morally ambiguous accommodation to the established powers of Nazi Germany. But it also reveals something more. Frankl's logotherapy has been promoted as an effective way to alleviate suffering. As a youthful Socialist, and a doctor by profession, Frankl undoubtedly exhibited a deep humanism. He apparently believed that he could overcome the reductionist materialism of Freud and Adler by turning to a spiritualized psychotherapy. In 1937, Frankl's solution to nihilism posited an anthropologically grounded responsibility. But, as we have seen, Frankl remained relativistic because he refused to provide content to the sense of responsibility. On to these relativistic grounds Frankl hoped to direct Nazi psychotherapy, which was his tactical accommodation of both Nazi ideology (and we might add Austrofascism). The contradiction here is that it was only from this position of relativism that Frankl could involve himself with the movement in the first place. From historical hindsight his aspirations appear exceptionally naïve. But the case of the humanist Frankl seems to suggest that the spiritualistic third path, taking historical institutional form as under fascism and Nazism, at least initially appeared to represent the possibility of fulfilling the urge for Meaning by overcoming materialism. More than one European intellectual was taken in.

Notes

1. For an excellent in-depth history of these events see Jürgen Gehl, *Austria, Germany, and the Anschluss: 1931-1938* (New York: Oxford University Press, 1963).

2. In the Wien Landes Stadt Archiv there are four references between 1934 and 1938 to Dr. Viktor Frankl. The citations from 1934 (no. 830) and 1935 (no. 1018) are missing, but we can conjecture that the former was his promotion and the latter either a promotion or, more likely, the extension of his contract. From the 1936 citation (no. 1779) we know that Frankl agreed to have his job extended for the "last time" one more year. Thus, on "November 18, 1937 after four years of service," Frankl was let go. See Index of Psychiatric Krankenhaus Baumgartnerhöhe 1934-1938, Wien Landes Stadt Archiv.

3. Klingberg, *When Life Calls Out to Us*, 73.

4. Ibid., 81.

5. Harriet Pass Freidenreich, *Jewish Politics in Vienna: 1918-1938* (Bloomington: Indiana University Press, 1991), 195.

6. See PB 7223 Staatsarchiv,Vienna.

7. See Klingberg, *When Life Calls Out to Us*, 79.

8. For a description of how anti-Semitism, although never an official policy of the corporate state, nevertheless had a widespread effect, see Sylvia Maderegger, *Die Juden im österreichischen Ständestaat 1934-1938* (Vienna: Geyer-Edition, 1973), and Doron Rabinovici, *Eichmann's Jews: The Jewish Administration of Holocaust Vienna, 1938-1945*, trans. Nick Somers (Cambridge: Polity Press, 2011).

9. George Berkley, *Vienna and Its Jews: The Tragedy of Success* (Boston: Madison Books, 1988), 245.

10. Herbert Rosenkranz, "The Anschluss and the Tragedy of Austrian Jewry 1938-1945," in *The Jews of Austria*, ed. Josef Fraenkel (London: Vallentine and Mitchell, 1970), 486.

11. See Frankl, *Was nicht in meinen*, 55.

12. See Berkley, *Vienna and Its Jews*.

13. Freud, quoted in Elke Mühlleitner and Johannes Reichmayr, "The Exodus of Psychoanalysts from Vienna," in Weibel and Stadler, *The Cultural Exodus from Austria*, 111.

14. Ibid., 113.

15. Frankl, *Was nicht in meinen*, 52.

16. Ibid., 53.

17. See *Wiener Medizinische Wochenschrift* no. 32 (1936): 854.

18. Frankl, quoted in Bericht: über die Tätigkeit der seminaistische Arbeitsgemeinschaft zwischen der Wiener psychologischen Schule (Führung Professor Dr. Karl Bühler) und der Wiener psychiatrisch-hirnpathologischen Schule (Führung Professor Dr. Otto Pötzl) im Wintersemester 1934/35. Herausgeber vom Auguste Flach and Karl Theodore Dussik (Vienna: Verlag von Moritz Perles, 1935).

19. Frankl, "Ein häufiges Phänomen bei Schizophrenie," *Zeitschrift für Neurologie und Psychologie* no. 152 (1935): 161–162.

20. Frankl, "Ein haüfiges Phänomen bei Schizophrenie," 161.

21. See Mauczka's file at the Dokumentationsarchiv des österreichischen Widerstandes. Also, Mauczka was involved in the euthanasia program (as "Kriegsteilnehmer" suggests) but his exact role is unclear.

22. See "Die National Socialist Beamtenschaft der Heilanstalt, Am Steinhof," Dokumentationsarchiv des österreichischen Widerstandes, Doc. 4486. (Dolfuss outlawed the NDSAP in the spring of 1933 and it remained illegal until the *Anschluss* in March of 1938.)

23. Frankl, *Frühe Schriften*, 149.

24. Ibid., 150.

25. Klingberg, *When Life Calls Out to Us*, 80.

26. See *Zentralblatt für Psychotherapie* 10 (1936): 7. Also, Mühlleitner, *Medizinische Psychologie und Psychotherapie*, 135.

27. As Peter Fritzsche depicted, "The Nazis were modernists because they made the acknowledgement of the radical instability of twentieth-century life the premise of relentless experimentation." See Peter Fritzsche, "Nazi Modern," *Modernism/Modernity* 3.1 (1996): 1.

28. Matthias Göring, *Zentralblatt für Psychotherapie* (1933), quoted in Geoffrey Cocks, *Psychotherapy in the Third Reich: The Göring Institute* (New York: Oxford University Press, 1985), 117.

29. For the details, see Cocks, *Psychotherapy in the Third Reich*, 3–10. Also, for how the Göring Institute related to the Freudians, see Karen Brecht, F.Volker, M.H. Ludger, J.I. Kaminer, and D.H. Jülich, eds., *Here Life Goes on in a Most Peculiar Way: Psychoanalysis before and after 1933*, trans. Christine Trollope (Hamburg: Kellner, 1995).

30. Cocks, *Psychotherapy in the Third Reich*, 116.

31. See *Zentralblatt für Psychotherapie* 10 (1937): 7–8.

32. We will recall Frankl left Adler's group with Allers. Frankl also dedicated his book *Psychotherapy and Existentialism* to Allers in 1967. Allers was also anti-Freudian and a supporter of the "Ständestaat"; see Rudolf Allers, "Die neue Zeit und die Heilerziehung," *Der Christliche Ständestaat* (4 March 1934).

33. On Jung's ethically questionable role in the movement, see Cocks, *Psychotherapy in the Third Reich*, 127–135.

34. Cocks, *Psychotherapy in the Third Reich*, 128. Obviously, Jung's citing of Allers in defense was rather disingenuous given Allers's politics and commitment to Catholicism.

35. See Alexander Batthyány, *Mythos Frankl? Geschichte der Logotherapie und Existenzanalyse 1925-1945, Entgegnung auf Timothy Pytell* (Wien; Berlin; Münster: 2008), 37.

36. Cocks, *Psychotherapy in the Third Reich*, 102–103.

37. After the war Stransky and Pötzl edited the *Wiener Zeitschrift für Nervenheilkunde* and Frankl contributed three papers.

38. Frankl, "Zur geistigen Problematik," 33–45.

39. Joseph Fabry and Elisabeth Lukas, "In Pursuit of Logos: Correspondence with Viktor Frankl," translation of Prologue and first chapter of the book, *Auf den Spuren des Logos—Briefwechsel mit Viktor E. Frankl aus der Pionierzeit der Logotherapie, Journal des Viktor Frankl Instituts* 3, no. 1 (Spring 1995): 50.

40. See Frankl, "Viktor Frankl," 188.

41. See Cocks, *Psychotherapy in the Third Reich*, 159.

42. Frankl, "Zur geistigen Problematik," 34.

43. Ibid., 33.

44. Ibid., 34.

45. Ibid., 35.

46. Ibid.

47. Ibid.

48. For a description of their role in the Göring Institute, see Cocks, *Psychotherapy in the Third Reich*, 72–86.

49. Frankl, "Zur geistigen Problematik," 36. Also, instead of "existential analysis" Frankl will later use the term logotherapy to avoid confusing his work with Binswanger's.

50. Ibid.

51. Ibid.

52. All three were members of the General Medical Society for Psychotherapy founded in 1926. This became the German General Medical Society after 1933, and in 1936 the Göring Institute. But citing Prinzhorn on this account was slightly disingenuous because Prinzhorn considered the psychotherapist a "Priesterdilettant" (amateur priest). See Cocks, *Psychotherapy in the Third Reich*, 6–8, 56.

53. Frankl, "Zur geistigen Problematik," 36–37.

54. Cocks, *Psychotherapy in the Third Reich*, 131. But Jung's anti-Freudianism often took on racial overtones.

55. Ibid., 130.

56. Frankl, "Zur geistigen Problematik," 37.

57. See Cocks, *Psychotherapy in the Third Reich*, 103.

58. Frankl, "Zur geistigen Problematik," 38.

59. Ibid.

60. Ibid., 39.

61. Ibid., 39–40.

62. Ibid., 40.

63. Ibid., 41.

64. Ibid.

65. Ibid., 43.

66. Ibid., 44.

67. Ibid., 43.

68. Cocks, *Psychotherapy in the Third Reich*, 89–90.

69. It is important to note that the goal of unifying the schools was also a pre-Nazi phenomenon.

70. Cocks, *Psychotherapy in the Third Reich*, 5, 177.

71. Geoffrey Cocks, personal correspondence with author (13 January 1997).

72. As noted, from the Göring Institute's perspective there could be a variety of reasons why they published the article. But there were difficult and problematic circumstances. For example, in 1937–1938 only one volume of six issues of the *Zentralblatt* appeared, and "although C.A. Meier has asserted that this was a result of his editorial policy of quashing 'Nazi nonsense' before publication, it is more likely the journal's difficulties stemmed from lack of funding." Cocks, *Psychotherapy in the Third Reich*, 146.

73. See Friedrich Stadler, "The Vienna Circle and the University of Vienna," in Weibel and Stadler, *The Cultural Exodus from Austria*, 57. Hildebrand fled to the United States after the *Anschluss*.

74. See Alfred Low, *The Anschluss Movement* (New York: Columbia University Press, 1985), especially "Austria on the Brink," 383–399.

75. Leonard Seif, "Erziehungder Erzieher," in dem, *Wegeder Erziehungshilfe*, 32, quoted in Cocks, *Psychotherapy in the Third Reich*, rev. 2d ed., 83.

76. Frankl, "Seelenaerztliche Selbstbesinnung," 8.

77. Frankl, "Seelenaerztliche Selbstbesinnung," 8. The full text in German is as follows: Sehen wir uns bloss einmal stichprobenweise im einschlägigen Schrifttum um: Gerade unter den modernen Autoren, die innerhalb der psychotherapeutischen Arbeit eine weltanschauliche Ausweitung, wie wir es oben nannten, fordern, finden sich solche, die bereits eine bestimmte Richtung vertreten und—im Rahmen der Krankenbehandlung—auch verfechten. Ich beschränke mich auf wenige Beispiele und Zitate. Karl Häberlin etwa ("Die Bedeutung von Ludwig Klages und Hans Prinzhorn für die Psychotherapie") schreibt: "So wird Psychotherapie zum Dienst an den Mächten des Lebens..., dass dem Leben und seinen Werten die Führerschaft bleibt, dass der Geist in Lebensabhängigkeit gehalten wird". Auch einer der führenden reichsdeutschen Psychotherapeuten, Gauger, ist einer ähnlichen Auffassung: "Der Sinn des Lebens ist nichts anderes als das Leben selbst". (Gauger, "Politische Medizin".) Ein anderer, Prof. M.H. Göring, spricht schliesslich offen davon, "...die 'Deutsche allgemeine aerztliche Gesellschaft für Psychotherapie'...hat die Aufgabe, ...zusammenzufassen...vor allem...diejenigen Ärzte, die willig sind, im Sinne der nationalsozialistischen Weltanschauung eine seelenaerztliche Heilkunst auszubilden und auszuueben." (*Zentralblatt: für Psychotherapie*. 1933).

78. Cocks, *Psychotherapy in the Third Reich*, 84.

79. See Carl Häberlin, "Die Bedeutung von Ludwig Klages und Hans Prinzhorn für die Deutsche Psychotherapie," *Zentralblatt für Psychotherapie* 7 (1934): 38–51.

80. See Kurt Gauger, *Politische Medizin: Grundriss einer Deutschen Psychotherpie* (Hamburg: Hanseatische Verlagsanstalt, 1934). George Mosse included an outake of *Politische Medizin*, to exemplify the intellectual crudity and pathetic "world-view" of Nazi psychotherapy, in George Mosse, *Nazi Culture*, trans. Salvator Attanasio (New York: Grosset and Dunlap, 1966), 215–227.

81. Frankl, "Seelenärztliche Selbstbesinnung," 8.

82. Quoted in Cocks, *Psychotherapy in the Third Reich*, 70. For Eliasberg's comments on these times, especially his rejection of Jung's anti-Semitism, see Wladimir Eliasberg, "Allgemeine Ärztliche Gesellschaft für Psychotherapie, 1926-31," *American Journal of Psychiatry* 112 (1956): 738–740.

83. See Batthyány, *Mythos Frankl?*, 45–51.

84. Cocks, *Psychotherapy and the Third Reich*, 4.

CHAPTER FIVE

The Doctor Perseveres

*We knew we would have to emigrate, but had not the faintest idea to
what place. I went from one consulate to the other, from one legation
to the next and from one steamship company to the other, wrote letters
to all countries under the sun ... all to no avail.*
— Victor Spira, quoted in Peter Eppel,
"Exiled Austrians in the USA"

After the *Anschluss* in March of 1938, disaster hit the Austrian Jews. No longer able to deny the threat of Nazism, they faced a reality much worse than anyone expected. The Nuremberg laws were implemented. Jews suffered almost every kind of humiliation: they were urinated and spat on, they were forced to scrub the streets, and their homes and businesses were plundered. Persecution was rampant, and many were murdered. Austrian anti-Semitism was so intense the Nazi authorities appealed to the people to moderate their enthusiastic persecution of the Jews. Consequently the emigration of Austrian Jews began. In the process of relocation they were prodded by the so-called specialist in Jewish affairs, the infamous Eichmann. By May of 1939 the census revealed that 84,000 Jews had left Austria. But strangely many more refused to leave. Even Sigmund Freud hesitated to leave—considering the possibility of suicide first. Not surprisingly, "hundreds of Austrian Jews committed suicide amidst the open Nazi violence" and in the ten days after the *Anschluss* nearly 100 Viennese Jews killed themselves.[1]

Notes for this section begin on page 96.

After the *Anschluss*, Frankl lost both his connection with the Göring Institute and his burgeoning private practice.[2] Although unemployed, Frankl continued his intellectual production. In 1939 he published two articles in Switzerland. The first was on the use of medication in the psychotherapeutic process. The medication, Benzedrin, was a methamphetamine that had been approved for use in the United States in 1937. It appears therefore that Frankl was again on the cutting edge of psychiatric research. There was also significant debate among medical experts concerning Benzedrin's effectiveness, but Frankl considered the drug useful in treating depression, melancholy, compulsive neurosis, and stuttering. Frankl claimed Benzedrin removed the symptoms of these afflictions, which made therapeutic intervention possible. He backed his claims with four case studies.[3]

Sustaining the Vision

Frankl's next article revealed that these events had not dramatically changed his perspective on psychotherapy. Although he retained his essential ideas, the reality of Nazi occupation had destroyed any hopes of working within the confines of the Göring Institute and therefore this article was devoid of any reference to the "leading German psychotherapists." The article was entitled "Philosophy and Psychotherapy: On the Foundation of an Existential Analysis" and Frankl stated that it was originally an outline to a book he conceived of in 1926. He also contended that Oswald Schwarz had praised the outline as having the same impact on psychology that Kant's *Critique of Pure Reason* had had on philosophy.[4]

In the article, Frankl repeated the distinction between Freudian and Adlerian psychotherapy and his criticism of reductionism. But now "relativism and psychologism" that "deprive things of their value" were "just like the diverse modern collectivisms that try to deprive humans (their freedom) their dignity ..."[5] For Frankl, psychoanalysis, individual psychology, Nazism, and Bolshevism were all part of the same intellectual tradition that "renders things worthless."

Frankl obviously wanted to avoid this reductionism. But in order to claim he was promoting a form of psychotherapy, not a philosophy, he focused on delineating how this new psychology of world views was a "supplement" to psychotherapy. "If ... we would like to evade psychologism we have ... to transcend it by means of logicism—and that means to supplement psychotherapy with logotherapy."[6] Although less ambitious, one might even say humble, based on the term "supplement," these were essentially the same ideas he presented in 1937. Now, he took a more philosophical approach, and conceived of logotherapy as a philosophical dialogue. Basically, Frankl's psychology of world views avoided Freudian and Adlerian reductionism by taking a phenomenological ap-

proach to therapy. In order to exemplify this approach, Frankl asked: "Since fear once in a while can be attributed to unconscious sexual causes, or 'tendencies to secure,' for that reason supposedly fear, such as fear of life and death—or fear of conscience does not exist?"[7]

Frankl also returned to the problem of the therapist's authority. In order to contextualize this problem, we should note that in traditional psychoanalysis the therapist represented a blank slate upon which the patient transferred neurotic tendencies. It was then left to the therapist to unpack and make conscious the transferences. Logotherapy, as a philosophical dialogue, was not interested in issues of the patient's transference. But Frankl did want to keep the therapist from "transferring" his values onto the patient. Under the rubric of the Göring Institute this value neutrality was clearly the most "pragmatic" stance. Now, Frankl used this value neutrality to distinguish his philosophical therapy from religious counseling, stating: "The physician ... does not have the right to transfer a given hierarchy of values onto the patient like a pastor who has been authorized to do so."[8]

Frankl summarized his new psychotherapy and again relied on the notion of responsibility and finding a unique mission as the universal ground for existential analysis. In Frankl's words: "we originally demanded to advance beyond the psychological field into the spiritual one, that is to integrate the totality of human existence into psychotherapy. Now we claim one last thing: to put the essence of human existence—to be responsible, to have a mission—into the center of psychotherapy. In this way psychotherapy becomes an analysis of existence in a double way: it becomes an analysis of the whole existence (Eros, Logos, and Ethos) and it becomes an analysis in regard to existence (to be human, being as responsibility)."[9]

Frankl therefore maintained his prescription for therapy articulated in 1937. The only significant changes were the conception of his existential analysis/logotherapy[10] as "supplemental," and a toning down of the "vitalized heroism" that marked his earlier article. Notably, he criticized the "modern collectivisms" and connected this reproach with his criticism of Adler and Freud. The article was also absent of any discussion of meaning fulfillment through the community. Since Frankl maintained the central thrust of his vision, let us step back from the political implications of Frankl's thought and frame his development within the context of his biography and intellectual trends within modernity.

The Mandarin

Frankl's theoretical construction of logotherapy was deeply tied to his personal struggle to find Meaning. By the late 1930s Frankl had come to view reductionism, especially as represented by Freud and Adler, as the source of what he took to be the nihilistic tendencies in Western modernity. In order

to counteract these reductionist trends he absorbed the "spiritual" perspective of existential phenomenology, onto which he grafted a theory of human responsibility and values. But Frankl's existential perspective, which relied on the individual accepting responsibility and choosing values, left open the question of ultimate meaning and values. Frankl therefore remained trapped in relativism, because he identified no transcendent "categorical imperatives"—only "missions," which were no more than acts of individualistic commitment. In this way, his existentialist solution to human meaning was not grounded in any universal values. As he recognized, his position as therapist rather than priest did not allow him to posit values, only point the way. There is one caveat here because Alexander Batthyány argues that Frankl "held the position that values are absolute, though their realization, i.e. their *offer* to being lived, takes an individual form." Batthyány claims Frankl's position is somewhat similar to Scheler's position that "there is the good as such for me. *As such* = absolute; *for me* = in relation to me."[11] Batthyány's explication of Frankl's position is helpful, but it seems that Frankl posits absolutes that remain dependent on the individual's conviction that absolutes exist. As Izenberg pointed out, devoid of Freud's positivism there are simply no solid epistemological grounds in which existentialism can base absolute values. Frankl's (and Scheler's) difficulties with values and psychotherapy are therefore reflective of a broader cultural crisis. His dilemma was strikingly similar to the problem of science and values well articulated by Max Weber in his speech "Science as a Vocation."[12] Weber claimed that "the task of the teacher is to serve students ... not to imprint upon them his personal political views." On the issue of "the 'value' of culture," Weber claimed such issues should be avoided in the lecture room, "because the prophet and the demagogue do not belong on the academic platform."[13] The task of the teacher was therefore to "force the individual ... to give an 'account of the ultimate meaning of his own conduct.'" According to Weber, the "teacher who succeeds ... stands in the service of 'moral' forces..."[14]

Weber also argued that science could not ground values and that in the age of rationalization, intellectualization, and disenchantment of the world, "the ultimate and most sublime values" had disappeared.[15] But Weber did not argue that values were impossible or that a neutrality of values could be maintained outside a scientific domain. Although Weber "denied that he or anyone else could objectively justify value choices, [he maintained that] the necessity of choice, of commitment to one's 'Daemon,' was an ethical imperative."[16] Weber's rejection of the possibility of objective values, combined with a call for ethical responsibility and commitment to one's "Daemon," seemed to correspond with Frankl's call for responsibility and discovering individual missions. Was Weber then also falling victim to the same relativism and ethical decisionism that plagued Frankl? This critique has been suggested because Carl Schmitt "took up Weber's idea and built a political philosophy of decisionism on it," and then "became a leading spokesman for German fascism." But in Weber's defense he

was an archenemy of such messianic currents, and for him "meaningful choice always involved accountability to the social and political forces of one's age."[17] It is vain speculation to question whether Weber would have been sympathetic to Nazism.[18] But one explanation for Frankl's attempt to solve the intellectual tensions in the Nazi Psychotherapy movement is perhaps found in the fact that Frankl never mentioned Max Weber and instead claimed to be influenced by Max Scheler.

As mentioned, Frankl described how in the late 1920s Max Scheler's *Formalism in Ethics*, which was a phenomenological work on objectivity and values, was like "a bible" for him, and essentially shook him free from "psychologism."[19] Despite this proclaimed influence, Frankl rarely cited Scheler in his writings. However, in 1937, he did quote Scheler's claim that "the fulfillment of man's highest possible values" is beneficial.[20] Once described as a "Catholic Nietzsche," Scheler was heavily influenced by the phenomenology of Husserl. Scheler also agreed with Weber that science must remain value neutral. But for Weber philosophy was considered under the rubric of science, and therefore the task of the scientist-philosopher was simply to analyze and catalog.[21] For Scheler though, the task of the philosopher was not to compare, but to decipher and choose the correct world view.[22] Scheler claimed "that 'value precedes and is independent of being.'" Thus, "the ideal is teleologically prior to the real, ... 'in the realm of essences' beyond the physical world of man's experience." Scheler's philosophical idealism led him to the conviction that "man has the responsibility to attempt to shape his physical and social world," and "bring it into conformity with the world of transcendental ideals."[23]

Although Frankl's theory of values shared some similarities with Scheler's, what is pertinent to our concerns is Scheler's "belief" in a realm of transcendent and knowable values. A not-so-hidden element in Frankl's logotherapy was the same conviction about objective values. Frankl seemed to be taking this leap of faith in objective values when he stated, "*Formalism in Ethics* became a bible for me." But given the situation of the therapist, a necessary distinction had to be made between instilling an "attitude" of responsibility and the valuation that took place after responsibility was accepted. Frankl was therefore correct to note that if not for this claimed value neutrality the therapist would resemble a priest. Conceivably, the key to understanding Frankl's thinking and activity in the 1930s is contained in Scheler's conviction about the objectivity of values. Following Scheler, Frankl seemed confident that the focus on responsibility would lead the patient to transcendent values. In a sense Frankl was a "false priest" confident that by leading people nowhere specific in terms of valuation, they will nevertheless find the right way. Clearly, Frankl's existentialism, along with his search for professional standing and Meaning, had led him far from his affirmation (in 1926) of the Adlerian values in which the therapist had "to push the patient so far that he sees clearly that there is no counter argument towards good will, work and love."[24]

But Frankl maintained his neutrality and his belief in a transcendent realm of values that was accessed through the "higher realm of responsibility," the realm of the conscience, throughout his life. Even in 1969 he claimed: "If I am asked, as I am time and again, whether this neutralism would have to be maintained even in the case of Hitler, I answer in the affirmative, because I am convinced that Hitler would never have become what he did unless he had 'suppressed' within himself the voice of conscience."[25]

Frankl therefore maintained his value neutrality and a "belief" in transcendent values within a "conscience." But this led to a position where he couldn't tell Hitler—in a therapeutic situation—that his mission of genocide was wrong. Apparently Frankl comprehended and accepted the relativism lurking behind his call for individual missions because he believed in a universal conscience. But he was in the existential impasse, because he had no grounds to argue against Hitler's genocidal "mission." The problem that Izenberg pointed out, and Frankl apparently failed to fully understand, is that authenticity is really "only a negative moment in which the self suddenly [becomes] aware of the irrationality of all 'necessary' beliefs and the self-constituted nature of permanent identities."[26] But beyond this disengagement and distancing, the concept of authenticity is unable to offer anything positive. The moment of authenticity in logotherapy was the realization and acceptance of responsibility. But, as Frankl admitted in his claim about Hitler, his existential analysis had no grounds to argue against finding "authenticity" in the totalizing movements of Nazism, communism, or Christianity.

Stumbling Through

In 1939, Frankl remained convinced about the value of his "pioneering" work in psychotherapy. He also had a significant professional track record and seemed well connected in the medical field despite the treacherous historical circumstances. Most Jews who had the opportunity emigrated. For example, of the fifty members of the Viennese Psychoanalytic Society who still resided in Vienna in 1937, all but three, August Aichhorn, Alfred Winterstein, and Richard Nepalleck, emigrated.[27] As is well known, Eichmann was ruthless in his drive to expunge and to force Austrian Jews to emigrate.[28] Not surprisingly, Frankl also applied for an emigration visa on 18 May 1938. His emigration questionnaire reveals that he aspired to immigrate to the United States. In response to the question of what other capacities he had beyond his medical degree and training as a psychotherapist, he sarcastically replied "possibly a house painter."[29]

The aspirations that the *Anschluss* would allow for a limited Austrian autonomy were quickly dashed as the Nazis took over Austria.[30] In the process of "Gleichschaltung" (coordination) the indigenous Austrian Nazis soon dis-

covered they were to play only a small role.[31] In these circumstances, the initial Austrian euphoria after Hitler's arrival soon dissipated.

The Nazi "takeover" of Austria obviously affected Frankl. For example, he described a confrontation with Nazis where he narrowly missed being shipped to Dachau. Apparently, Frankl and his father were called to the police station. Because of his age, Frankl's father was sent home, but officers retained Frankl. Eventually he approached a policeman and claimed he needed to leave in order to proceed with institutionalizing a patient who was in a state of excitation. Another time, he escaped deportation by administering short-term therapy (paradoxical intention) to a Gestapo official.[32] In terms of his family, both Frankl's sister and brother escaped Austria. His sister traveled to Australia while his brother took refuge in Italy (he was later captured and sent with his wife to Auschwitz and killed).

Frankl eventually received his visa to the United States in November 1941—but he let his request lapse.[33] His reasons for not emigrating vary. According to the standard interpretation he stayed to protect his parents.

> The day that his visa was approved by the United States, he agonized over whether he should accept the visa with the hope that his parents and his fiancée would be able to follow him. Covering the yellow star that he was compelled as a Jew to wear, he entered Saint Stephen's Church in the center of Vienna, where an organ concert was taking place. He sat in a pew and prayed silently, "O God, give me a sign." Should he stay with his family with the hope that they could be saved, or should he go to the United States, where he believed he could continue his pioneer work in psychology? When he came home he found his father in tears. When Frankl asked what had happened, his father replied, "Viktor, the Nazis have destroyed the synagogue" and showed him a fragment of marble he had salvaged. The fragment of the Torah his father held in his hands had one letter engraved on it, the beginning of the commandment "Honor thy father and thy mother." Frankl called the American embassy and canceled his visa. He had received his sign.[34]

Beyond this allegedly mystical sign, and his commitment to his parents, there were other possible reasons behind Frankl's decision to stay in Vienna. He told a friend that times of crisis require good doctors. Along these lines he relayed the following story: "… I have never told anyone this—But about this time I had a strange dream, one that belongs to my deepest experiences in the realm of dreaming. I dreamed that people were lined up—psychotics, patients—to be taken to the gas chambers. And I felt that I must do something and working as a psychotherapist in a concentration camp, supporting the people there mentally, would be incomparably more meaningful than just being one more psychiatrist in Manhattan."[35]

Under the Nazis, Frankl was unable to practice as a doctor. Eventually he took a job as *Judenbehandler* (Caretaker of Jews) and then became a *Judischer Fachbehandler* (Jewish Specialist) at the Rothschild hospital. Frankl was the "Director of Neurology," and his curriculum vitae from 1947 at the university archive in Vienna listed his employment at Rothschild from 1939 to 1942. In a

1993 interview with Dr. Wolfgang Neugebauer and Dr. Elisabeth Klamper he was asked if he "was there in 1938?" and replied "no, 1940–42." Other sources also listed his employment as 1940–1942.[36] The date is significant because the hospital was supposedly taken over by the Nazi authorities in April of 1939.[37] Frankl was therefore unemployed from the *Anschluss* until he began work at Rothschild, but the exact date and circumstances of his employment remain unclear.[38]

After the *Anschluss* the Rothschild hospital functioned as the communal center for Jews. The hospital was also one of the few places Jews could work, and therefore Frankl must have felt lucky to have employment. He likely replaced one of the doctors who had fortuitously managed to emigrate.[39] We know very little about the Rothschild hospital in this period, but apparently the hospital originally had 250 beds, which was increased to 450 in 1941, and in that same year treated 45,141 outpatients.[40] However we do know that the hospital was "raided" intermittently by the SS.[41] At the Nazi-controlled Rothschild, in these years of extremity, we can only surmise the types of pressure Frankl was under.

Frankl described three significant events that stemmed from this period. First, he combined with Pötzl in a proclaimed sabotaging of Nazi attempts at euthanasia. Second, he met and eventually married his first wife, Tilly Gosser. Third, while working as director of the neurological wing, he conducted medical research. The research took the form of experimental operations on suicidal Jewish patients who had been given up for dead.

Pötzl and Tilly

In his autobiographical work Frankl took great pride in narrating how Pötzl helped him save some Jewish psychotics from the Nazi euthanasia program. Apparently, Frankl and Pötzl combined to have psychotics rediagnosed so they appeared to be suffering from physical problems, not psychotic. In this way they were able to place them in a Jewish home for the aged. Pötzl was able to help Frankl save some patients, but not all, because "each and every patient who was regarded as incurable.… Even the relatives … of high-ranking party functionaries were gassed. And Pötzl could not help them."[42] We know Frankl was deported to Theresienstadt in September of 1942, which means they were sabotaging euthanasia sometime between 1939 and early 1942. It seems odd then that despite the pressure to perform euthanasia, Pötzl applied for official membership in the Nazi party on 2 November 1943 and claimed he had paid party dues between 1930 and 1933. His application was approved on 31 December 1943.[43] But strangely, in September of 1944, he had his membership reconsidered and redated to 1 January 1941—around the same time the sabotaging of euthanasia occurred. What is clear is that the act of sabotaging means

both Pötzl and Frankl were being pressured to participate in the euthanasia program.

Perhaps Pötzl was forced to join the party due to the extremity of the situation and his position as the head of the university clinic. On the other hand Pötzl seemed to share some of the Nazi's views on health. For example, in 1938 he accepted the sterilization of the mentally ill on the grounds that "it is indispensable for the future of the people."[44] Also in 1940, "Pötzl spoke of the need for psychiatrists and psychotherapists to cooperate in meeting the country's urgent demand for increased productivity by strengthening the physiological and psychological elements that comprise the human will."[45] Also in his de-Nazification file one key charge against him included in the summary of charges—and likely the one that led to his dismissal from the university—was made by his students, who claimed that "Professor Pötzl made no statements against the euthanasia program and he also sent patients to institutions where the procedures were being carried out."[46]

Frankl's first wife, Tilly Gosser, was a nurse under Professor Donath at the Rothschild hospital. She was nearly twenty years younger than Frankl, and they were married in December of 1941. The date of her death is unknown but she perished late in the war at Bergen-Belsen. When Frankl returned to Vienna, he learned of his wife's death from Emil Tuchman, the former Director of the Rothschild hospital.[47] Frankl described how Tuchman wept when he told him the news about his wife.[48] Although Frankl did not specifically mention it, we can surmise from the following that Pötzl must have also known Tilly. After learning of his wife's death Frankl immediately went to visit Pötzl: "… my old teacher was the first one that I wept in front of. But unfortunately I could not help him: On the same day he was, as a former National Socialist, irrevocably released from his position."[49] This disjointed passage reveals a few things. For one, Frankl's immediate visit to Pötzl, and then his open weeping over Tilly in front of him, seemed to suggest that Pötzl had emotionally, at the very least, invested himself in the well-being of both Frankl and Tilly. The emotional pain Frankl felt over Tilly's death must have been profound, and it is a theme we will revisit. But why would Frankl feel a responsibility and desire to help Pötzl? In his autobiographical work Frankl described how Pötzl confused his umbrella with Frankl's after their visit. Pötzl first took Frankl's umbrella, then both umbrellas, and finally only his own umbrella. It is strictly conjecture, but it seemed like Frankl was suggesting there was confusion over who was playing the role of protector.[50] Frankl, along with seventeen others, gave a deposition in defense of Pötzl in his de-Nazification proceedings. Frankl's statement that described their sabotaging of euthanasia was a critical element because the commission was concerned about Pötzl's clear affinity for National Socialism and he surrounded himself with a number of SS assistants. He also spoke highly of Hitler and was enthusiastic with the *Anschluss*.[51] From his writings and actions it seems clear that at the very least Pötzl was a political opportunist if not an outright Nazi.

Whatever the case, Frankl and Pötzl maintained their connection postwar, and collaborated on two articles.[52] Frankl also contributed to Pötzl's Festschrift.[53]

Frankl described how although Tilly was "beautiful," he married her because of her character. As a testament to Tilly's character Frankl related the following: when Tilly's mother lost her protection from deportation, they were all quite fearful. But Tilly's mother wasn't deported. At the last minute she fortuitously received a job cleaning out the apartments of just deported Jews. Tilly described the repristination of her mother's status as the work of God. Frankl characterized Tilly's response as "the most beautiful and shortest 'summa theologiae' ... he had ever heard."[54]

Frankl also recounted the moment he decided to marry. It seems he interrupted his lunch to rush to the hospital and perform experimental surgery. Upon returning, Frankl, to his surprise, was not admonished by Tilly for missing lunch. Instead, she asked how the operation went. At this moment he decided to marry her. It is a revealing association. That she understood the importance of the medical research for Frankl was apparent. But the concern also revealed she supported the research when some of her colleagues were questioning the wisdom of Frankl's procedures.[55]

How Can I Help?

Under normal circumstances, experimental efforts to revive suicidal patients would fulfill the Hippocratic Oath to preserve life. But under the circumstances of Nazi occupation, and in a Jewish hospital under Nazi control, these experimental operations conducted on people who had chosen suicide to counteract their plight (deportation) seem morally questionable on a number of levels. But we must remember that these were extreme times in Vienna. This extremity was certainly the necessary precondition for Frankl to practice brain surgery.

Also, for those readers that may find the following medical experiments by Frankl shocking, it is important to first note that these aggressive medical efforts by Frankl fit the time-honored Viennese medical tradition in experimental and inventive research. Both Frankl's and Pötzl's medical work in the latter 1930s and early 1940s exhibited an experimental character.[56] Pötzl is credited with co-inventing and testing on a large scale insulin shock therapy.[57] For his part, Frankl described treating the schizophrenic and melancholic patients he rescued from euthanasia with "Cardiazolschocks."[58] Both Frankl and Pötzl performed lobotomies and shock therapy, and Frankl apparently initiated drug therapy for psychosis on the continent.[59] Finally, Frankl's boss at Am Steinhof and member of the Göring Institute, Alfred Mauczka, was tried after the war and accused of "physical mishandling" and using "brutal force" with patients (although apparently these atrocities occurred after Frankl had been terminated).[60] From all of

this we can conclude that the medical practice of Viennese doctors between the wars was characterized by experimental and often violent techniques.[61]

Frankl claimed he was justified in trying the experimental research because there were up to ten Jewish suicides a day in the early 1940s. We know that approximately twelve hundred Viennese Jews killed themselves during the Nazi era,[62] and suicide, or the "Masada solution," was very popular, especially among assimilated, upper-middle-class, elderly Austrian Jews faced with deportation. Normally the motivation for suicide is loneliness, grief, and advancing age, and no doubt these factors were part of the decision by Austrian Jews. But the deeper motivations of suicide, anger, and aggression against an unloved self were absent under the circumstances—essentially people killed themselves to avoid deportation and losing control of their lives to the Nazis.[63] Often the suicide was done at the deportation centers, no doubt to disturb the Nazis. Also, "those reflecting on the suicides of relatives or friends often admired the courage it took to end one's own life."[64] Under the circumstances it was a dignified act. Cyanide, sleeping pills, or poison were the most common methods of suicide and therefore drugs were in high demand.[65]

Apparently, whenever patients had taken an overdose of pills and then had been given up for dead by other doctors, Frankl felt "justified in trying something." First, "some injections intravenously ... and if this didn't work I gave them injections into the brain ... into the Cisterna Magna. And if that did not work I made a trepanation, opened the skull ... inserted drugs into the ventricle and made a drainage so drug went into the Aquaeductus Sylvii.... People whose breathing had stopped suddenly started breathing again." But he "could only keep them alive for 24 hours no longer."[66] Frankl administered the stimulants Pervitin and Tetrophan.

Pervitin, also known as the "chemical whip," was a widely used amphetamine in Nazi Germany. The Nazis were also interested in the applications and misuse of the drug. For example, concern over the side effects of Pervitin on mental acuity (along with the death of an SS member by overdose) led the Nazis to first closely regulate the drug and then conduct "human experiments with Pervitin on the effects of the drug on altitude sickness ... at the Dachau concentration camp from 1942-45." Also, in "November 1944 the SS tried out a combination of Pervitin, Eukadol, and synthetic cocaine at the Sachsenhausen concentration camp on prisoners forced to march around for long periods of time with overloaded packs on their backs."[67] There was also a "second wave" of Pervitin use late in the war by civilians and so-called "attack Pervitin" was replaced with "work Pervitin."[68]

According to Alexander Batthyány, Frankl first described his experiments in a lecture in 1947 at the Austrian Society for Neurology. However, he made no mention of his research in his original biographical statement in 1973,[69] although he did mention the "experiments" in his 1981 interview with Tom

Corrigan. He did however give a full description of the research in his 1993 interview with Dr. Neugebauer and Dr. Klamper as well as in his 1995 autobiography. Never one to express much self-doubt, Frankl proudly recounted his research efforts. Frankl narrated that although he had no training in brain surgery, and was denied access "to even look on" when Professor Schönbauer performed surgery, he was still able to conduct the surgery. Frankl also remarked that the primary surgeon Reich refused to do the operations (it is not clear why he refused to do surgeries), and therefore Frankl decided to perform the brain surgery techniques after reading about them. He published an article in *Ars Medici* documenting the experiments in September of 1942 (ironically, just as he was deported to Theresienstadt).

The work that Frankl cited as having read on brain surgery was "Dandy."[70] Walter E. Dandy and his mentor, Harvey Cushing, were probably the two most influential figures in the field of modern brain surgery. Dandy was a famous American brain surgeon noted for his work on ventriculography and brain tumors. Ventriculography is the term "for a diagnostic procedure utilizing the injection of air or some other gas as a contrast medium into the ventricles of the brain, in order to make the brain tissue visible in contrast to the less opaque gas. In the absence of air or gas, the chambers cannot be seen on an x-ray plate because they are filled with cerebrospinal fluid having the same x-ray capacity as the surrounding brain tissue."[71]

Dandy's great contribution was a technique for allowing the brain to be clearly x-rayed, which facilitated the detection and removal of brain tumors. Dandy made this discovery at a young age and then became a renowned surgeon. But what exactly is the relationship between Dandy's work and Frankl's experimental procedures?

Since Dandy never mentioned inserting amphetamines directly into the brain cavity we can surmise this was Frankl's idea. Indeed, in the article on the research, Frankl began by addressing this point, and "the possibility to give and to bring a medication more quickly and closer to the place of action."[72] As mentioned, the medication that Frankl was administering was Pervitin and the usual transmission of the drug would occur from the blood to the cerebral spinal fluid. Normally, one would inject Pervitin intravenously and Frankl's initial research did just that.[73] But Frankl thought he could bypass the bloodstream and apply the drug directly into the cerebrospinal fluid. Dandy's work on ventriculography suggested there were two ways of achieving this. One was via the spine or "lumbar puncture," and the other was through a trepanation of the skull and insertion into the cisterna magna or ventricles. For injecting air, Dandy rejected the use of lumbar puncture "as superfluous … because a ventricular puncture gives the same and much additional information and entails much less risk."[74] Frankl used both lumbar puncture and trepanation to administer the drug. But as he remarked, and the article revealed, the results of his research were inconclusive. Nevertheless, he decided to publish it.

If Frankl had read Dandy's original article on the discovery of ventriculography, he might not have been surprised that his patients never came out of a coma. In 1918 Dandy wrote:

> The various solutions … thorium, potassium, iodide, collargol, argyrol, bismuth subnitrate and subcarbonate … were injected into the ventricles of dogs, but always with fatal results owing to the injurious effects on the brain…. The severe reactions that are sometimes encountered after the intraspinous injection of the most therapeutic remedies indicate the dangers even from carefully prepared solutions. A slight acidity or alkalinity may result even in death. It seems unlikely that any solution … will be found which is sufficiently harmless to justify its injection into the central nervous system.[75]

Apparently, in this extreme situation, Frankl felt justified in trying something. But, as Frankl admitted, he had no training, and his limited knowledge was based in spotty reading rather than clinical experience. Frankl was therefore testing the limits of proper medical practice and ethics. Preferably, this research would have been first tried on animals for an extended time period, and ideally there also would have been a strong basis in clinical observation and experience. But neither was the case. Since Frankl had been interested in suicide prevention since the late 1920s it is certainly possible that he was simply committed to rescuing suicidal patients whatever the circumstances. But he used questionable medical practices to achieve that end, and it is likely that he did these experiments in an attempt to ensure his own professional status.

The use of extraordinary measures to save Jews who had freely chosen suicide to take their own lives was looked down on by one of Frankl's own colleagues at the hospital. Frankl described how his female "assistant Dr. Rappaport protested against his attempts to save those persons who had undertaken suicide." Frankl then claimed that this very Dr. Rappaport later attempted suicide when she had been called up for deportation—and he saved her.[76] But Frankl was apparently very aware of the moral and ethical dilemmas posed by these experiments, because at the end of his article documenting the research he stated: "It incidentally may be worth mentioning, that for the treatment of suicide we stand on the position, that all that is therapeutically possible, should be done. We do not share the opinion that destiny should take its course…. We are of the opinion, that we have to rescue, when we can … and claim it is not the job of doctors to decide over the being or non-being of people."[77]

This concluding statement reveals Frankl's defensive posture concerning his efforts. Also, his justification that the doctor does not have the right to play God put him a difficult if not slightly contradictory position when defending his radical measures.

But how then did a "Jewish Specialist" manage to get this article published in 1942? There are number of explanations. At times he suggested that because of the Nazis he could only publish the article in Switzerland. In his last autobiographical statement he claimed the article was "approved by the Jewish

advisor to the National Socialist medical board."[78] Interestingly, on 20 February 1972 at the United States International University Frankl made these remarks to his students: "I was put in the concentration camps before I could finish the research. This by the way was published, and the National Socialists hoped that this could be tried and used in war, in combat, in the case of their soldiers. That is why they even encouraged me to publish it in Switzerland, so that they may read it in a journal. Only for this, I thank this possibility to publish it."[79]

The uncensored honesty of his description before his students made it clear that this suicide intervention was supported by the Nazis. Also, the fact that the Nazis were experimenting on prisoners in concentration camps with the same drug is deeply troubling. An honest appraisal suggests that at the very least the research allowed him to appear "useful" in the Nazi war effort.

Suicide in the Face of Nazis

Frankl's decisions and medical research starkly contrasted with those of other Jewish doctors who faced similar choices. For physicians in Berlin the debate over Jewish suicide turned on the issue of whether or not to provide "the patient" with the means (pills) to facilitate their own suicide. This was more than just a moral dilemma for the doctors, because the Gestapo "wanted to find out where the individuals concerned had procured the means for their attempted suicide."[80] Most significantly, when doctors in Berlin discussed the suicide wave, "no voice was raised against the proposal that the last will of those who had attempted to take their own lives should be respected by allowing them to die."[81] In the circumstances of Nazi oppression this resignation, as difficult and tragic as it was, seemed a "reasonable" response.

Also, suicide in response to Nazi oppression usually had a political element. But the political side was obscured because the majority of those who chose suicide, in the face of forced collaboration or deportation, did so silently and stoically.[82] In these circumstances suicide was not an act of resignation, but rather an act undertaken to retain some dignity. But there was the "'violent protest' ... of one Jew who rushed into a Vienna coffee-house screaming 'Heil Hitler' then cut his throat before the eyes of the customers."[83] This tragic and desperate act serves to point out that suicide under the circumstances of Nazi occupation often had a political content. The profoundly difficult decision to commit suicide is subject to a plethora of motivations. However, under the circumstances of Nazi brutality and oppression, retaining dignity and an attempt to *resist* total indignity is the prime motivation. This is because faced with the Nazis in the 1940s, Jews in Austria had extremely limited choices. They could try (if possible) to emigrate, go underground, accommodate or collaborate, or take the most desperate act, suicide. These extremely limited possibilities, and

especially suicide, clarify in an exceptional way the magnitude and totality of Nazi ruthlessness and domination.

Micheal Geyer has argued that understanding resistance requires "an exploration of the shifting grounds of cooperation, affirmation, self-defense, rebelliousness, and outright resistance."[84] Taking this perspective, Geyer has argued that "resistance emerged from some kind of integration and involvement in the machinations of the regime." According to Geyer "the reality of resistance … is one of turning involvement into refusal as opposed to participation."[85] It is important to note that a person cannot compromise or collaborate without first being a victim of the Nazis. Therefore, Frankl will always be first and foremost a victim of the Nazis. But following Geyer, we can attempt to contextualize Frankl's activities in Vienna under the Nazis.

Viewed from the "shifting grounds" of resistance, accommodation, and collaboration, Frankl's desperate activities can be conceived as *bordering on collaboration*. There are three reasons behind this assertion. First, Frankl refused to recognize as legitimate his colleague's resistance to his actions. Likely she questioned not only his lack of training but the "wisdom" of such procedures under the circumstances. Second, he was breaking Jewish attempts to *resist* succumbing completely to the Nazis and retain minimal dignity through suicide. Also, those he saved would later be deported and probably feared "falling into Frankl's hands" after they made such a desperate decision to commit suicide. These two points elucidate Frankl's breaking of Jewish communal solidarity. That is, unlike the Berlin doctors who viewed the issue as one of community, and debated whether or not to *facilitate* Jewish suicide in the circumstances— Frankl stood outside such a communal vision. He did not respect, much less support, the decisions of his fellow victims. Third, because he shared the Nazi conviction that Jewish suicide must be averted, he had the approval of the Nazis. Apparently, Nazi approval also stemmed from the fact they thought the research might be useful for military purposes.

On this last point there is an important distinction. Frankl's rejection of suicide stemmed from his position as a doctor and preserver of life (the need to save himself and a religious conviction might have also been a consideration, although he never said so) while the Nazis based their opposition to Jewish suicide in terms of ideology and power—an important differentiation. On the other hand the Nazis approved of them. Clearly, though, Frankl did not consider his activities as a doctor a form of compromise or collaboration. There is one caveat here because in his 1993 interview with Dr. Neugebauer and Dr. Klamper he admitted that the experiments seemed *nazistische* (Nazi-esque) and then added "that was the atmosphere of the time."[86] It seems Frankl had absorbed enough of the "atmosphere" that even he recognized his activities were bordering on collaboration. Nevertheless at all other times Frankl suggested that his activities were a legitimate medical response to the difficult choice of suicide chosen by the persecuted. Apparently Frankl never considered suicide a

legitimate choice under any conditions. Although the experiments fit with the experimental culture of Vienna and we might imagine, Nazi medicine, perhaps his actions are best understood as an attempt to survive under unfathomable circumstances. At Rothschild it appears that Frankl was willing to cooperate with the Nazi regime in order to save himself and his family, and in his accommodation he apparently never engaged in active resistance.[87]

The rise of Nazism had a profoundly disruptive impact on the life of Frankl. Depending on one's perspective, he tried valiantly or questionably to find a path of professional development. In the process he appears to have gone to great lengths to accommodate the regime, but it did not matter; just as his article on the experiments was published in September of 1942, he was sent to Theresienstadt. The "third attempt" had failed miserably, and "the mandarin" could only desperately continue "to stumble through."

Notes

1. Goeschel, Christian, *Suicide in Nazi Germany* (London: Oxford University Press, 2009), 101.

2. After the *Anschluss*, Jewish doctors lost their positions and licenses to practice. In the rare circumstances they were allowed to practice, they were restricted to Jewish patients. For a discussion of these issues, see Ludwig Popper, *Soziale Medizin* (Bremerhaven: Wirtschaftsverlag NW, 1991), 80–101. This was a widespread phenomenon because "Jewish families were impoverished and torn out of their social context" after the *Anschluss*. See Rabinovici, *Eichmann's Jews*, 29.

3. Frankl, "Zur medikamentösen Unterstützung der Psychotherapie bei Neurosen," *Schweizerisches Archiv für Neurolologie und Psychiatrie* no. 43 (1939): 26–31.

4. Frankl, *Was nicht in meinen*, 43.

5. Frankl, "Philosophie und Psychotherapie, Zur Grundlegung einer Existenzanalyse," *Schweizerische Medizinische Wochenschrift* no. 31 (1939): 26.

6. Frankl, "Philosophie und Psychotherapie," 25.

7. Ibid., 26.

8. Ibid., 27.

9. Ibid., 28.

10. During the 1930s Frankl vacillated between existential analysis, logotherapy, and height psychology for designating his brand of therapy. After the war he identified logotherapy as a brand of existential analysis.

11. Alexander Batthyány Personal correspondence, 12 June 2009.

12. Max Weber, "Science as a Vocation" (1919), *From Max Weber: Essays in Sociology*, trans. and ed. C. Wright Mills and Hans Gerth (New York: Oxford University Press, 1958), 129–156.

13. Ibid., 146.

14. Ibid., 152.

15. Ibid., 155.

16. Arthur Mitzman, *The Iron Cage* (New Jersey: Transaction, 1985), 229. For a new reading of the political and religious significance (rupture and revelation) of this crisis of values in the 1920s and 1930s and in particular what it means for us today, see *The Weimar Moment: Liberalism, Political Theology, and Law*, ed. Leonard V. Kaplan and Rudy Koshar (Lanham, Md.: Lexington Books, 2012).

17. Ibid.

18. Hans Gerth and C. Wright Mills argued that Weber's "philosophy of charisma ... might have given him such affinities. But his humanism, ... and his unceasing campaign against racism and anti-Semitic demagoguery would have made him at least as sharp a 'critic,' ... of Hitler" as his brother Alfred was. See Weber, *From Max Weber*, 43.

19. Frankl, *Was nicht in meinen*, 42.

20. Frankl, "Zur geistigen Problematik der Psychotherapie," 36.

21. For an example of Weber's cataloging and comparing, see Weber, "The Social Psychology of Religion," in *From Max Weber*, 267–301.

22. For an outline of Scheler's thought and his differences with Weber, see Ringer, *The Decline of the German Mandarins*, 423–425.

23. John Rapheal Staude, *Max Scheler 1874-1928* (New York: The Free Press, 1967), 210–211.

24. Frankl, "Zur Psychologie des Intellektualismus," ftn. no. 1, 327.

25. Viktor Frankl, *The Will to Meaning: Foundations and Applications of Logotherapy* (Cleveland, Ohio: World Publishing, 1969), 67.

26. Izenberg, *The Existentialist Critique of Freud*, 259.

27. Mühlleitner and Reichmayr, "The Exodus of Psychoanalysts," 116.

28. See Rabinovic, *Eichmann's Jews*.

29. See Frankl's Emigration Questionnaire, Archiv der Israelistischen Kultusgemeinde Wien. I have Anatol Steck from USHMM to thank for this citation.

30. For an excellent discussion of this issue, see Maurice Williams, "German Imperialism and Austria, 1938," *Journal of Contemporary History* 14 (1979): 139–153.

31. On the Austrian Nazis' failure to gain positions of power and their subsequent disillusionment, see Pauley, *Hitler and the Forgotten Nazis*, 217–229.

32. See Frankl, *Was nicht in meinen*, 62, and Corrigan Interview (GTU).

33. Frankl's decision was surprising because so many Jews were desperate to leave and did not have the opportunity. Walter Langer, an American analyst in Vienna during the *Anschluss*, struggled to get people out. He described his efforts as a "soul-searching experience. There were all these fine people whose lives were in jeopardy and yet I could only help a limited number of them." See Walter Langer, "An American Analyst in Vienna during the Anschluss," *Journal of the History of the Behavioral Sciences* no. 14 (1978): 37–54.

34. Gould, *Viktor E. Frankl*, 21. Also see Frankl, *Was nicht in meinen*, 61–62. Since Frankl did not marry until December of 1941, his wife would not have been able to emigrate with him.

35. Frankl, quoted in Mary Hall, "Conversation with V.E. Frankl of Vienna," *Psychology Today* no. 9 (February 1968): 57.

36. Viktor Frankl. Interviewed by Dr. Wolfgang Neugebauer and Dr. Elisabeth Klamper, 1 February 1993, available at the Dokumentationsarchiv des Österreichischen Widerstandes no. 832. Also see Frankl, in Herausgegeben vom Kürschners, *Deabohe Gelehrtenkalender* (Berlin, New York: 1992).

37. See Norman Bentwich, "The Destruction of the Jewish Community in Austria 1938-1942," in *The Jews of Austria*, ed. Josef Fraenkel (London: Valentine and Mitchell, 1970), 475–476. Bentwich's article is based on personal remembrance.

38. The records of the hospital were moved to Jerusalem after the war, and are now stored at the Central Archive in Jerusalem.

39. On the emigration of the Rothschild doctors, see Eric Stern, *Die letzten 12 Jahre Rothschild-Spital Wien: 1931-1943* (Vienna: Europäischer Verlag, 1974), 7–8.

40. The central work, Stern, *Die letzten 12 Jahre Rothschild-Spital*, was written in 1974 by Dr. Erich Stern. Stern, who was a doctor at Rothschild, covered the entire period in a mere twenty pages. There was no mention of Frankl, nor of the hospital's director, Emil Tuchman, who at his postwar trial was disparagingly labeled the "Jewish Hitler." The Rothschild hospital's archive was moved to Jerusalem after the war. Brief mention of the hospital was made in Herbert Rosenkranz, *Verfolgung und Selbstbehauptung: Die Juden in Österreich 1938-1945* (Vienna; Munich: Herald, 1978), and it was also briefly mentioned in Rabinovici, *Eichmann's Jews*, 139.

41. See Stern, *Die letzten 12 Jahre Rothschild-Spital*, 14.
42. Frankl, quoted in Hall, "Conversation with V.E. Frankl," 63.
43. See Pötzl's Nazi Party file, Dokumentationsarchiv des Österreichischen Widerstandes, Vienna.
44. See Micheal Hubenstorf, "Medizinische Fakultät 1938-1945," in *Willfärige Wissenschaft: Die Universität Wien 1938-1945* (Vienna: Verlag für Gesellschaftskritik, 1989), ftn. no. 92, 275. In the same article Hubenstorf questioned whether Pötzl "knew" of the euthanasia, 251.
45. Cocks, *Psychotherapy in the Third Reich*, 98.
46. See Umschlagbogen 194 Otto Pötzl, Staatsarchiv Vienna. Despite this summary statement, the actual testimony of the students is missing from the file.
47. Tuchman was put on trial after the war for collaboration with the Nazis and his role in the deportations. But the trial was interrupted and halted by Ralph Segalman, the director of the American Joint Distribution Committee in Vienna. See Emil Tuchman, file no. 17142 at the Dokumentations archiv der Österreichischen Widerstandes, Wien.
48. See Wolf Interview (FPÖ).
49. Frankl, *Was nicht in meinen*, 81.
50. See Frankl, *Was nicht in meinen*, 48–49.
51. See Umschlagbogen 194 Otto Pötzl, Staatsarchiv Vienna. Significantly, Frankl's testimony was listed as the fifth point of the five key points in Pötzl's defense.
52. See Viktor Frankl and Otto Pötzl, "Analyse einer transitorischen temporalen Aphasia," *Wiener Zeitschrift Nervenheil* no. 11 (1955). Also, Frankl and Pötzl, "Über die seelischen Zustände während des Absturzes: eine psycho-physiologische Studie," *Monatsschrift Psychiatrie und Neurologie* no. 123 (June 1952).
53. See Hurbert Urban, *Festschrift: Zum 70. Gerburtstag von Prof. Dr. Otto Pötzl* (Innsbruck, Austria: Universitätsverlag Wagner, 1949).
54. Frankl, *Was nicht in meinen*, 63–65.
55. On the last point see ibid., 58.
56. For example note the inventiveness, violence, and experimental character revealed in Pötzl's description of shock therapy:

> Prof. O. Pötzl reports.... Even one deep shock may make the mind lucid temporarily, but the isolated points of lucidity only begin to fuse after a number of shocks.... The mortality is low.... The treatment should be begun with 5 units ... and the dose increased ... until the maximum shock dose (occasionally 150 units and more are required!) is reached. The symptoms are: somnolence, outbreak of sweat, myoclonic twitchings, epileptic seizures etc. The dose should be so arranged that the shock lasts 4 hours and that severe symptoms only supervene in the last hour. The shock is then, on principle, checked ... irregularities of the pulse, spasm of the glottis, respiratory disturbances ... occasionally make it urgent to check it sooner.... The patient should have six shocks a week; a permanent cure is at times only achieved after 50 shocks.

Pötzl, *Ars Medici* no. 5 (1938): 209. To this we can add that Else Pappenheim said Pötzl was interested in shock therapy because he hoped it would lead to a Nobel prize. Else Pappenheim, interview by author, New York City, 15 July 1996.
57. See Manfred Sakel, "Über die Einführung der sogenannten Schocktherapie und Pötzl's Verdienst um ihre Einführung," in Urban, *Festschrift*, 404–409.
58. Frankl, *Was nicht in meinen*, 60.
59. See Frankl, "Zur medikamentösen Unterstützung der Psychotherpie."
60. See Alfred Mauczka's "Volksgericht," no. 21866/45, at the Dokumentations Archiv für österreichischen Widerstandes.
61. These attitudes were also quite pervasive throughout the German and Austrian medical establishments. For instance, Robert Lifton connected the general absence of empathy among German psychiatrists to their critique of psychoanalysis and to their development of violent techniques. Thus, the psychiatrist's "doctrine of an absence of empathy ... contributed to the development of violent somatic treatment procedures ... such as insulin and metrazol shock therapy,

electroshock therapy, and lobotomy." Robert Jay Lifton, *The Nazi Doctors: Medical Killing and the Psychology of Genocide* (New York: Basic Books, 1986), 113.

62. See Berkley, *Vienna and Its Jews*, 265.

63. See Marion Kaplan, *Between Dignity and Despair: Jewish Life in Nazi Germany* (New York: Oxford University Press, 1998), especially 173–201.

64. Ibid., 181.

65. Goeschel, *Suicide in Nazi Germany*, 101.

66. For a verbal description of these experiments, see Corrigan Interview (GTU). Frankl's written documentation is Viktor Frankl, "Pervitin Intrazisternal," *Ars Medici* no. 1 (1942): 58–60.

67. Geoffrey Cocks, *The State of Health: Illness in Nazi Germany* (New York: Oxford University Press, 2013), 167–168.

68. Ibid., 169.

69. Frankl, "Viktor Frankl," 177–204.

70. See Frankl, *Was nicht in meinen*, 57–58.

71. W.L. Fox, *Dandy of John Hopkins* (Baltimore, Md.: Williams and Wilkins, 1984), 44.

72. Frankl, "Pervitin Intrazisternal," 58.

73. Ibid.

74. W.E. Dandy, *Neurosurgery* (Hagerstown, Md.: 1945), 73. This is an outake from Dandy's 1936 *Brain Surgery*, which was translated and published in German.

75. W.E. Dandy, "Ventriculography Following the Injection of Air into the Cerebral Ventricles," *The Annals of Surgery* (July 1918): 39.

76. See Frankl, *Was nicht in meinen*, 58. Dr. Rappaport was later deported.

77. Frankl, "Pervitin Intrazisternal," 60.

78. Frankl, *Was nicht in meinen*, 57.

79. Lecture at San Diego International University (1972).

80. Konrad Kwiet, "Suicide in the Jewish Community," *Leo Baeck Yearbook* 38 (1993): 160. Kwiet also described how different doctors were in Hamburg. When the Gestapo was expected to arrive, patients would be given large doses of "Dolantin" in order to simulate suicide attempts. "However, such measures effected nothing more than a postponement, for those patients had to reckon with all the greater certainty to be included in the next transport." Interestingly, Kwiet criticized Frankl for downplaying the magnitude of suicide in the concentration camps.

81. Ibid., 159–160.

82. See Rosenkranz, *Verfolgung und Selbstbehauptung*, 41.

83. Kwiet, "Suicide in the Jewish Community," 149.

84. Michael Geyer, "Resistance as Ongoing Project: Visions of Order, Obligations to Strangers, Struggles for Civil Society," *Journal of Modern History* 64 (December 1992): 221.

85. Ibid., 231.

86. Viktor Frankl. Interviewed by Dr. Wolfgang Neugebauer and Dr. Elisabeth Klamper, 1 February 1993, available at the Dokumentationsarchiv des Österreichischen Widerstandes no. 832.

87. The hospital was often raided by the SS but there was also some resistance to the Nazis. Stern described how some patients were diagnosed with ailments that did not exist to avoid deportation. Stern, *Der letzten 12 Jahre Rothschild-Spital*, 13. This was confirmed by Ernest Seinfeld, who had his appendix removed at Rothschild to avoid deportation in 1940. Ernest Seinfeld, interview by author, Connecticut (9 July 1996).

Surviving and Working
Through to Redemption

Life itself teaches most people we are not here to enjoy ourselves.
—Viktor Frankl, *The Doctor on the Soul*

Frankl's sport of choice was mountain climbing, and apparently he was fairly adept at technical climbing. He was an accredited member of the alpine club "Donauland" in the mid 1930s, and he kept climbing into his eightieth year. Frankl's experience as a mountain climber led Elisabeth Kubler-Ross[1] to describe him as the "first European physician, psychiatrist, and scientist to study out-of-body experiences in the thirties, when it was still in the drawers of the obscure." According to Kubler-Ross, Frankl "studied the time" required for a falling mountain climber, "to review his life experiences which out of the body can be done in the fragment of a moment as time does not exist."[2] One may wonder if out-of-body experience is out of the drawers of the obscure, or how one "studies" time that "does not exist," but Kubler-Ross certainly held Frankl in high regard.

As we have seen, Frankl liked pushing and testing limits. His "height psychology" investigated the border territory between psychotherapy, philosophy, and religion, his medical work was experimental, and he also pushed the limits of his chosen sport and experimented beyond the "normal" parameters of mountain climbing. For anyone who has experienced it, the rush of overcoming one's physical limitations and fear of heights to ascent a mountain is quite a "high." And for those who have fallen, or come close "by seeing their life flash," the "rush" down is even more intense than the high. Arguably, Frankl's climb-

Notes for this section begin on page 126.

ing was a way to investigate the aesthetics of fear—the fear of death. Other comments on climbing by Frankl reveal his fascination with testing limits:

> we discover that this theory of mine on man's need for something such as sport holds ... only for the first three degrees of difficulty in rock climbing. From the third degree the situation changes. No ape has ever climbed such steep cliffs because there was never a need ... man is challenging his organism to give more than its best to cope with the fourth, fifth and sixth degrees of climbing ... the official definition of the sixth degree ... reads 'Close to the ultimate limits of human possibility'.... The wish is [for man] to explore the limits of his potential, the ultimate possibility.[3]

In 1942, Frankl hid his yellow star and went climbing after a two-year absence; he was so overjoyed he "kissed the rock."[4] Frankl also divulged that the last possession he abandoned upon entering Auschwitz was his leadership pin from the alpine club Donauland, his "highest pride."[5] Finally, Frankl's pursuit of "limit experiences" was exemplified when he remarked that there were three "breathtaking things ... a first ascent, gambling in a casino and a brain operation."[6] Frankl's fascination with limits was reflected in all dimensions of his existence when he combined gambling and climbing with brain operations. These characteristics suggest Frankl was a "counterphobic" character (a person who confronts their fears) or, in the vernacular, had an attitude of "no fear."

Surviving

Frankl, his wife (Tilly), and his parents (Elsa and Gabriel) were all deported to the "model ghetto" of Theresienstadt on 25 September 1942.[7] At the time, the Jewish population of Vienna had been reduced to about 22,000, or one-tenth of its pre-*Anschluss* figure.[8] Since Jewish doctors were no longer able to practice after the *Anschluss*, many of Frankl's colleagues had emigrated.[9] As Eichmann pressed for the removal of all of Vienna's Jews, those still left were residents of old-age homes, high-ranking war veterans, and Jewish partners in mixed marriages. In September of 1942 these prominent Jews received their deportation notices.[10] Before deportation, Frankl and his family were taken to the Gymnasium on Sperlgasse, where Frankl and his father had the profoundly humiliating experience of having their heads shaved completely bald.[11] As they were deported, Frankl and his father (like all deportees) documented their monetary wealth, which was subsequently confiscated.[12] Frankl described his journey to Theresienstadt on a special medical train, with a carload of patients who were under his care.[13] Apparently the head of the Jewish community in Vienna, Emil Tuchman, arranged for this special transport.[14]

The history of Theresienstadt is macabre. In June of 1942 reports appeared in the German press that "the Führer was presenting an entire city to the Jews." But "only some Jews would benefit from the ... gift."[15] Eligible Jews were the

elderly, the culturally prominent, those who had political positions, employees of Jewish organizations who had worked under the Nazis, and doctors and nurses from Jewish hospitals. Most of these hospitals were now being shut down and their patients sent to Theresienstadt as well.[16] The Rothschild hospital was also evacuated, and in some sense Frankl probably felt "lucky" to be sent with his family to Theresienstadt. Although as he was soon to discover this was just one more ruse used by the Nazis to manipulate the Jews.

The Nazis established Theresienstadt as a model ghetto in November of 1941. At Theresienstadt privileged Jews "were to live out their remaining years in comparative comfort." Thus, "residents were allowed facilities and activities unheard of elsewhere in the Reich. There was a nursery, an infirmary, a bandstand, and for a while even a coffee house."[17] There was also a significant amount of culture produced, the most renowned being the art of the children in the camp. But the *reality* of Theresienstadt was "a joke hatched in hell." Overcrowding led to horrendous housing conditions, lack of food created malnutrition, and elder residents often starved to death. The so-called "privileged ghetto" was actually more akin to a concentration camp. In 1943 and 1944 the Nazis used Theresienstadt as a propaganda camp for the International Red Cross to visit. This "sprucing up" that fooled the Red Cross allowed the camp to function as a "coverup" for the Holocaust.[18]

At Theresienstadt, Frankl described having "the most wonderful feeling you can imagine" when he was able to ease the suffering of his dying father by giving him a shot of morphine.[19] Likely Frankl's father was one of the countless elderly that starved to death. Also, from the monthly reports that Frankl wrote for the Public Health department in March and June 1944, it appears that he was involved in the mental hospital and "psychic-hygiene." It seems his duties included providing psychotherapy, and he discussed the need for "committing the psychopathic."[20] Apparently there was an insane asylum/mental hospital in what was once the horse stables but the conditions were extremely inhumane and decrepit. It is also possible that these monthly reports, which were written in the spring of 1944, were part of the "show" put on for the International Red Cross. This is confirmed by Theresienstadt survivor and Holocaust scholar the late Charlotte Opfermann, who claimed there was no functioning mental hospital and the "horse stables" where the mentally ill were left to suffer were avoided at all costs.[21]

Under "public health" was also the promotion of cultural programs, which included distribution of cards for the "lending library, theater and Kaffeehaus."[22] As a doctor Frankl was quartered with five or six other doctors and with these living conditions he managed limited conjugal visits. There was also some degree of mail service in the ghetto.[23]

Frankl met Rabbi Leo Baeck in Theresienstadt. Nathan Grossman described that although both men had "opportunities to escape," they both chose to remain, in order to "console, aid, comfort, and succor." They also gave lectures in

"secret, in an attic," and "once they lectured together."[24] Frankl gave at least ten lectures while interned in Theresienstadt.[25]

Also, at the urging of Dr. Karl Fleischman, Frankl set up a *Stosstruppe* (shock troop) that helped "new arrivals overcome the shock of Theresienstadt life." He then developed this into a suicide intelligence service where "any expression of a suicidal idea or intention would be immediately reported to him. He would then contact the would-be suicide and seek to dissuade him\her."[26] Frankl and his team members would console the prisoners, who were often sick and elderly, with logotherapeutic techniques that focused on maintaining a desire to live.

According to the historian George Berkley, Frankl's work in Theresienstadt was "a major reason for a steep drop in the suicide rate after the first year." And suicides did drop, from 254 in 1942 to 164 in 1943.[27] Nevertheless, Frankl's humanitarian efforts were also vital for the "proper" function of the ghetto, because at Theresienstadt: "Suicide was strictly prohibited. Offenders who survived were taken to the ill-famed 'small fortress,' and the same punishment was meted out to others. Relatives were punished in keeping with the principle of 'kingship liability;' fellow prisoners who kept silent about a suicidal act, contrary to camp regulations, which made reporting such events mandatory, were called to account. This affected the camp doctors in particular, who frequently hushed up suicides by stating 'heart failure' as the cause of death."[28]

These regulations suggest that Theresienstadt was indeed more akin to a concentration camp. One can imagine that under these conditions prisoners had to conform to expectations; lived in constant fear of deportation; competed for status and privilege; and at times of reprieve, bonded and comforted each other.

After Frankl's two-year internment in Theresienstadt, his life took a dramatic turn for the worse. The ghetto was "only five-eighths of a mile square and had only 219 houses ... by late fall of 1942 ... the population had grown to nearly sixty thousand."[29] In order to reduce the population strain, the Nazis began running a "shuttle train" to Auschwitz. Between 26 October 1942 and 28 October 1944, the Germans deported 46,750 Jews from Theresienstadt to Auschwitz in 27 transports. The first twelve transports, involving between 20,168 and 20,204 persons each, arrived at Auschwitz between 26 October 1942 and 20 March 1944.[30] In this way, Theresienstadt began to play a key role in the liquidation of European Jewry.[31] The deportations reached a climax in the fall of 1944. Frankl and his wife were on the so-called "Es" transport to Auschwitz on 19 October 1944, and his mother followed four days later.[32] Survivors of this ordeal related that the Nazis disguised the destinations of these transports in order to get the prisoners to "volunteer." Although suspicious, the prisoners could not be certain these trains were going to Auschwitz. Frankl apparently also had suspicions that the "transport east" was to Auschwitz.[33] Upon arrival at Auschwitz, Frankl described being separated from his wife, and how

he beseeched her to stay alive "at any price," even if that meant she had to pros-
titute herself. Frankl wanted her to know he absolved her, "a-priori."[34] Frankl's
absolution no doubt reflects the fact that at Theresienstadt "sexual barter" was
a well-known survival strategy.[35]

At Auschwitz, Frankl recalled (although he sometimes wondered if he had
imagined it) being selected by Joseph Mengele "to the left for the gas chamber."
But he "switched behind Mengele's back" to the right line, where he recog-
nized his friends.[36] In *Was nicht in meinen Büchern steht*, Frankl suggested he was
quickly transported out of Theresienstadt to Auschwitz.[37] But we know he was
in Theresienstadt for two years. Also, after reading *Man's Search for Meaning*, the
reader is left with the impression Frankl spent a substantial length of time in
Auschwitz.[38] But in 1991 Frankl told the American preacher, Robert Schuller:
"I was in Auschwitz only three or four days.... I was sent to a barrack and
we were all transported to a camp in Bavaria."[39] This fact is substantiated by
the prisoner's log from the sub-camp of Dachau, Kaufering III,[40] which listed
Frankl's arrival on 25 October 1944, exactly six days after his deportation from
Theresienstadt.[41] The usual travel time was two days from Theresienstadt to
Auschwitz, although Frankl described the journey as lasting "several days and
nights."[42] Frankl also described his journey out of Auschwitz to Kaufering III
as lasting "two days and three nights."[43] Frankl was therefore interned in Aus-
chwitz for two or three days. According to the research assistant Joseph White
at the United States Holocaust Memorial Museum, Frankl was likely a "depot
prisoner" held in the unfinished *mexico* (BIII) section of Birkenau. These pris-
oners were never registered in Auschwitz and were transported elsewhere in
the *concentration camp universe* of Europe.[44] Therefore it is highly unlikely Frankl
was selected by Josef Mengele, although it is possible that Mengele visited the
depot section to find twins.[45] We know Frankl was "processed" and numbered
in Dachau. This is confirmed by the Dachau archive and he also signed his affi-
davit in Pötzl's de-Nazification file "Dr. Viktor Frankl, Dachau prisoner num-
ber 119104." However, as the tenure of Frankl's testimony attests, two or three
days in depot at Auschwitz surely must have been an eternity.

In his testimony Frankl described numerous selections that apparently oc-
curred at Auschwitz, and how "in those few minutes fate had passed [him] in
many forms." In the next paragraph Frankl recounted that when a transport
was arranged a "second time" for "sick patients," for a "rest camp," Frankl put his
"name (that is, number) on the list" as a doctor. But no one knew if this transport
was just a "ruse" to get more work out of the sick or really a trip to the ovens.
Frankl decided to risk it, claiming he "had learned to let fate take its course."[46]

At Kaufering III Frankl was put to work digging ditches. In his words: "I
was Number 119,104, and most of the time I was digging and laying tracks for
railway lines. At one time, my job was to dig a tunnel, without help, for a water
main under a road. This feat did not go unrewarded; just before Christmas 1944,
I was presented with a gift of so-called 'premium coupons.'"[47]

Eventually Frankl volunteered for duty as a doctor in a typhus ward. "On my fourth day in the sick quarters … the chief doctor rushed in and asked me to volunteer for medical duties in another camp containing typhus patients. Against the urgent advice of my friends … I decided to volunteer. I knew that in a working party I would die in a short time. But if I had to die there might at least be some sense in my death."[48]

We therefore get a sense of the desperate reality Frankl was experiencing in the winter of 1944–1945. Frankl also depicted how "in the winter and spring of 1945 there was an outbreak of typhus which infected nearly all the prisoners."[49] Living conditions at Kaufering were horrendous. Although Frankl was able to warm himself temporarily in the evenings in the barracks of a privileged prisoner named Reynolds, he also described the pervasive winter cold, feeling deep despair and his sinking into "dangerous malaise" of a loss of hope.[50]

The Kaufering camps were the largest of all the sub-camps of Dachau and by the end of April 1945 thirty thousand people were held in the Kaufering system. The Kaufering complex was designated for the production of aircraft. Prisoners were used to build concrete bunkers and railway supply embankments. Under the atrocious conditions prisoners "became incapacitated within a very short period of time." For example, in September and October of 1944, 1,322 prisoners were selected and deported to Auschwitz, where they were gassed. Typhus, spotted fever, and tuberculosis were widespread.[51]

The camp Frankl volunteered for was Türkheim (also known as Kaufering VI), since the prisoner logs from Kaufering III show no. 119104 being transported to Türkheim on 8 March 1945.[52] Frankl therefore spent just under five months (25 October to 8 March) in the work camp at Kaufering III. When he was deported to Türkheim it must have been clear to him that he would not have survived much longer under the conditions at Kaufering III. It was certainly his most difficult test physically; he was undoubtedly "lucky" to have survived.

Klingberg describes that at Türkheim "conditions improved" for Frankl in the "nick of time." He had access to aspirin and "rested better and took nourishment."[53] At Türkheim Frankl was in charge of fifty patients, and he was designated the senior block warden. "I was forced to keep straightening blankets, picking up bits of straw … and shouting at the poor devils who … upset all my efforts at tidiness and cleanliness. Apathy was particularly increased among the feverish patients, so that they did not react at all unless shouted at. Even this failed at times, and then it took tremendous self-control not to strike them."[54]

Frankl gave the date of his liberation as 27 April 1945.[55] Therefore, it seems that his confrontation with the vast terror of the concentration camps occurred for about six months (19 October 1944 to 27 April 1945).

In this period, Frankl described numerous near death experiences. Along with his fortunate escape from Auschwitz and overcoming typhus, he recounted being rescued from the gas chamber by a "Viennese gangster." Frankl described

how he originally met the gangster while he was being beaten at the "small fortress" in Theresienstadt (he never mentioned why he was sent there).[56] This gangster saw Frankl in line for a transport and replaced him with another prisoner because that "group was ill-fated."[57] Also while in the Kaufering system Frankl recalled "being protected" by a Kapo. Finally, at the end of the war, Frankl and his friend were not evacuated from Türkheim by the SS and instead remained in the camp as the front approached. The SS took their "other friends who had thought they were traveling to freedom" and locked them in huts and burned them to death.[58] In the winter of 1944–1945 Frankl experienced an incredible ordeal full of angst, anxiety, fear, and moral dilemmas. Like many survivors, Frankl expressed a deep remorse when he stated: "We know: the best of us did not return."[59]

After his liberation Frankl worked for two months as the head doctor in an American-controlled displaced persons hospital at Bad-Wörrishofen (Bavaria). Because the borders were closed between the American sector of southern Germany and the Soviet control over Austria, it was illegal for Frankl to return to Vienna. However, as concern for the fate of his wife and mother enveloped him,[60] he decided to return to Vienna. Before returning to Vienna he spent two months in Munich, where he was employed by the U.S. Army to give radio talks on psychological problems of reconstruction. However, the day before his transport to Vienna he learned that his mother had died in the gas chambers of Auschwitz. At this point the crestfallen Frankl considered suicide.[61]

Upon his return to Vienna he quickly learned his wife had expired of disease and hunger—like thousands of others—at Bergen-Belsen shortly after the British liberated the camp. From his letters, especially one written to his sister on 7 November 1945, Frankl was clearly in the depths of despair, stating "there is no joy in living" and "I live only for work."[62]

The work Frankl was referencing was the manuscript that had been taken from him at Auschwitz. Frankl also described to his sister how during his internment at Türkheim, and "near death" from typhus, he began to reconstruct the manuscript *Ärztliche Seelsorge* (The Doctor and the Soul).[63] In the book Frankl described how the process of reconstruction began by writing on scraps of paper that his friend had given him for his fortieth birthday.

> We know of the following case: In a barrack in a concentration camp lay several dozen men down with typhus. All were delirious except one who made an effort to avert the nocturnal deliria by deliberately fighting back sleep at night. He profited by the excitement and mental stimulus induced by the fever, however, to reconstruct the unpublished manuscript of a scientific work he had written, which had been taken away from him in the concentration camp. In the course of sixteen feverish nights he had recovered the whole book—jotting down, in the dark, stenographic cue words on tiny scraps of paper.[64]

This passage contains the embryo of the heroic version of survival that made *Man's Search for Meaning* so popular. Arguably, on a psychological plane writing

in the third person also allowed Frankl to begin to disassociate and put his traumatic experiences behind him. Later he described the book as his "spiritual child," which helped him offset the delirium of typhus and continue living.[65] From his statements and letters it is clear his book continued to give Frankl a goal as he tried to put his shattered life back together in the fall of 1945.

Interpreting the Holocaust

In one widespread view the Holocaust is understood as a unique representative of human evil that destroyed any notion of human Meaning. The nihilistic and irrational destruction of millions is viewed as *the* rupture in Western historical consciousness. This rupture is interpreted as causing the failure of modernity's faith in reason, progress, and human Meaning. Theodor Adorno initiated this view of the Holocaust with his conceptualization that "after Auschwitz poetry cannot be written."

On the issue of rendering Holocaust experience, Adorno's claim implied that the incomprehensible horror of the Holocaust cannot be aestheticized without normalizing it. Adorno warned of the barbarism inherent in attempts to represent the Holocaust artistically because "any such representation 'contains the power … to extract pleasure out of it…. Through aesthetic principles of stylization …'" The danger is that the inconceivable reality of death-camp experience appears as if it had "some meaning; it is transfigured and stripped of some of its horror …"[66] Echoing Adorno, Auschwitz survivor Primo Levi argued that language lacked the capacity to portray the experience appropriately.[67] In opposition to Adorno, Berel Lang argued that although one may inevitability fail to adequately depict the evil of the Holocaust, "writing is still justified—because of the menace of the alternative; that is, the silence into which the Holocaust otherwise would disappear."[68]

One of the best-known writers on the Holocaust, Lawrence Langer, has described the Holocaust as a "rupture in human values" that:

> after the war left stunned minds staring blankly at alien modes of living and dying in the monstrous milieu of ghettos and camps. One response to this scenario might be to accept the Holocaust as a warrant for futility, a witness to the death of hope … another … is to regard the calamity as a summons to reconsider usual views of the self, its relation to time and memory, its portrayal in literature born of the Holocaust, its use and abuse by culture, and its role in reshaping our sense of history's legacies from the past and bequests to later generations. Such probing may not transform our present or even improve our prospects, and certainly will not redeem our past, but it can help us to live with clearer eyes. Clarity has a virtue of its own in murky times.[69]

Langer offered sound advice for those thinking about Holocaust literature. Therefore, Langer's measured call for the necessity of "probing" and "clarity" will guide our interpretation of Frankl's version of the Holocaust. Nevertheless,

our deference for those who managed to survive does not mean we should attribute to them an almost "religious aura." As Elie Wiesel argued, the "sacredness of the event" must center on remembering the dead. There is no need to give the survivors a moral role and an undeserved intellectual acumen.[70] Also, as Irving Howe claimed, we can submit Holocaust memoirs to "critical judgment" because "[o]ur awe before the suffering and our respect for the sufferers does not disable us from making discriminations of value, tone, authority." Howe was making the simple point that in choosing to become writers, survivors have no choice but to accept the burden of our scrutiny.[71] But we must be sensitive, because for the survivor, who has been traumatized and is often beset with guilt for just being alive, memory is both problematic and treacherous. For anyone, but especially a trauma survivor who has been profoundly victimized, an honest engagement and reckoning with the past is a rare achievement.

Working Through

Frankl's output in his first year out of the camps was truly prolific.[72] He "dictated and dictated, ... three stenographer-typists worked in shifts to capture it all" and "the floodgates had opened."[73] Within a year of the war's end, he had published *The Doctor and the Soul: From Psychotherapy to Logotherapy*, and *From Death-Camp to Existentialism: A Psychiatrist's Path to a New Therapy*, which in 1963 was retitled *Man's Search for Meaning*. Frankl also gave a lecture series shortly after the war, which became the book *The Unconscious God*. In addition, immediately after the war Frankl wrote some poems and a play entitled *Sychronisation in Birkenwald*. This play, originally published in the Catholic journal *Der Brenner* in 1948 under the pseudonym Gabriel Lion (his father's first and his mother's last name combined), was translated by Joseph Fabry and performed at the Graduate Theological Union in Berkeley in 1977. This intellectual outburst reflected Frankl's initial working through of his experiences. Undoubtedly, the working through of a traumatic experience has the effect of objectifying and distancing the immediacy of the experience and thus resolving a certain amount of the anxiety.

In 1946, Frankl explained the "apparent paradox that some prisoners of a less hardy make-up often seemed to survive camp life better than did those of a robust nature" with the claim that these "sensitive people ... were able to retreat from their terrible surroundings to a life of inner riches and spiritual freedom."[74] In 1968, over twenty years after his internment, Frankl was interviewed by *Psychology Today* and described his survival in these terms: "I was lucky. And I survived better as a person because I had a rich intellectual background, an inner life on which to draw. And I had a mission, to counsel other inmates. Do you know what my fantasy and finally compulsion became in those years? I wanted to live to go mountain climbing again. Can you understand that?"[75]

It seems luck, character, training, and the desire for the "normal" limit experience of climbing were the reasons Frankl survived. As mentioned, Frankl also attributed his survival to his desire to reconstruct the manuscript, his "spiritual child" that was taken from him at Auschwitz.[76] Strangely these claims by Frankl portrayed the Holocaust as a "manageable" experience that (with luck) was survivable. In order to understand why Frankl viewed survival in these terms, we need to unpack and reflect on the relationship between Frankl's character, his world view, his actual camp experience, the conditions under which he wrote, and the subsequent version of survival. The concept of working through implies that the Holocaust represented a new intellectual problem for Frankl, thus the discontinuity. But obviously there is continuity between Frankl's thinking before the war and his intellectual outburst in the mid 1940s.

Frankl took two different stances on how the experience of the concentration camps affected his psychological theory. Frankl remarked that "people think I came out Auschwitz with a brand-new psychotherapy. This is not the case."[77] Since the mid 1960s Frankl has claimed that the concentration camps validated his brand of psychotherapy because "the tenets of logotherapy were justified by the acid test of the concentration camp."[78] But Frankl should not have been surprised that "people" thought his therapy originated in his concentration camp experience, because the original English subtitle to his Holocaust testimony was *A Psychiatrist's Path to a New Therapy*. Also, in 1959 his publishers promoted his testimony on the Holocaust with his claim that: "What is most important is that this psychotherapy was, as the *author points out*, 'not concocted in the philosopher's arm chair nor at the analyst's couch; it took shape in the hard school of air-raid shelters and bomb craters; in concentration camps and prisoner of war camps.'"[79] (My italics.)

Frankl's statement, along with the publisher's promotion, was deleted from later editions, and his testimony was retitled *Man's Search for Meaning*. But in 1963 a similar statement appeared on the back cover of *Man's Search for Meaning*: "After three grim years at Auschwitz and other Nazi prisons, Dr. Frankl gained freedom only to learn almost his entire family had been wiped out. *But during, and indeed partly because of*, the almost incredible suffering and degradations of those years, he developed his theory of logotherapy." (My italics.) Also, in 1949, in the *American Journal of Psychotherapy* Frankl's good friend Paul Polak described "Frankl's Existential Analysis" as a "'new start'... that integrated the specific physical and mental suffering this generation had to endure during the last decade."[80] Clearly in his own writing and publisher's marketing there was an oscillation between the camps as where his ideas "took shape," and the camps as the testing ground that "justified" his preconceived notions. It may be that both the publisher and Frankl simply wanted to use his survival of Auschwitz to promote his therapy. Frankl's testimony also includes a theoretical synopsis of logotherapy, and many readers felt Frankl's therapeutic legitimacy stemmed from his survival. For example, Gordon Allport made this statement about the source of

Frankl's intellectual legitimacy in the Preface to *Man's Search for Meaning*: "How could he—every possession lost, every value destroyed, suffering from hunger, cold and brutality, hourly expecting extermination—how could he find life worth preserving? A psychiatrist who personally has faced such extremity is a psychiatrist worth listening to."

Resolving Trauma

Frankl's trauma and loss is unfathomable. As mentioned, Frankl's mother was gassed at Auschwitz; his father died starving in Theresienstadt.[81] His wife, who followed him on her own initiative to Auschwitz from Thereseinstadt, died in Bergen-Belsen. His brother died in Auschwitz. He lost a number of close friends as well. Given the magnitude of his loss, Frankl's personal prescription for coming to terms with this trauma deserves our unmitigated respect. However, when his resolution is extended to the cultural realm, we have a responsibility to engage him, and work through—for ourselves—the Holocaust.

As mentioned, while he was writing under the duress of typhus, Frankl's working through began as his internment in the camps was ending. Since he was reconstructing and revising a work conceived and put down on paper before the Holocaust, there existed a deep continuity between his prewar and postwar work. *The Doctor and the Soul* was dedicated to Tilly and contained his previous intellectual concerns. According to Alexander Batthyány, the main ideas of *The Doctor and the Soul* are contained in the prewar draft, but not "as concise[ly]" and not with the same "urgency."[82]

In the book he recapitulated his criticisms of Freud and Adler, and once again turned to his central intellectual preoccupation—life's meaning. Citing the phenomenological work of Heidegger and Binswanger, Frankl articulated what made humans unique and different from animals. According to Frankl, "human existence takes the form of historical existence. It is—in contrast to the existence of animals—always placed in a historical space."[83] For Frankl, history opened the possibility for life to have meaning. Simply, history is what gives life a base in the past and directs us toward the future. To this idea Frankl added that any attempts to live in a "presentist condition" by intoxication in work or play may be considered neurotic unless this escape is consciously chosen. Frankl's conception of human uniqueness, which was grounded in responsibility, now had a heightened focus on the experience of temporality.

Frankl continued his evaluation of the human condition by revisiting the problem of the transitoriness of existence. Now, after catastrophe had struck his family, his ideas seem more concise and urgent. For example he writes that transitoriness cannot be conceived as making life meaningless because: "having been is also a kind of being—perhaps the surest kind. And all effective action in life may, in this view, appear as a salvaging of possibilities by actualizing them.

Though past, these possibilities are now safely ensconced in the past for all eternity, and time can no longer change them."[84]

Frankl's response to the transitoriness of existence, and subsequent problem of meaninglessness, was to make the past permanent. The question arises—to what degree did this interpretation of the past help Frankl work through his trauma? By making the past and those in it permanent, and thus "eternal," undoubtedly eased his sense of loss. In terms of the future, Frankl claimed "the future—happily—still remains to be shaped; that is, it is at the disposal of man's responsibility."[85]

Frankl then connected the conception of the past as eternal, to Jaspers's description of man as a "deciding being." According to Frankl, humans were responsible for giving form to "eternity" by the choices they made in the present. He also claimed that "it is fearful to know that at this moment we bear the responsibility for the next, every decision ... is a decision for all eternity ... we bring to reality—or miss—a possibility that exists only for a particular moment."[86] As we saw in his 1937 article Frankl was focused on the issue of responsibility, but now he plumbs the depths of responsibility. He asks: "But what is responsibility? ... in truth there is something about responsibility that resembles an abyss. The longer and the more profoundly we consider it, the more we become aware of its awful depths—until a kind of giddiness overcomes us ... there is something fearful about human responsibility. But at the same time something glorious!"[87]

Before the war, Frankl considered responsibility a foundational feature of human existence. Now the articulation has a new seriousness where responsibility equals an abyss that must be faced until one is consumed by giddiness. Prefacing the passage, Frankl claimed that "so long as life remains, all guilt and all evil is still 'redeemable.'" This claim about guilt and evil, along with the heightened focus on time, choices as eternal, and individual responsibility conceived as an abyss leading to giddiness, are insightful depictions of his psychological state. The heightened reflection on guilt and responsibility was likely attributable on some level to the trauma of his own survival when so many others, including his family, perished. Responsibility, originally conceived pre-war as an anthropological principle, is now perceived as an "abyss" with "awful depths." But contemplation of the abyss leads to "giddiness," to something "glorious." Once this past is faced, then one is capable of taking action and choosing what will be stored for all eternity. These insights are summed up by the maxim that Frankl took to guide "the post-Auschwitz period" of his life: "Live as if you were living for the second time—and as if you had acted the first time as wrongly as you are about to act now."[88] Frankl's relief for having survived is apparent in the statement "live as if you were living for the second time." But in order to counteract the insight into the burdensome depth of responsibility and guilt, Frankl derived an ethic that would seem to lead to a life of repentance. That is, "act as if you had acted the first time as wrongly as you are about to act

now." At the heart of this ethic is the realization that a guilt-ridden past leads
to a burdensome present. Therefore the reason to act properly stems from a
heightened awareness of the guilt, or shame experienced when acting improp-
erly. It seems that after the Holocaust, the ethic by which Frankl guided his life
focused on avoiding the accruement of guilt.[89]

With this ethic as backdrop, we can conclude that the following passage
represented Frankl's initial working through of his trauma, loss, and guilt of
survival. It is worth quoting at length:

> To mourn for anything irrevocably lost must seem useless and foolish from the
> point of view of 'sound common sense,' and this holds also for repenting an ir-
> redeemable wrong. But for the inner biography of a man, grief and repentance
> do have meaning. Grieving for a person whom we have loved and lost in a sense
> continues his life, and repentance permits the culprit to rise again freed of guilt.
> The loved person whom we have grieved for has been lost objectively, in empir-
> ical time, but he is preserved subjectively, in inner time. Grief brings him into the
> mind's present. And repentance … has the power to wipe out a wrong; though
> the wrong cannot be undone, the culprit himself undergoes a moral rebirth. This
> opportunity to make past events fruitful for one's inner history does not stand in
> opposition to man's responsibility, but in a dialectical relationship. For guilt pre-
> supposes responsibility. Man is responsible in view of the fact he cannot retrace a
> single step; the smallest as well as the biggest remains a final one. None of his acts
> of commission or omission can be wiped off the slate as if they had never been.
> Nevertheless, in repenting man may inwardly break with an act, and in living out
> this repentance—which is an inner event—he can undo the outer event on a spir-
> itual, moral plane.[90]

This measured passage, blending loss and guilt with grief and repentance,
seems to be Frankl's initial resolution of some of the more profound trauma
surrounding his Holocaust experience. Since he was reworking a book con-
ceived before the war it may be that these positions originated before his trauma.
However, from the articulation it does appear that these conceptions are aiding
in working through his trauma. The grief and mourning obviously had to do
with the magnitude of Frankl's personal loss. But what Frankl meant by "acts of
commission or omission" or repentance as "an inner event" is not clear. These
claims were likely tied to his ethic to live "this time" properly, since he claimed
that ethic guided the "post-Auschwitz" period of his life. But the repentance
also allowed him to "inwardly break with an act" and thus resolve his past. Once
this was achieved he had the "opportunity to make past events fruitful for …
[his] inner history."

Frankl's resolutions to his traumatic experience seem to confirm Aharon
Appelfeld's description of how "[t]he survivor's testimony is first of all a search
for relief; and as with any burden, the one who bears it seeks also to rid himself
of it as hastily as possible."[91] Although Frankl's first work was not specifically
a testimony, Appelfeld's characterization of the survivor's psychological needs
appears apt. Also, in 1981 Frankl described the "relief" he felt when he first
conceived of "time as permanent."[92] After the Holocaust, Frankl continued to

affirm responsibility as a key component of human existence. But he could have just as easily taken the opposing interpretation and claimed that the Holocaust destroyed choice and thus responsibility. But this would have left him viewing human existence as essentially absurd and tragic, which was the response of many intellectuals but an unlikely conclusion for Frankl to draw since he had spent his life in search of Meaning. Also, if Frankl viewed the past as absurd and tragic he would have faced unending grief. On the other hand, accepting responsibility had all the "abysmal" terror of irresolvable guilt. But he was able to side-step this issue and begin to resolve this loss and guilt by making the past permanent, and thus a repository of meaningful experiences. It seems Frankl's combining of the past as eternal with responsibility was his initial resolution of the guilt and pain he was feeling for "luckily" surviving.

This solution also allowed Frankl to conceptualize his Holocaust experience as meaningful, and not only that, but as a repository of meaningful experiences that were eternal. In this version, repentance occurred through looking at the past as a lesson in self-improvement in order to make better choices in the present. Although emotional angst was clearly evident in his first post-Holocaust work, Frankl did seem to be quickly resolving the terrifying horrors of the camps. This rapid working through is exemplified on the opening page of his Holocaust testimony when he made the strange claim in that "this tale is not concerned with great horrors, which have already been described often enough." It may be that Frankl's suggestion that his training as a psychiatrist helped him survive the camps is also applicable to his post-Holocaust experience. From this perspective, his training and the focus on responsibility allowed him to "quickly" work through and objectify his camp experience. It seems that by the time Frankl dictated his popular testimony, he had already initially "worked through" the great horrors and deep despair in his first work.

Along with his initial working through of his trauma we can also reconstruct Frankl's "existential reality" when he dictated his testimony. That Frankl's spirit was not completely destroyed by his camp experience is reflected in his recollection that when he returned to Vienna after the camps he told his friend Paul Polak that he "had a feeling … that something was expected of me, that I am destined for something."[93] Although Frankl debated numerous emigration opportunities in the winter of 1945–1946, including Brazil, the United States, and even Australia to be with his sister,[94] he eventually decided to stay and make a life in Vienna. According to Klingberg, in late August of 1945 Frankl spent a number of weeks in deep despair in a pension. But apparently Frankl began to recover because Klingerg describes that already by the end of September 1945 "it is clear that Viktor was not only writing but making a professional reentry." This reentry was abetted by Dr. Bruno Pitterman (Frankl knew him from Socialist circles in his school days). Pitterman not only procured a living space for Frankl on Mariannegasse (where he would live for the next fifty-three years), he also found Frankl a position (even though Frankl had "no interest in getting

a job"[95]). Pitterman gave Frankl a choice between running the state hospital Am Steinhof where Frankl worked in the 1930s or serving as director of neurology at Vienna's small city hospital the Policlinic. Frankl accepted the position at the latter and began working there in February of 1946, around the same time *The Doctor and the Soul* was published.

In 1983 Frankl described that he wrote *Man's Search for Meaning* because: "I had wanted simply to convey to the reader by way of concrete example that life holds a potential meaning under any conditions, even the most miserable ones. And I thought that if the point were demonstrated in a situation as extreme as that in a concentration camp, my book might gain a hearing. I therefore felt responsible for writing down what I had gone through, for I thought it might be helpful to people who are prone to despair."[96]

We can conclude that although Frankl was still in despair when he set out to dictate his testimony, it also seems he was no longer suicidal and the worst was over.[97] He had finished his "spiritual child," he had a place to live, and was reestablishing himself professionally. No doubt the process of writing/dictating was therapeutic for him, but it also seems that his deep humanistic urge to heal others was a prime motivation.

The Camps

It is clear that Frankl's training as a doctor and psychiatrist was helpful to him in the camps. His medical degree gave him a role in caring for the sick, and promoting his vision of psychology imparted the all-important sense of a mission. Also, his background in psychology, especially his focus on attitudinal values, provided a perspective from which he could come to terms with what he was experiencing.

Although Frankl initially wanted to publish *Man's Search for Meaning* anonymously, at the urging of his friends he decided he "should accept responsibility" for the book.[98] In the book Frankl used a sober analytic tone that attempted to capture the desperate conditions of the camps. The reader certainly experiences a feeling of impending apocalypse.

The testimony is structured like a long essay, and is a very fluid ninety-page read. In the preface, Gordon Allport presented Frankl's testimony as a "gem of dramatic narrative" that is "artfully constructed and gripping." Captivated by Frankl's style, Allport described how his "mixed flow of emotion and apathy is arresting." He also saw how Frankl rendered "hunger, humiliation, fear and deep anger at injustice ... tolerable by closely guarded images of beloved persons, by religion, by a grim sense of humor, and even by glimpses of the healing beauties of nature ..." Allport also understood the appeal of Frankl's ability to make "larger sense out of his apparently senseless suffering" by facing "fully the ubiquity of suffering and the forces of evil," and thus deriving "a surprisingly

hopeful view of man's capacity to transcend his predicament and discover an adequate guiding truth." Finally, Allport considered Frankl's testimony "a compelling introduction to the most significant psychological movement of our day."[99]

Allport's uncritical praise combined with Frankl's moving narrative made the work into a worldwide best seller. Apparently, Allport was not interested in providing a critical reading of Frankl's testimony because he felt "Dr. Frankl's words have a profoundly honest ring, for they rest on experiences too deep for deception."[100] But a critical reading is justified because there are some misleading statements and contradictions. Langer, who was unaware of Frankl's actual camp experience, picked up on the contradictions when he argued it is "as if Frankl himself were unconsciously committed to a dual vision, torn between how it really was and how, retrospectively, he would like to believe it had been."[101]

Frankl also began with the erroneous claim that "many factual accounts about the concentration camps are already on record." He then added, "here, facts will be significant only as far as they are part of a man's experience." It is not clear why the facts were not central because Frankl wanted to describe the "exact nature" of the experiences of "an ordinary prisoner."[102] Also, most readers of *Man's Search for Meaning* will be surprised to discover that Frankl spent only a few days in depot at Auschwitz. In the book, Frankl made no reference to his two-year internment in Theresienstadt. Instead, he began his testimony with his arrival in Auschwitz and movingly imparted the details of his experiences.

According to Frankl, the first phase a prisoner experienced was shock. He gave the example of "the circumstances of [his] admission" and described how a "cry broke from the anxious passengers, ... Auschwitz!"[103] He then related the initial selections, shaving, delousing, and showers that occurred upon admission to Auschwitz. But the reader is led to believe that Frankl was actually interned at Auschwitz by his descriptions of enduring sleep deprivation, of the inability of prisoners to clean their teeth (yet they "had healthier gums than ever before"), and of the wearing of "the same shirts for half a year," etc.[104] He also claimed that "the prisoner of Auschwitz, in the first phase of shock, did not fear death. Even the gas chambers lost their horrors for him after the first few days."[105] This is an odd claim not only because Frankl was in Kaufering III after the first few days but because it defies what we know about living and dying in Auschwitz.

We know that Frankl spent two to three days in Auschwitz, and on the opening page of *Man's Search for Meaning* he honestly asserted that "most of the events described here did not take place in the large and famous camps, but in the small ones where most of the real extermination took place." The problem is that he begins by detailing his experiences in Auschwitz. But again he was held in depot and never selected at Auschwitz. In addition, Frankl also seemed oblivious to the fact that the death camps were where "the real extermination

took place." There were also work camps and ghettos, where Frankl was interned. Although Frankl's experience was certainly atrocious, his claim to have knowledge of "where the real extermination took place" is incorrect.

Frankl also understated the horrors of the camps. For example, he described being handed a picture of the concentration camp prisoners and being asked, "Isn't this terrible, the dreadful staring faces—everything about it." Frankl responded: "'Why?' I asked, for I genuinely did not understand. For at that moment I saw it all again: at 5:00 a.m. it was still pitch dark outside. I was lying on the hard boards in an earthen hut where about seventy of us were 'taken care of.' We were sick and did not have to leave camp for work; we did not have to go on parade."[106]

Frankl's stoic response to the camp experience has emotional appeal. Frankl also described the death of a young woman he witnessed in the camps:

> … it may sound as if I had invented it; but to me it seems like a poem.
> This woman knew she would die in the next few days. But when I talked to her she was cheerful in spite of this knowledge. "I am grateful that fate has hit me so hard," she told me. "In my former life I was spoiled and did not take spiritual accomplishments seriously."[107]

Frankl even presented the dehumanization of Auschwitz in similar terms. According to Frankl, dehumanization led to a necessary detachment from reality through "a grim sense of humor" and "curiosity" because prisoners knew they "had nothing to lose except [their] ridiculously naked lives." He then related this process of detachment to his previous experience of climbing. "Apart from a strange kind of humor, another sensation seized us: curiosity. I have experienced this kind of curiosity before, as a fundamental reaction toward a certain strange circumstance. When my life was once endangered by a climbing accident, I felt only one sensation at the crucial moment: curiosity, curiosity as to whether I should come out of it alive or with a fractured skull or some other injuries."[108]

Apparently Frankl's peculiar preparation for the concentration camp was his previous confrontation with death in a climbing experience. This capacity for self-detachment was also a key component of his therapeutic techniques (dereflection and paradoxical intention). He also recalled that his friends said he was not initially affected by the camp experience.

Frankl then delineated how this detachment, although necessary and normal, could lead to a feeling of apathy. Thus, "the prisoner passed from the first to the second phase; the phase of relative apathy, in which he achieved a kind of emotional death."[109] According to Frankl, the root of the apathy was the feeling that present reality was unbearable and the realization that there was no future in sight because camp life destroyed not only hope in the future, but also any sense of normality. "His life seemed to him absolutely without future. He regarded it as over and done, as if he had already died. This feeling of lifelessness was intensified by other causes: in time, it was the limitlessness of the term of

imprisonment which was most acutely felt; in space, the narrow limits of the prison. Anything outside the barbed wire became remote—out of reach and, in a way, unreal."[110]

Frankl's solution to this apathy relied on the promotion of attitudinal values. Therefore, even in these extreme circumstances, Frankl heroically claimed that one can overcome the apathy by choosing to place meaning in the suffering. "Fundamentally, therefore, any man can, even under such circumstances, decide what will become of him—mentally and spiritually. He may retain dignity even in a concentration camp. [Also] If there is meaning in life at all, then there must be meaning in suffering.... Here lies the opportunities of attaining the moral values that a difficult situation may afford him. And this decides whether he is worthy of his sufferings or not."[111]

Frankl's existentialist attitude helped him find meaning in the oppressive and dehumanized situation of the concentration camp. His testimony is peppered with such uplifting statements, and is certainly one reason why the book is popular. Frankl even found a certain "freedom" in his aestheticization of death. Thus: "for us, the meaning of life embraced the wider cycles of life and death, of suffering and dying. [Also] Suffering had become a task on which we did not want to turn our backs. We had to realize its hidden opportunities for achievement. [and] ... to find us suffering proudly—not miserably—knowing how to die."[112]

As we have seen, Frankl developed this notion of attitudinal values in his pioneering work in psychology during the 1930s. Langer has described Frankl's prescriptions for suffering and dying in Auschwitz as "almost sinister, certainly ... insensitive."[113] Langer also questioned how entering a gas chamber could "represent a hidden opportunity," and how, could one "suffer proudly" and "know how to die" while being asphyxiated. But we must recognize that Frankl's claims, insensitive as they seem, represented his own peculiar way of coming to terms with his experience. For example, Frankl's heroic version helped him resolve the psychic turmoil caused by, among other things, the knowledge of *how* his beloved mother died: "Once those people—including my own mother by the way—had been crammed into gas chambers and they saw the canisters of Cyclone B gas thrown into a crowd of naked people, they saw there was no help. Then they began to pray, saying the Shema Israel, and surrendered themselves to what God had bestowed on them—the Communists singing the 'Marseillaise,' the Christians saying the Our Father, the Jews saying Kaddish upon each other."[114]

There are no words to adequately depict the experience of dying in a gas chamber. But Frankl's rendition, full of religious connotation, certainly stylized the horror, and his description misleadingly suggested that Jews, Christians, etc., died together. However, the affirmation of suffering and death overcame the meaninglessness only in a philosophical sense. On a more practical level, Frankl claimed that survival required retaining a sense of the future. Obviously, the

predecessor of this idea is the call for finding a mission. In this light he became fond of repeating Nietzsche's prescription that "[h]e who knows a why for living, will surmount almost every how."

Frankl maintained that his future was sustained by two things. One was obviously the hope of seeing his wife again. The other was his career and continual promotion of his "height psychology." Thus in a telling and strangely prescient comment he imagined himself lecturing about his camp experiences. When Frankl found himself reflecting upon "the trivial things" of daily survival he described how:

> I forced my thoughts to turn to another subject. Suddenly I saw myself standing on the platform of a well-lit, warm and pleasant lecture room. In front of me sat an attentive audience on comfortable upholstered seats. I was giving a lecture on the psychology of the concentration camp! All that oppressed me at that moment became objective, seen and described from the remote viewpoint of science. By this method I succeeded somehow in rising above the situation, above the sufferings of the moment, and I observed them as if they were already of the past. Both I and my troubles became the object of an interesting psychoscientific study undertaken by myself.[115]

Frankl's scientific training allowed him to distance himself from his circumstances and take flight into a future possibility, one that ironically became true.

Frankl also demonstrated the necessity of "believing" in the future by recounting the following story. His senior block warden confided to him that he had a dream that the war would come to an end on 30 March 1945. On 29 March 1945 the man fell ill, and he died on the thirty-first. Frankl gave this interpretation of his death: "Those who know how close the connection is between the state of mind of a man—his courage and hope, or lack of them—and the state of immunity of his body will understand that the sudden loss of hope and courage can have a deadly effect ... the ultimate cause of my friend's death was that the expected liberation did not come and he was severely disappointed."[116]

Putting aside whether or not Frankl's interpretation is true, or even has elements of truth, the pitfalls of such a rendition is that it equates survival with having the proper attitude. Frankl seems to be suggesting that those who died were not strong enough to bear the conditions of the camps. Langer had this response to similar claims by Frankl: "Frankl avoids the difficulty of altering his reader's consciousness so that it can contend with the moral uncertainties of the Holocaust. His own moral view is clear-cut, precise, almost self-congratulatory: 'One could make a victory of those experiences ... or one could ignore the challenge and simply vegetate, as did a majority of prisoners.' It comes as no surprise to the reader, as he closes the volume, that the real hero of *Man's Search for Meaning* is not man, but Viktor Frankl."[117]

Langer recognized that Frankl failed to contend with the moral uncertainties of living (and surviving) in the camps. Langer also understood that Frankl made the Holocaust comprehensible within the grounds of traditional morality. As Langer pointed out, the problem with Frankl's version is that it served to

lessen the horror by making the Holocaust seem survivable and thereby denied the moral and physical terror at the heart of the Holocaust. Langer was certainly correct to argue that Frankl's heroic story was an attempt "to bring the Holocaust into line with familiar experience by making it verbally manageable," and thus set "the Holocaust solidly into the bedrock of spiritual history ..."[118] Langer therefore recognized that Frankl's claims made Holocaust "survival a matter of mental health."[119] But Langer went further. On Frankl's claim that everyone needs a specific mission, he stated: "So nonsensically unspecific is this universal principle of being that one can imagine Heinrich Himmler announcing it to his SS men, or Joseph Goebbels sardonically applying it to the genocide of the Jews!"[120] On Frankl's claim that attitudinal values will help you to turn tragedy into a triumph through transcendence, Langer wrote: "If this doctrine had been more succinctly worded, the Nazis might have substituted it for the cruel mockery of *Arbeit Macht Frei*."[121] Langer recognized the close connection between Frankl's claims and the cynicism of Nazi ideology. Langer didn't go so far as to claim that Frankl was identifying with his oppressors, but Frankl's empty heroics did seem to mirror the Nazi world view.

Less critical readers have accepted Frankl's version and have been completely taken in. Subsequently the comments deferring to and lionizing Frankl are abundant. For example, note these comments on his testimony: "Frankl's experiences in the four concentration camps he survived, and the human heights which he reached in that setting, are almost legendary."[122] Or more to the point: "The problem one faces in appreciating Frankl's courage is that his heroics seem almost super-human, a model of reaction reserved for a saint."[123]

Frankl's rendition attempted to overcome the nihilistic evil of the Holocaust by aestheticizing it into a stoic and heroic suffering. In order to inspire people and put the pain of his loss and lingering trauma further behind him, he constructed a narrative of meaning. He personalized this by suggesting his preparation in psychology and rock climbing had given him the necessary attributes to survive. The Holocaust then became a story of heroic survival that had proven his theories. The intellectual anchor for this vision was the "will" to derive meaning from human evil. Undoubtedly Frankl's own psychological "health" required just such intellectual gymnastics. His counterphobic character served him well, and despite the erroneous conception of Holocaust reality it appears that Frankl had found a key to psychological resilience. On the other hand it also appears that he successfully repressed the real tragedy of the Holocaust for himself and his followers.

To Redemption

Frankl's focus on the psychology of world views led to his conclusion that one must retain an affirmative attitude toward life even when confronted with hor-

rendous loss. In an excerpt arguing for this point, it is easy to see that this was how Frankl came to terms with the loss of his wife.

> ... someone who had lost a loved one around whom his life revolved, and who then despairingly raises the question of whether his own life any longer has meaning. There is something particularly pitiable about the man whose faith in the meaningfulness of his own existence totters in such a crisis. He has been left without moral reserves. He lacks that spiritual fiber which can be supplied only by a world-view unqualifiedly affirmative attitude toward life. Lacking this fiber ... he is unable in difficult times to 'take' the blows of fate and to set his own strength against them.[124]

Frankl's devastating loss of his wife was overcome by the "unqualifiedly affirmative world-view." He derived this optimism, from an experience in the camp. As he stated: "that brought thoughts of my wife to mind ... my mind clung to my wife's image, imagining it with an uncanny acuteness. I heard her answering me, saw her smile, her frank and encouraging look. Real or not, her look was then more luminous than the sun which was beginning to rise ... for the first time in my life I saw truth as it is set into song by so many poets ... I grasped the meaning of the greatest secret that human poetry and human thought and belief have to impart: 'That salvation of man is through love and in love.'"[125]

Frankl's longing for his wife obviously preoccupied him during his camp experience. This longing eventually led him to have semi-mystical experiences. "The guard passed by, insulting me, and once again I communed with my beloved. More and more I felt that she was present, that she was with me; I had the feeling that I was able to touch her, able to stretch out my hand and grasp hers. The feeling was very strong: she was there. Then, at that very moment a bird flew down silently and perched in front of me, on the heap of soil which I had dug up from the ditch, and looked steadily at me."[126]

In coming to terms with the loss of his wife, Frankl began to turn toward mysticism and religion. The unspoken anchor for Frankl's affirmative world view, and sense of salvation, was a belief in a "super-meaning" or God. Frankl claimed "for a good many men learned in concentration camp, and as a result of concentration camp, to believe in God again."[127] Frankl also revised his theory of values along religious lines. He claimed his three categories of values were analogous to the "three principal branches of Occidental religion." Therefore creative values were connected to the "moral urge springing" from "mosaic monotheism." Experiential values were equated with Protestantism and the concept of grace. Attitudinal values were realized by taking "the perspective of the cross, of the Crucified one, a freely chosen imitation of Christ."[128] Langer, recognizing the Christian vocabulary and world view in Frankl's testimony, commented that it seems as if "Frankl secretly yearned for a transfiguration of Auschwitz into nothing more than a test of the religious sensibility."[129]

Frankl was quite aware that the criticism easily leveled at his religious conviction is that it was born under rather dire circumstances, and is thus only

a "foxhole" religion. He countered that this is true, that in dire circumstances the religious conviction is heightened (he also described attending séances in the camps),[130] but this in no way delegitimized the religious conviction.[131] Therefore, in response to the tragic loss of his wife, a vicious and nonsensical evil, Frankl offered religious sentiment as the normative cure. Eventually he extended this prescription to be inclusive for everyone. Thus, "It is self-evident that belief in a super-meaning—whether as a metaphysical concept or in the religious sense of Providence—is of the foremost psychotherapeutic and psychohygienic importance."[132]

In a speech to a youth meeting on 15 June 1947, published a month later as the "The Place of Religion in Today's World," Frankl made an argument for the necessity of monotheism and the reality of "the concrete God of the Bible, the living God ... which we have spoken to in the ditches of the concentration camps and in the bombshelters."[133] The article also revealed that the origins of Frankl's convictions about God were not only grounded in the circumstances of the concentration camps. In order to buttress his claim for monotheism, Frankl called for a rejection of the "Gods we have come to know and learn in the last few years: Volk—Reich—Fuehrer; Blood and Soil; Race—and perhaps also Class."[134] Frankl wanted to replace the false gods of ideology with the one true and "living God."

Nazi Evil

After Auschwitz, Frankl affirmed the existence of God to provide grounds for human meaning. But these religious convictions seemed uneasy when confronting the novel evil of Nazism. Frankl resolved Nazi evil for himself in his play *Synchronization in Birkenwald*. He wrote the play in a few hours, reflecting, "It was as if something deep inside me dictated the play. I could hardly write fast enough."[135] The play provides quite an insight into Frankl's consciousness, especially about how he was working through the trauma of his experiences and the guilt of survival. Set in heaven, the play began with a discussion between Socrates, Spinoza, and Kant, three great philosophers of morality. The philosophers had decided to intervene in history to once again provide a moral lesson for humanity. Although remaining outside of time and space, they arrived as observers at the concentration camp just as Franz (who clearly represented Frankl), his brother Karl, and one other prisoner arrived.

Karl began by describing Franz's rejection of his emigration visa. Karl had "had it up to here" with Franz's "eternal self-sacrifice.... You could have gone to America—but no: you didn't want to leave your family." But in this version told by Karl, Franz didn't appear heroic because "look what happened. To save you from the Gestapo, our sister sacrificed herself. And grief about Evi's death killed father. And then it was *my* turn. And now mother is gone..."[136] This ren-

dition didn't completely reflect Frankl's biography because we know Frankl's sister survived the Holocaust by immigrating to Australia.[137] Thus it is not clear how she sacrificed herself. Nor is it clear what was meant by "*my* turn." Nevertheless, it was quite apparent that Frankl was feeling guilty about the fate of his entire family.

Frankl quickly turned to a more heroic story of his sacrifice. The heroics were told by his mother, who, along with the philosophers, looked down upon her sons from heaven. She claimed Franz "stayed, with my husband and me. I know why: he didn't want to leave us behind—yes, that was it. We implored him to go. No, he said, I want to remain.… He didn't want us to know that he only stayed because of us."[138] Since Frankl was writing in his mother's voice, the last sentence has a slightly bitter ring, and rightfully so, as his attempt to protect his family from the Nazis had failed and he had barely escaped death.

Reflecting on her sons, the mother asked the philosophers if they could join her in heaven. She beseeched the philosophers, showing the prayers and thoughts that her sons had directed toward her in the form of packaged gifts. And when her sons questioned whether she was alive, the mother asked the philosophers to reassure them that she was fine.

In order to fulfill the mother's request to be with her sons a new character emerged—a black angel. The black angel was upset and frustrated because he had been sent on a mission at the petition of the mother. The angel was directed to test her sons, and he was to be dressed as an SS man. His mission was to torture Karl for information about who switched numbers at the train station. (In his autobiographical work Frankl recalled switching lines at two different times to avoid the gas chamber.) If Karl talked under torture they were "all finished." Karl therefore decided to adhere to Franz's theory and stated: "Today I'll give meaning to my life—according to your theory. Today I'll catch myself a meaningful death! … I'll stand the test."[139] When Franz realized that his brother had allowed himself to be beaten to death by the Gestapo in order to protect him, and in so doing fulfilled his theory of a meaningful death, he began to feel overwhelming guilt. Then he articulated the irresolvable dilemma of survival guilt. He recalled how he traded a piece of bread for a coat that could have kept another alive in the winter. But then he extended the ubiquitous guilt to everyone because "we have to make our choices, over and over again, every moment. None of us starts out as a devil, either—not even the SS-men."[140]

For Frankl, the guilt-ridden dilemma of survival—which meant others died—was conflated with the evil perpetuated by the Nazis. In this version, Frankl made no distinction between the immorality required to survive and the evil done by the SS. Everyone was initially innocent and the circumstances created the guilt. But evil was also depicted as an opportunity sent from heaven in the form of the black angel. Frankl's suggestion that the confrontation with Nazi evil was an opportunity for the attainment of heroic meaning was now

rendered as a gift from heaven in the form of a black angel. Therefore, the SS man was not endemically evil, but actually an "angel," a "gift from God," sent at the request of his mother. Undoubtedly, Frankl was justified in whatever manner he chose when coming to terms with his survival guilt. He was truly innocent. But in this rendition he seems also to be resolving responsibility for those who chose to become Nazis. Frankl even had Karl and the black angel reconcile in heaven. Given the tact of the play it is not surprising the Catholic journal *Der Brenner* chose to publish it.

Frankl concluded the play with a glorification of death that revealed it was not the philosophers who were providing a moral lesson for humanity—but Frankl himself. As the philosophers watched Karl be put to death by the black angel, Socrates said to Kant and Spinoza: "Was this not our fate, too? … At least, this was the way it worked with me: I became effective not through my dialogues but through my death."[141] Frankl then connected his brother's heroic death to his work on suicide prevention. Frankl used the character of Immanuel Kant to work through the lingering issue of suicides. Kant, who remained outside of time and space, was teaching a course to those who had died by committing suicide. He excitedly described how he was planning to use Karl's meaningful death as an example of the proper way to die. Kant also described, how, after finishing the course, those who chose suicide were being punished and "regrouped into transports" that were destined for "Concentration Camp Sun-Planet Earth."[142] Suicide to escape the camps therefore led to Concentration Camp Sun-Planet Earth, not heaven. It was slightly bizarre for Frankl, as a Holocaust survivor, to select a concentration camp as "punishment" for those who chose death in such circumstances. The suggestion is that they were cowards and that their deaths were lessons in the wrong way to die. They did not pass the test and have a meaningful death. Arguably by "criminalizing" the suicidal, Frankl could work through and over his questionable medical experiments at Rothschild. The "lesson" also placed Frankl as a moral philosopher, in the company of Socrates, Spinoza, and Kant.

Along with this literary presentation, Frankl rationalized his suicide prevention in the *Doctor and the Soul* when he claimed that "suicide is never ethically justifiable." Frankl deflected the criticism "that the doctor who intervenes in an attempt at suicide is taking on the role of an arbiter of destiny," by arguing "if 'destiny'—or Providence—were intent on letting a person weary of life die, it would have found ways to make the doctor's intervention come too late."[143] As mentioned above, Frankl was interested in suicide prevention before the war and likely would not have countenanced suicide under any conditions, but since the context is absent, we need to recall that at the Nazi-controlled Rothschild Frankl's suicide prevention was conducted on people given up for dead by other doctors and often whose breathing and pulse had stopped. Frankl's rationalizations and conviction that Providence was the ultimate arbitrator appears to have eased his conscience.

The Mountain Top

Frankl's resolution of Nazi evil and belief in God is a somewhat surprising re-sponse to the events. The dehumanization and the novel display of human evil in the Holocaust led many but certainly not all intellectuals to conclude "God is dead." If there were a "God" how could six million people be put senselessly to death? How could a "God" not intervene?

Elie Wiesel had a different position on Holocaust significance and remem-brance. For Wiesel, the Holocaust offered no Meaning or possibility for re-demption. The key point for Wiesel was remembering the dead. For Wiesel the prescription was not to place the past "in the storehouse of time," but rather to somehow remain united with the past. That is, to give voice to the silence of the dead, in order to not succumb to the process of forgetting. Against Frankl's celebration of his strategies of survival, Wiesel focused on those who did not survive, and thus died for no apparent reason. For Wiesel, like Adorno, Auschwitz represented a rupture in historical consciousness: "Auschwitz signi-fies not only the failure of two thousand years of Christian civilization, but also the defeat of the intellect that wants to find meaning—with a capital M—in history. What Auschwitz embodied has none. The executioner killed for noth-ing, the victim died for nothing.… At Auschwitz the sacrifices were without point, without divine inspiration. If the suffering of one human being has any meaning, that of six million has none."[144]

As we have seen, for Frankl, Auschwitz did not represent the failure of Christianity, nor defeat his pursuit of Meaning. Both Frankl and Wiesel were in agreement that after Auschwitz there was no Meaning to be found in history. But unlike Frankl, Wiesel did not turn to God for Meaning. Wiesel claimed that "God died in the concentration camps." In response, Frankl claimed that if belief in God is unconditional "it will stand and face the fact that six million died in the Nazi Holocaust; if it is not unconditional it will fall away if only a single child has to die…"[145] When justifying his belief in God, Frankl refused to make a distinction between the meaningless death of one or six million. Frankl also used his survival of Auschwitz to justify his claim. He argued "my personal experiences offer evidence—religion did not die in Auschwitz, nor 'after Auschwitz,' to allude to the title of a book that was authored by a rabbi (who incidentally had not been there)."[146] Frankl's disparaging remark was di-rected at Richard L. Rubenstein's controversial *After Auschwitz*, which rejected "the traditional biblical theology of covenant and election" in the name of a "death-of-God theology."[147] But for Frankl working through the reality of Auschwitz did not require a profound reevaluation of theological propositions.

On a cultural level, the "working through" of the Holocaust has right-fully been rather slow. But the distancing, and numbing of emotional response, is nevertheless unavoidable and perhaps "healthy." Nevertheless, a catastrophe of world-historical proportions such as Auschwitz continues to reverberate in

contemporary consciousness—be it individual or collective. Thus, for every working through and "resolved repression," there is subsequently a constant return of the repressed. No event of such magnitude comes to a completed resolution for either an individual or a culture, nor should it.[148]

Frankl is a peculiar representative of the Holocaust. His testimony, far and away one of the most popular, was also misleading. Based on his optimistic version he was able to promote his vision of logotherapy on a global scale. Clearly his mendaciousness was not intentional and instead was a product of long-standing intellectual interests, and the desire to heal himself and others. It also appears that Frankl's trauma led to a degree of repression and denial, but also reflected a psychic resilience that seems to have stemmed from his counterphobic character and prescriptions. However, his testimony, which was dictated in nine days, and his white heat literary production *Synchronization in Birkenwald* do not appear to be a measured working through of the traumatic experience.

His intellectual commitment to God, and his attitudinal values of "taking the cross," led to his positing the highest meaning in suffering and death. In this vision a deity provided "ultimate" meaning. Frankl extended his prescription of meaning, derived from the Holocaust, to the level of everyday existence when he stated: "Such men are not only in concentration camps. Everywhere man is confronted with fate, with the chance of achieving something through his own suffering."[149]

At the end of *Man's Search for Meaning*, Frankl had shed his burdens and claimed that the survivor "had nothing left to fear but his God." If we consider his fear of God equivalent with his multi-layered trauma, it follows that Frankl's confrontation with God/judgment and his subsequent conquest allowed for the assertion of an ultimate meaning to his life and survival. After working through his fear of God, Frankl could claim this about the difference between a religious and irreligious man. "On his way to find the ultimate meaning of life, the irreligious man, as it were, has not yet reached the highest peak, but rather has stopped at the next to highest.... And what is the reason the irreligious man does not go further? It is because he does not want to lose the 'firm ground under his feet.' The true summit is barred from his vision; it is hidden in the fog, and he does not risk venturing into it, into this uncertainty. Only the religious man hazards it."[150]

For the counterphobic Frankl, confronting God, the Holocaust, and his tortured past was another limit experience he heroically conquered. Rather than a leap, his transcendence allowed him to lose the firm ground under his feet, and he was no longer burdened with the conscience that had to find meaning through aestheticized suffering. Now Frankl was once again deriving meaning from heroic mountain climbing and the painful pangs of his conscience were objectified as representative of a "real" religious urge, reaffirmed by the "real" mystical experience of the camps. For Frankl, God did not die in Auschwitz, he was reborn.

Notes

1. Kubler-Ross was considered the founder of the American thanatology movement. See Elisabeth Kubler-Ross, *On Death and Dying.*

2. Elisabeth Kubler-Ross, "Behüt Dich Gott," *International Forum for Logotherapy* no. 3 (Spring 1980): 49. Frankl also referenced these experiments with "Absturzerlebnis" and claimed Pötzl was interested in his work. See Frankl, "Der Alpinismus und die Pathologie des Zeitgeistes," 12. Also, Frankl and Pötzl, "Über die seelischen Zustände während des Abstürzes."

3. Viktor Frankl, "Cosmos and the Mind, (How Far Can We Go?)," *Pace* 5, no. 8 (August 1969): 35.

4. Corrigan Interview (GTU).

5. Frankl, *Was nicht in meinen*, 71.

6. Ibid., 15.

7. *Totenbuch Theresienstadt* (Wien: 1971), 32. This was the so-called eleventh transport.

8. Berkley, *Vienna and Its Jews*, 294.

9. See Popper, *Soziale Medizin*, especially 87–113. On the emigration of doctors from Rothschild and Erich Stern's failure to get out, see Stern, *Die letzten 12 Jahre Rothschild-Spital*, 8–9.

10. Berkley, *Vienna and Its Jews*, 295. Also see Rabinovici, *Eichmann's Jews*, 158.

11. See Klingberg, *When Life Calls Out to Us*, 110.

12. According to their Dermoegensderzeichnis, Frankl brought 68 Reichsmarks with him and had 180 Reichsmarks in the bank, while his father brought 282 Reichsmarks and had 282 Reichsmarks in the bank. Staatsarchiv Vienna documents no. 62/1068 and 62/1072.

13. Lecture given at San Diego International University, 1973.

14. Klingberg, *When Life Calls Out to Us*, 110–111.

15. George Berkley, *The Story of Theresienstadt* (Boston: Branden Books, 1993), 8.

16. Ibid., 9–11.

17. Berkley, *Vienna and Its Jews*, 297.

18. On these issues, see Berkley, *The Story of Theresienstadt*, 41–60. Also, Zdenek Lederer *Ghetto Theresienstadt* (New York: Fertig, 1993), 35–57. Finally, the 900-page tome, H.G. Adler, *Theresienstadt 1941-1945* (Tübingen: 1960).

19. Frankl, *Was nicht in meinen*, 6.

20. I have Ernest Seinfeld to thank for providing these monthly "Tätigkeitsbericht."

21. Personal Correspondence with Charlotte Opfermann (Spring 2004). For a description of the medical facilities and conditions in the camp, see Vera Schiff, *The Theresienstadt Deception* (New York: Mellen Press, 2013). Schiff survived the camp and was a nurse in the hospital.

22. Berkley, *The Story of Theresienstadt*, 92.

23. See Klingberg, *When Life Calls Out to Us*, 118, 120.

24. Nathan Grossman, "Rabbi and the Doctor of the Soul," *Jewish Spectator* 34, no. 1 (January 1969): 11.

25. Frankl lectured on the "Psychologie des Alpinismus," "Ärztliche Seelsorge," "Soziale Psychotherapie," "Lebensmüdigkeit und Lebensmut in Theresienstadt," and "Das Existenzproblem in der Psychotherapie." I am grateful to Ernest Seinfeld for providing a list of Frankl's lectures. Also see Klingberg, *When Life Calls Out to Us*, 117–118.

26. Berkley, *The Story of Theresienstadt*, 123. Also see Frankl's description in Frankl, "Psychohygiene im Notstand," *Hygiene* (October 1952). Frankl also described his suicide prevention activities in a lecture given at the International Congress for Psychotherapy in Leyden, Holland, in September of 1951. Also see Klingberg, *When Life Calls Out to Us*, 122–123.

27. See Adler, *Theresienstadt 1941-1945*, 316.

28. Kwiet, "Suicide in the Jewish Community," 163. Kwiet based his claims on a "personal communication with Dr. Edith Kramer," and he made no mention of Frankl's suicide prevention squad.

29. Berkley, *Vienna and Its Jews*, 298.

30. See Theresienstadt, Concentration/Transit Camp for German and Austrian Jews, United States Holocaust Memorial Museum, http://www.ushmm.org/wlc/en/article.php?ModuleId=10007507.

31. For a list and a description of the outcome of transports from Theresienstadt, see Lederer, *Ghetto Theresienstadt*, 192–242.

32. See *Totenbuch Theresienstadt*, 32. According to Lederer (241), only 250 men of the 1,500 prisoners on this transport survived selection by Dr. Mengele. Frankl's wife also survived selection, but later died.

33. Frankl, *Was nicht in meinen*, 68.

34. Ibid.

35. See Anna Hájková, "Sexual Barter in Times of Genocide: Negotiating the Sexual Economy of the Theresienstadt Ghetto," *Signs* 38, no. 3 (Spring 2013): 503–533.

36. Ibid., 71.

37. Note this passage: "Nine months later we arrived in Theresienstadt. Tilly was given a two year exemption from deportation because her work in the munitions factory was important for the war effort. But I was summoned to be transported 'to the east' to Auschwitz." Frankl, *Was nicht in meinen*, 68.

38. See Frankl, *Man's Search for Meaning*, 16–32.

39. Robert Schuller, "Dr. Robert Schuller Interviews Viktor Frankl: How to Find Meaning in Life," *Possibilities: The Magazine of Hope* (March/April 1991): 10.

40. The camps of the Kaufering group had numbers from I to XI and were established around Landesberg. Kaufering III was a work camp established in June of 1944, and held up to 2,000 prisoners. See *Das nationalsozialistische Lagersystem*, ed. Martin Weinmann (Frankfurt: Zweitausendeins, 1990), 195, 558.

41. I am grateful to Ernest Seinfeld for this citation.

42. Viktor Frankl, *From Death-Camp to Existentialism: A Psychiatrist's Path to a New Therapy*, trans. Ilse Lasch (Boston: Beacon Press, 1959), 6.

43. Ibid., 44.

44. Personal communication with author, Fall 2009.

45. Also, Frankl does recall a number of selections at Auschwitz. See Klingberg, *When Life Calls Out to Us*, 134.

46. Frankl, *From Death-Camp to Existentialism*, 54.

47. Ibid., 5.

48. Ibid., 48–49.

49. Ibid., 33.

50. See Klingberg *When Life Calls Out to Us*, 137–140.

51. See Geoffrey P. Megargee, ed., 0315-0208 Dachau/Kaufering I-XI, *The United States Holocaust Memorial Museum Encyclopedia of Camps and Ghettos, 1933–1945—Volume I Early Camps, Youth Camps, and Concentration Camps and Subcamps under the SS-Business Administration Main Office* (Indiana: Indiana University Press, 2009).

52. I have Ernest Seinfeld to thank for this citation.

53. Klingberg, *When Life Calls Out to Us*, 143.

54. Frankl, *From Death-Camp to Existentialism*, 64.

55. See Marianne Gruber, "Der Wille zum Sinn," *Die Pestsäle* (December 1974): 224.

56. Frankl, *Was nicht in meinen*, 71.

57. Ibid., 72.

58. Frankl, *From Death-Camp to Existentialism*, 62.

59. Ibid., 4.

60. See Frankl's letter to the director of the D.P. hospital in Frankl, *Gesammelte Werke: … trotzdem Ja zum Leben sagen und ausgewählte Briefe (1945-1945) Band 1*, ed. A. Batthyany, K. Biller, and E. Fizzotti (Vienna: Böhlau Verlag), 121–122. It is also clear from the letter and Klingberg that Frankl was contemplating returning from Vienna to work for the Americans. See Klingberg,

When Life Calls Out to Us, 148. Also see Viktor Frankl, "There is No Collective Guilt," *Austrian Information* 41, no. 6 (1988): 5. Frankl's cv from the Archiv Universität Wien reveals that he worked at the D.P. hospital.

61. Klingberg, *When Life Calls Out to Us*, 148.

62. Frankl, *Gesammelte Werke, Band 1*, 142.

63. Frankl continued to work on reconstructing the book while working the in the displaced persons hospital. We also know that a copy of the original manuscript survived in Vienna in the care of Paul Polak and that Frankl was able to use it in reconstructing his book.

64. Frankl, *The Doctor on the Soul*, 90–91.

65. Frankl, *Was nicht in meinen*, 73–77.

66. Micheal Bernstein, *Foregone Conclusions: Against Apocalyptic History* (Berkeley: University of California Press, 1994), 43.

67. See Primo Levi, *Survival in Auschwitz*, trans. Stuart Woolf (New York: Collier Books, 1961), 22. Also, I have tried to explain the radically different tenor of Levi's and Frankl's versions of surviving Auschwitz in "Typology of Gray Flowers: Levi and Frankl on Surviving Auschwitz," in *The Legacy of Primo Levi*, ed. Stanislao G. Pugliese (New York: Palgrave Macmillan, 2004).

68. Berel Lang, *Writing and the Holocaust* (New York: Holmes and Meir, 1988), 3.

69. Lawrence Langer, *Admitting the Holocaust* (New York: Oxford University Press, 1995), 3.

70. The Bettleheim controversy revealed this phenomenon. For an excellent discussion of this tendency toward deification, see Terence Des Pres, "The Bettleheim Problem," in *Writing into the World* (New York: Penguin, 1991).

71. Irving Howe, "Writing and the Holocaust," in Lang, *Writing and the Holocaust*, 185.

72 For a description of the concept of "working through" and the Holocaust, see Dominick LaCapra, *Representing the Holocaust* (Ithaca: Cornell University Press, 1994), especially 205–211. Also, Saul Friedlander, "Trauma, Memory, Transference," in *Holocaust Remembrance: The Shapes of Memory*, ed. Geoffrey Hartman (Cambridge Mass.: Blackwell, 1994), 260–261. La Capra derived his idea from psychoanalysis and subsequently the notion of the unconscious. My use of the term will be less psychoanalytical and instead will focus on how Frankl came to terms with his traumatic Holocaust experience and then used his particular world view to confront and work through the trauma to restore his dignity and sustain his search for meaning. For his part, Friedlander was concerned with how the historian "works through" the testimonies and documents "without giving into the temptation of closure." This is a concern we will heed when reflecting on Frankl's production.

73. Frankl, *Was nicht in meinen*, 83.

74. Frankl, *From Death-Camp to Existentialism*, 35.

75. Frankl, quoted in Hall, "Conversation with V.E. Frankl," 63.

76. Frankl, *Was nicht in meinen*, 77.

77. Frankl, quoted in Cohen, "The Frankl Meaning," 60.

78. Frankl, quoted in Hall, "Conversation with V.E. Frankl," 58.

79. Frankl, *From Death-Camp to Existentialism*. This passage is quoted from the jacket cover. Also see 104.

80. Paul Polak, "Frankl's Existential Analysis," *American Journal of Psychotherapy* 3 (1949): 518.

81. Gabriel Frankl died on 3 February 1943; see *Totenbuch Theresienstadt*.

82. Personal exchange in the fall of 2009. Batthyany also remarked that the main focus of the prewar book was responsibility.

83. Frankl, *The Doctor on the Soul*, 27.

84. Ibid., 33.

85. Ibid., 35.

86. Ibid.

87. Ibid.

88. Frankl, "Facing the Transitoriness of Human Existence," *Generations: Aging and the Human Spirit* 14, no. 4 (Fall 1990): 7. Also see Frankl, *The Doctor and the Soul*, 64.

89. For an informative discussion of survivor's guilt, see Robert Jay Lifton, *Death in Life: Survivors of Hiroshima* (New York: Random House, 1967).

90. Frankl, *The Doctor and the Soul*, 108–109.

91. Aharon Appelfeld, "After the Holocaust," in Lang, *Writing and the Holocaust*, 84.

92. Corrigan Interview (GTU).

93. Frankl, *Was nicht in meinen*, 82.

94. Frankl, "Letter to Oswald Schwarz February 1946," in *Gesammelte Werke Band 1*, 127.

95. Frankl, quoted in Klingberg, *When Life Calls Out to Us*, 156.

96. Frankl, *Man's Search for Meaning* (Preface to the 1984 edition), 12.

97. By April 1946 Frankl had met his future wife, Elly Schwindt, a nurse at the Policlinic. See Klingberg, *When Life Calls Out to Us*, 205. By August 1946 Frankl had returned to climbing again. See his letter to his sister in Frankl, *Gesammelte Werke Band 1*, 148.

98. Frankl, *Was nicht in meinen*, 84.

99. Gordon Allport, preface to Viktor Frankl, *From Death-Camp to Existentialism*, ix-xii.

100. Ibid.

101. L. Langer, *Version of Survival*, 10.

102. Frankl, *From Death-Camp to Existentialism*, 4.

103. Ibid., 7.

104. Ibid., 14–16.

105. Ibid., 16–17.

106. Ibid., 47.

107. Ibid., 68–69.

108. Ibid., 14.

109. Ibid., 18.

110. Ibid., 71.

111. Ibid., 66–67.

112. Ibid., 78–83.

113. L. Langer, *Versions of Survival*, 20.

114. Frankl, quoted in Cohen, "The Frankl Meaning," 61.

115. Frankl, *From Death-Camp to Existentialism*, 73–74.

116. Ibid., 75. Ironically, this is probably when Frankl became block warden. Also see Frankl, *The Doctor and the Soul*, 101.

117. L. Langer, *Versions of Survival*, 24.

118. Ibid.

119. Ibid., 26.

120. Ibid.

121. Ibid., 28.

122. Reuven Bulka, "Logotherapy as a Response to the Holocaust," *Tradition* 15 (1975): 86.

123. Irving Halperin, *Messengers from the Dear* (Philadelphia: Westminster Press, 1972), 32.

124. Frankl, *From Death-Camp to Existentialism*, 29.

125. Ibid., 36.

126. Ibid., 40.

127. Frankl, *The Doctor and the Soul*, 104.

128. Ibid., 59–60.

129. L. Langer, *Versions of Survival*, 22–23.

130. Also, he lectured at Theresienstadt on "Wonderful People and Strange Mysterious Facts."

131. See Viktor Frankl, "Group Psychotherapeutic Experiences in a Concentration Camp," in *Psychotherapy and Existentialism: Selected Papers on Logotherapy* (New York: Washington Square Press, 1967), 103.

132. Frankl, *The Doctor and the Soul*, 33.

133. Frankl, "Der Platz der Religion in der Welt von heute," *Mahnruf: Für Freiheit und Menschenrecht* no. 6 (July 1947): 2.

134. Ibid., 1.

135. Viktor Frankl, *Synchronization in Birkenwald*, trans., Joseph Fabry (Berkeley: Institute of Logotherapy Press), i.

136. Ibid., 9.

137. Frankl's sister, Stella, fled to Australia to escape the Nazis and Frankl dedicated his book *The Unconscious God* to her.

138. Frankl, *Synchronization in Birkenwald*, 10.

139. Ibid., 17.

140. Ibid., 23.

141. Ibid., 18.

142. Ibid., 19.

143. Frankl, *The Doctor and the Soul*, 49.

144. Elie Wiesel, *Legends of Our Time* (New York: Schocken Books, 1982), quoted in L. Langer, *Versions of Survival*, 141.

145. Frankl, *The Unconscious God*, 15–16.

146. Frankl, *Man's Search for Ultimate Meaning*, 152.

147. See Richard Rubenstein, *After Auschwitz: History, Theology, and Contemporary Judaism*, 2d. ed. (Baltimore, Md.: Johns Hopkins University Press, 1992), especially "Part III. Theology and Contemporary Judaism," 157–293.

148. For an excellent discussion of these issues, see Hartman, *Holocaust Remembrance*.

149. Frankl, *From Death-Camp to Existentialism*, 67.

150. Frankl, *The Unconscious God*, 56–57.

The Flight into the Spiritual

*energizing or animating guilt … always connects with an image
beyond the guilt and beyond the atrocity…*
—Robert Jay Lifton, "Questions of Guilt"

In the late 1940s and early 1950s Frankl began to flesh out the theory behind his vision of the "unconscious God." In many ways Frankl's intellectual trajectory is similar to Heidegger's. It is no surprise then that Frankl was fond of quoting how "the really big ones," like Heidegger, thought highly of his work. Frankl had a great deal of respect for Heidegger, and also had a personal relationship with him. At the end of his seminars at San Diego International University in the 1970s, Frankl narrated a slide show on his visit to Heidegger's home.[1] Frankl also described how Heidegger expressed a special desire to visit him on his trip to Vienna in the 1950s.[2] Since Heidegger was an "unrepentant" Nazi,[3] the question arises: What was the substance of their relationship?

Apparently, Heidegger found Frankl's "teaching worthy of support,"[4] and once wrote in his guest book: "To the remembrance of a beautiful and instructive visit."[5] Clearly there was a mutual affinity of some intellectual substance. But we know little of their personal relationship, and most likely it was only of limited significance.

Interestingly, postwar they shared a common conception of the past. Frankl quoted Heidegger's statement: "Das Vergangene geht. Das Gewesene kommt." Frankl translated this as: What has passed, has gone: What is past, will come.[6] He also claimed that Heidegger wrote these lines "in my guest book, in order

to show how much he agreed with me" and "my optimistic views on the past."[7] We know Heidegger's conception of the past was somewhat optimistic, because he argued that a genuine "beginning … is always a head start, in which everything to come is already leaped over … a beginning already contains the end latent in itself."[8] That is, a genuine origin is not an event but the promise of something to come. Since Heidegger considered the "inner truth and greatness of the [Nazi] movement"[9] as something that was lost, the question arises: Was this the context for their mutual optimism that the past will come again? For Frankl's part, he continually reaffirmed his turn toward responsibility, will, and the spiritual realm that he first conceptualized in the 1930s.

Frankl's affinity and identification with Heidegger also had an intellectual aspect. Although Frankl first read Heidegger in the late 1920s, in his books citations of Heidegger were sparse. There was also no in-depth analysis of his ideas. For example, in Frankl's book on the intellectual foundations of logotherapy, the discussion focused on Heidegger's concept of "Being in the world." Frankl claimed that Heidegger's concept was wrongly interpreted as subjectivist. He argued that he knew this because he "discussed it in a personal conversation." Frankl then described how he fooled an audience by asking them to distinguish between the mad rumblings of a schizophrenic and Heidegger's writing. An "overwhelming majority" thought the quoted passage from Heidegger was the schizophrenic. Nevertheless, Frankl maintained, "by no means does it speak against the greatness of Heidegger—and let us take it for granted that he is as great as many experts believe."[10] Significantly, Frankl didn't seem to perceive himself as one of the experts on Heidegger. In the end we can only "tease out" Heideggerianism in his writings and it seems that Frankl was influenced by Heidegger and other existential currents, but his was a simplified and popularized version.

Logotherapy and Existentialism

From 1947 to 1956 Frankl produced ten books. No small feat for anyone, but there was a significant amount of repetition of a few key ideas. Nevertheless, this outpouring crystallized his psychological vision. Frankl's praxis of existential analysis or logotherapy was presented in *On the Theory and Therapy of Mental Disorders*. His theory that centered on a critique of nihilism was the focus of his books *Der unbedingte Mensch, Homo patiens, Logos und Existenz*, and *Der unbewusste Gott (The Unconscious God)*.

Frankl's theoretical conception of logotherapy was constructed in opposition to both Freud and Adler, and was based on the insights of existentialism and phenomenology. Frankl placed himself as an inheritor of the existential problem of human meaning first articulated by Kierkegaard and developed by

Bergson, Husserl, and Scheler. Frankl also claimed that "after the first world war, Heidegger, Jaspers and Jean Paul Sartre fully clarified existential philosophy."[11] Frankl's absorption of the existential perspective led him to focus analysis on the "existence" of the person. For Frankl, "existence" equaled no more than human reality. But the "reality" Frankl focused on was the consciousness of time, space, and the component of memory.

The Heideggerian perspective in Frankl was also apparent in his "ontology of man," which aimed to study "not the 'existing' man, but the being of the self."[12] Thus Frankl focused on *Dasein*, or "Being" human, as opposed to humans as beings or objects. This proclaimed rejection of subject/object dualism likely stemmed from his absorption of Heidegger's exhortations against metaphysics. In the simplest of terms, Heidegger claimed that to perceive humans as subjects with identities and substance was to engage in a process of reification. That is, to make human experience into "thingness." And, thingness, or more simply substance, was not a feature of "Being" human, but only of non-human things and experience. Instead, human experience (*Dasein*) was conceived as a radical openendedness or "throwness" in the world without any substantial grounds.[13] Thus, both Frankl and Heidegger conceived human existence as ungrounded, and therefore essentially performative (*Vollzugswirklichkeit*).[14] That is, "Being" was understood as the reality of performance, and an "unanalyzable and unreflectable phenomenon."[15] He therefore argued, since: "human existence cannot fully be reflected upon by itself, it cannot be fully analyzed either. That is why existential analysis can never be an analysis of existence but can only be an analysis toward existence. Human existence remains an 'Urphaenomene,' i.e. an unanalyzable, irreducible phenomenon."[16]

But Frankl still wanted to make sense of existence and posit a Meaning. Therefore, against the seemingly insurmountable intellectual barriers of human existence as unanalyzable and irreducible, Frankl turned to Heidegger and ontology to claim: "Within the plane of psychological immanence, both consciousness and responsibility are and remain unsolvable problems. However, as soon as we transpose them into the ontological dimension they cease to be problems. For then they are taken as 'Urphaenomene,' constitutive of human existence, or in Heideggerian terms, they are 'existentials,' attributes that belong to the very foundations of human existence."[17]

Therefore consciousness and responsibility become constituent features of human existence and following Heidegger these were considered man's unique and characteristic features.[18] Therefore the configuration of "Being" as openended performance, which was nevertheless grounded in "existentials," was Frankl's absorption of Heidegger's rejection of a metaphysical understanding of human experience. But as we shall see, in *reality*, Frankl was in stark contradiction to Heidegger's anti-metaphysical commitments, because he made constant reference to spirit, self, unconscious, and at times, even the ego and the id.

Spiritual Dimension

The Introduction described the theoretical impasse of existentialism as rooted in the concept of authenticity. That is, authenticity is "only a negative moment in which the self suddenly [becomes] aware of the irrationality of all 'necessary' beliefs and the self-constituted nature of permanent identities."[19] But beyond this disengagement and distancing, the concept of authenticity was unable to offer anything positive. The existentialists therefore could not say what is "natural," but only what is "authentic." Izenberg illustrated the dilemma when he described how Freud preserved the holist concept of health by grounding it in universal instincts, but the existentialists "had no such recourse to biological norms of health" and therefore "each took a different path out of their common dilemma." One strategy to solve this impasse was Sartre's attempt to blend existentialism with Marxism. For his part, Heidegger turned to Nazism and "historical activism in the form of nationalist renewal," and after the failure of the Nazi movement to "a mystical form of idealist absolutism that betrayed his original concept of Authenticity."[20] In a similar fashion, Frankl attempted to access authenticity through his "height psychology." After defeat of his hopes, and his traumatic war time experience, he turned toward "the concrete God of the Bible, the living God."

In the late 1940s and early 1950s Frankl constructed the theoretical backing to his belief in God with his concepts of an "unconscious God" and the "spiritual dimension." In the latter realm, Frankl located both morality and authentic existence. In a revision of Descartes's dictum, "I think therefore I am," Frankl claimed: "Provided that I exist, I exist spiritually and morally, provided that I spiritually and morally exist, I also exist with meaning and worth …"[21]

To construct this spiritual dimension, Frankl drew a binary opposition between material and spiritual existence. The first tack taken to assert the primacy of the spiritual attacked the reductionist, and according to him, nihilistic perspective of the human sciences. Frankl considered reductionism "the crisis of humanism," because humans were depicted "as 'nothing but' a product of biological, psychological or sociological conditioning."[22] For Frankl "all humanity is conditioned," but "authentic humanity" is "raised over its conditioning" and "exceeds" conditioning. "Thus, man is only man in so far as, and as long as he—as a spiritual being—is over and beyond his somatic and psychic being." In other words, "man is only existential in so far as he detaches and distances himself from the vital and the social."[23] The spiritual dimension was therefore constructed by marking off a realm "beyond" biological, psychological, and sociological conditioning.

Since, materialistic interpretations of human experience were conceived as reductionist and nihilistic, the spiritual dialectically became the realm of meaning and fulfillment. The biological and social were recognized as only "conditioners" of humanity, while authentic existence was achieved by a con-

quest of these material conditions. This interpretation allowed Frankl to place responsibility for nihilism on the perspective of the human sciences that denied the spiritual dimension, and viewed man as "nothing but" a bundle of drives or reflexes.

Before the war Frankl fought against what he considered the reductionist tendencies of psychology. After the war he expanded this criticism to all of the human sciences, and added the claim that reductionism is nihilistic. With this full definition of the spiritual dimension, Frankl was able to place Adlerianism within the framework of the "nihilistic" human sciences. According to Frankl, Adler's conception of meaning was imbedded in the social dimension (not the higher spiritual dimension). Consequently, Adler's "life tasks" fall victim to the same icy determinism as the Freudian pleasure principle.[24]

Frankl furthered his criticism of the human sciences by turning to discuss the evolution of humans. According to Frankl, "with the mutation, that suddenly 'endowed' the hominid with 14 billion neurons, we can date the unfinished development of man, or, if you will, the emergence of the sixth day of creation."[25] It is not exactly clear what exactly Frankl meant by the quasi-mystical "endowed." Apparently in order to overcome what he considered the nihilism of evolutionary theory that viewed humans as nothing but animals, Frankl asserted a subtle anthropomorphism, combined with an overt anthropocentricism. This comfortably closed the door—at least for Frankl—on the disturbing iconoclasm at the heart of a biological grounding of human experience. Frankl also added that animals *are* their instinctual life, while men only *have* instincts. That is, humans, unlike animals, can take a stand toward their biological urges and psychological experience.[26] Frankl called this the defiant power of the human spirit, or, as he titled his postwar lecture series, ... *Nevertheless say yes to life.*[27]

Frankl also revised traditional conceptions of inheritance and genetics based on his spiritual premises. He thus extended his ideas on the radical independence of the individual's spiritual realm from the somatic and psychic by claiming, "the parents transmit only their chromosomes to the children." According to Frankl, "the chromosomes determine the psychophysical organism, but not the spiritual person," and therefore "spiritual existence cannot be transmitted from the parents to the child. What alone can be transmitted, are the building stones—not the architect."[28] This denial of genetic influence on the spirit was another of Frankl's attempts to cordon off a realm of human experience that stood above biological determinism.

Frankl based his distinction between the spiritual and somatic on his understanding of brain pathology and the work of his old friend, Pötzl. Frankl argued "psychic functions can be condition by the somatic but not produced." Also "Pötzl, shows 'the function is not capable of being localized only the disturbance of the function.'"[29] In Frankl's, and apparently Pötzl's, vision, the somatic was denigrated to playing only a spiritually destructive role. That is, the

somatic was conceived as incapable of originating any positive psychic activity. If you think about it, this claim is spiritualism and uncontestable, and is perhaps more fitting for a priest than a brain pathologist. But this conviction fit Frankl's intellectual itinerary, and allowed him to claim that heredity "explains nothing." What mattered is what the individual did with "the available inherited disposition, with the psycho-physical mass of inheritance."[30]

Against possible criticism that Frankl was dividing man against himself, and thus abandoning the project of uncovering the "Being" human, he posited a holism in the spiritual dimension. From this perspective Frankl made the following claims: a person is unified and complete as an individual; this wholeness is established through the unity of the physical, psychological, and spiritual and represents the totality of human reality; and within the individual's lifetime these dimensions are interconnected and not separable.[31]

Frankl also claimed that there is a hierarchal holism in human experience. According to Frankl, there are three dimensions to human existence: somatic, psychic, and noological. Overarching and encompassing all three dimensions was theology. Therefore: "a higher dimension, by definition, is a more 'inclusive' one. The lower dimension is included in the higher one; it is subsumed in it and encompassed by it. Thus biology is overarched by psychology, psychology by noology, and noology by theology."[32]

From this quote it appears Frankl used religion and theology in order to unify human experience. "Thus the spiritual core, and only the spiritual core, warrants and constitutes oneness and wholeness in man."[33]

"Truth" and the Will to Meaning

Frankl's positing of a holism in the spiritual dimension was his attempt to overcome the reductionism and nihilism that he claimed to be at the heart of the human sciences. But the problem of how to locate and stabilize values and morals within the open-ended existential world view remained. Frankl therefore relied on the previously mentioned Heideggerian "existentials," which he considered to be the constituent features of human existence.[34] According to Frankl, the two essential existentials in the spiritual dimension were freedom and responsibility.

However, Frankl's metaphysics surpassed Heidegger's since he described both what the spiritual dimension consisted of and its *capacity*, namely, the ability to exceed, or reject the conditioning of materialism upon the self. In one of his first articles in English, Frankl described the connection between the spiritual dimension and freedom in these terms: "Freedom means freedom in face of three things: (1)the instincts (2)inheritance (3)environment." According to Frankl, "man has drives, but these drives do not have him." Therefore "man

is by no means a product of inheritance and environment" because "man ulti-
mately decides for himself."[35]

Despite the existentials, the notion of freedom continued to raise the prob-
lem of values. That is, what values and morals did man ultimately decide for
himself? What values governed this vision of radical individual assertion and
freedom? For his solution Frankl turned to the phenomenologists. Based on the
insights of phenomenolgy, Frankl posited a realm of objective values that was
beyond analysis. Thus, "spiritual acts are volitional in essence," and "are directed
toward transcendental goals." Spiritual acts have an object, but "this object, by
necessity, gets out of sight in the moment the acts themselves are considered to
be the objects."[36]

In order to cordon off a realm of objective values, Frankl drew a demarca-
tion (by analogy) between the role of existential analysis and phenomenology.
Thus, "just as only an existential analysis is capable of safeguarding the subjec-
tive character of the spiritual person, only a phenomenological analysis is ca-
pable of maintaining in sight the objective character of the realm of senses and
values (the 'objective spirit')."[37] By relying on a combination of existentialism
and phenomenology, Frankl was able to argue that the meaning of existence
comes from being responsible to something or somebody outside of oneself.
These people or things exist in the irreducible and apparently eternal realm of
objective spirit.

Frankl's turn to that which is external to human existence to locate meaning
was necessitated by his rejection of the concept of self-understanding because
"the self-understanding of existence is an irreducible phenomenon." Though
existence can know itself, "existence cannot understand its own self-under-
standing. This understanding, ... must itself namely take place in a higher di-
mension than the original self-understanding."[38] To explain this concept Frankl
used the analogy that as an animal cannot understand the intent of man, so we
cannot understand the intent of God.[39] These claims represented the culmina-
tion of his rejection of the human sciences and denied an immanent meaning
to human experience. Instead, Frankl turned to the "higher," spiritual dimen-
sion, and ultimately to God.

Frankl's solution to the problem of Meaning was to claim that since ex-
istence cannot understand itself it must be directed outward, not inward. As
an adolescent Frankl had abandoned the question of "What is the meaning of
life?" because the answer surpassed the capacity of human insight and under-
standing. Instead, he reversed the question, and claimed that life asked questions
of the person. Now, Frankl's theory of the spiritual dimension, which denied
Meaning to material existence, seemed to provide the answers to life's questions.

Despite the spiritual dimension, and the phenomenological claims, Frankl
was still beholden to the perspectivism of existential individualism. This is be-
cause he claimed every individual had to answer for himself the questions life

seemed to present. This contradiction between perspectivism and objective truth led Frankl to make theoretical claims that seem unfeasible. He therefore argued that objective truth can be achieved from his radical subjectivist position. Since this passage lays bare Frankl's inability to overcome the contradiction between his existentialism and his desire for absolute truth, it is worth quoting at length. "'One's truth is however never 'a' truth, but always 'the' truth—however that he in his perspective sees truth. It is still his perspective, that opens the truth up to him.... So lies the sole absolute, which truth allows to men, in the absolute uniqueness of the perspective, in which the truth is revealed to each individual person. And therefore perspectivism by no means falls into relativism."[40]

Given Frankl's intellectual honesty, his concluding claim seemed slightly disingenuous and a somewhat futile attempt to overcome, by denial, the radical uncertainty contained in his existential perspectivism. In this sense, Frankl's attempt to resolve the relativism of existential perspectivism failed.

But Frankl had found his solution to nihilism. In his view, the problem was the "nihilistic human sciences" that denigrated the spiritual dimension and God. Against this he used phenomenology to assert the reality of the higher spiritual dimension. But, "in truth," his existentialism continued to undermine the realm of objectivity.

This dilemma was even more apparent in Frankl's metaphysics, which asserted objective reality and values. For his revision, Frankl turned to Jaspers's conception of man as a "deciding being." Following Jaspers he claimed, "existence is ... the spiritual person with humanity characterized as deciding being."[41] He also connected this conception of man as a "deciding being" to authenticity. Thus: "the real criterion of authentic human existence only derives from discerning whether a given phenomenon is spiritual or instinctual—in contrast to the psychoanalytic concept—being human is not being driven but 'deciding what one is going to be' ..."[42]

By making subjective decision a characteristic of the spiritual person, Frankl tried to place metaphysics within human experience. But unlike Freud's instincts, or Adler's will to power, Frankl claimed a will for meaning existed. Therefore, the realm of "freedom and responsibility," combined with "the discovery of a will to meaning," affords the ability to realize objective values.[43] Ultimately, the "will to meaning" was anchored in religion because Frankl claimed that "there is, in fact, a religious sense deeply rooted in each and every man's unconscious depths."[44] This led to Frankl's conception of an unconscious God, which "refers to man's hidden relation to a God who himself is hidden."[45]

With the will to meaning, and the unconscious God, Frankl had the core features of his "height psychology" or spiritualized conception of human nature that he exported to America beginning in the late 1950s. But the continuing captivation of the human sciences that Frankl regarded as reflecting the nihilistic spirit of the age is that they have the capacity to explain much of human behavior and are scientifically verifiable. In contrast, Frankl's substantiations of

the spiritual dimension were rather strained. Ultimately, it cannot be denied the somatic grounds of existence represent not just conditions—but actually the cause—of mental and subsequently spiritual life. Frankl's denigration of heredity and somatic factors in the realm of "authentic" human existence seems to stem from deep seated needs to transcend the organic world view. Therefore in developing his prewar intellectual vision that he did *not* reject the spiritualistic tendencies in his thought. Instead, he seems to have attempted a "purification" of the spiritualistic view.

The claim that the spiritual realm existed above and beyond the material realm, and at the same time incorporated the material realm, is contradictory. Also, Frankl's positing of a spiritual dimension seemed to suggest he believed in the reality of a world that transcended time and space. Clearly this was the thrust of his play, his "communication" with his wife in his Holocaust testimony, and his belief in God. Arguably this flight from material reality was deeply reflective of how he responded to his traumatic wartime experience. After those experiences, Frankl posited a will—to meaning—that could only come from a transcendent source.

The "Praxis" of Death as Meaningful

In terms of praxis, Frankl extended the spiritual dimension and his heroic vision of not succumbing to the material conditions to treatment of psychotic patients. Frankl's prescription was that psychotics could counteract their disease by relying on the spiritual dimension, which could not be assaulted by somatic disease. According to Frankl, "the spiritual remains untouched even in the psychosis ... [because] neither somatic sickness nor the somatic treatment can approach the spiritual."[46] Logotherapy therefore suggested that even psychotics could counteract their condition, by mustering the "defiant power of the human spirit." The argument that the spiritual could stand beyond and determine the somatic was also used in Frankl's forsaking of euthanasia.

Frankl rejected euthanasia on the grounds that the way someone dies, "is an integral part of his life; it rounds that life out to a meaningful totality."[47] In this prescription Frankl was extending his notion of a meaningful death in the camps to deny arguments in favor of euthanasia. To buttress his critique of euthanasia against "opponents" that argued "a psychotically ill person is in no condition to look after his own interests" and therefore "doctors ought to take the step of destroying him," Frankl asked "whether we are entitled to deprive an incurably ill patient of the chance to "die his death, ... even though the only realm of action open to him is the realizing of attitudinal values."[48] Interestingly, instead of dismissing the arguments out of hand, Frankl took the claims of "opponents" seriously. This led him to the conviction that these people's lives must be maintained so they have the "chance to die their own death."

When the value of human existence is defined from the perspective of Frankl's spiritual dimension the door is open to the practice of euthanasia. This is because meaning, located in the spiritual dimension, is not considered to be *immanent* in life itself. Other commentators have pointed to this contradiction. Marius G. Schneider (O.F.M.) argued that "logotherapy is in no position to defend consistently the dignity of the human person. Its existentialist and spiritualistic concept of the human being serves a justification for the destruction of 'unworthy' human life rather than of its inviolability."[49] Schneider also added that "Frankl's conviction of the unique value of the human person is unquestioned."[50] It is interesting that Schneider recognized that the concept of man in Frankl's spiritualistic psychology was in accordance with the world view that led to Nazi euthanasia practices.

In Frankl's defense, in 1946 he used the example of a man who suddenly awakened after spending five years in coma as representative of the fact that the doctor never knows if the patient is "incapable of being healed."[51] But Frankl's statements against euthanasia reveal that he understood the "rationale" behind the practices and was aware that the Nazis perpetrated them. It comes as some surprise, then, that Frankl did not give testimony in the postwar euthanasia trials, especially since he claimed to "sabotage" the practices. He certainly had useful information.[52]

Frankl also argued from his position of the spiritual dimension that suffering and death allowed access to the highest values. For Frankl, the Freudian pleasure principle was "ethical nihilism."[53] (We should note that it was Frankl, not Freud, who was asking whether the pleasure principle could be a foundation for life's meaning.) According to Frankl, in order to survive the camps a prisoner had to derive meaning from a source outside of the purely pleasurable. From this he concluded that if "we set up pleasure as the whole meaning of life, we insure that in the final analysis life shall inevitably seem meaningless." This is because pleasure is only a "condition" of materialism, and "the materialist— and hedonism is generally linked up with materialism—would even say pleasure is nothing but a state of cells in the brain."[54]

The reason pleasure could not be the foundation of a meaningful life was also deeply tied to his existentialist focus on death. Frankl argued that because life is surrounded by death, pleasure cannot really offer ultimate and fulfilled Meaning. Because "all of life is confronted with death," pleasure is cancelled out. "Anyone holding this hapless view of life as nothing but a pursuit of pleasure would have to doubt every moment of such a life, if he were to be consistent."[55] Although the line of reasoning was difficult to follow, Frankl argued that the constant possibility of death denied ultimate Meaning to any pleasure experience. He used the example of the last meal of a condemned prisoner; why eat when you are about to die? Therefore the pleasure principle could not supply a meaningful life because in the face of death pleasure provided no

Meaning, much less solace. Meaning could only come from the spiritual realm that was ultimately anchored in the realization of death.

Frankl's construction of the spiritual realm, dependent on a binary opposition between the spiritual and organic, created a conception of human nature immersed in a tortured struggle. This led Frankl to devalue organic experience and to affirm Meaning through heroic suffering. This attitude was evident in his first article presented in the *American Journal of Psychotherapy* in 1953, with the statement: "It is our conviction that psychotherapy has also the task of making the individual capable of enduring pain."[56] In combination with this psychotherapeutic attitude, Frankl's medical practice did not hesitate to use extreme measures. In his "department at the Polyclinic," they used "drugs," and "electroconvulsive treatment." Frankl "signed authorizations for some lobotomies without having cause to regret it ... [he] even carried out transorbital lobotomy." But Frankl claimed "that the human dignity of our patients [was] not violated" by these practices. According to Frankl "what matters is never the technique or therapeutic approach ... but the spirit it is being carried out."[57] This is similar to the argument Frankl made in Pötzl's festschrift, where Frankl claimed that the school of psychotherapy was of less importance than the personality of the physician and his approach to the patient.[58] On these grounds Frankl was trying to defend some of the more excessive medical practices of the 1960s. Nevertheless, with this attitude Frankl could partially lobotomize someone, and claim that the spiritual dimension remained intact. For Frankl, the spiritual orientation justified medical practices that are at best an incredibly tragic necessity, and at worst, barbaric.

Finally, the spiritual dimension led to his interest in psychosomatic medicine and a claim for the determining power of the spiritual over the physical. Thus he flirted with the conception that "Only a 'glorified' body is representative of the spiritual person; the body of 'fallen' man, however, presents a shattered, and, therefore, distorted mirror."[59]

The Past Will Come Again?

Frankl's formation of height psychology deeply reflected his war time experience. But arguably Frankl did not purge his theory or his clinical work of the authoritarian tendencies. According to Frankl, "biologism led ... right into the gas chambers of Auschwitz." The concentration camps were "the ultimate consequence of the theory that man is nothing but a product of inheritance and environment, or, as they liked to say in those days, of 'Blood and Soil.'" Thus, "the gas chambers of Auschwitz, Treblinka, and Maidnek, were ... prepared ... at the desks and in the lecture halls of nihilistic scientists and philosophers."[60] In Frankl's view, Nazism and the Holocaust were products of the nihilism inherent

in the human sciences. He therefore conflated reductionism and materialism with Hitlerism and the Holocaust.

This version of the origins of Nazism and the Holocaust simplified things immensely. But it allowed Frankl to place the origins of Hitlerism within the enlightenment tradition of rational materialism. On a simplified level this was undoubtedly true. But this view overlooked the connection between the spiritualistic conception of human experience and Nazism.[61] This conviction also served to justify his "spiritual" understanding of human experience.

Frankl's interpretation of nihilism is somewhat similar to Heidegger's critique of the technological rationalism that stemmed from the enlightenment.[62] Following Nietzsche, Heidegger recognized that the dilemma of nihilism turned on the issue of values. Heidegger agreed with Nietzsche that "there is no longer any goal in and through which all the forces of the historical existence of peoples can cohere and in the direction of which they can develop."[63] For Nietzsche this dilemma was to be solved by the "overman," who was free enough to create his or her own values. But according to Heidegger, Nietzsche's framing and solution to the dilemma only perpetuated the problem. That is, the idea that we once had values, or are capable of positing values, is reflective of nihilism. Therefore the concern with values is also a form of nihilism.[64]

Heidegger would have undoubtedly found Frankl's will to meaning too simplistic as a solution to nihilism. Nevertheless, Frankl's claim that scientific reductionism led to the Holocaust would have stood easily with Heidegger's claim that Nazism failed because the "inner truth and greatness of the movement" had become overrun by the very technological orientation the movement had tried to overcome.[65] By perceiving the movement as a manifestation of the essence of technology Heidegger conveniently placed Nazism beyond anyone's control. For his part, Frankl blamed the "nihilistic scientists," and clearly he had Freud in mind. Interestingly, Heidegger even trivialized the Holocaust by claiming that "the motorized food industry ... is the same thing as the manufacture of corpses in gas chambers..."[66]

As mentioned, Frankl's relationship to Heidegger is difficult to unpack. Frankl used some of Heidegger's essential insights in a simplified fashion, and they shared a similar intellectual trajectory. But Heidegger was a committed Nazi, while Frankl only tried to accommodate spiritualistic trends in psychotherapy. Nevertheless, both Frankl and Heidegger saw possibilities in the movement (Heidegger in the cultural and political and Frankl in the focus on world views, will, and responsibility in National Socialist psychology), only to be disappointed. Both attributed Nazism to the scientific materialism stemming from the Enlightenment. For Heidegger this explained the failure of the movement. One could imagine that Frankl would have made a similar claim as to why the Göring Institute failed to take up the banner of his height psychology. In delineating their shared hopes and disappointments perhaps we have discovered the source of their mutual agreement that the "past will come again." Neither

seemed capable of an "honest" reckoning with the past. They both therefore turned to idealist abstractions for solutions to their existential quests. Therefore, Heidegger's claim that we must "prepare expectations" because "only a god can save us now"[67] is similar Frankl's turn toward the spiritual dimension and ultimately God.

As we shall see, Frankl's affirmation of a spiritual dimension in combination with his view of the past allowed him to fashion a professional life in Vienna after the war, and eventually, internationally in the American humanistic psychology movement.

Notes

1. Lecture given at San Diego International University (1972).

2. Frankl, *Was nicht in meinen*, 91.

3. Heidegger paid his party dues until 1945, although he apparently rejected the racialism of Nazi ideology; his "apology" was to claim that "the inner truth of the movement was lost." In addition, he never expressed any remorse for the fate of the Jews.

4. Viktor Frankl, "Existential Dynamics and Neurotic Escapism," *Journal of Existential Psychiatry* 4 (1963): 30.

5. Frankl, *Was nicht in meinen*, 91.

6. Frankl, "Existential Dynamics and Neurotic Escapism," 30.

7. Ibid.

8. Martin Heidegger, *Poetry, Language, Thought*, trans. Albert Hofstadter (New York: Harper and Row, 1971), 76.

9. For a discussion of the meaning and context of this statement, see "The Spiegel Interview with Martin Heidegger," in Gunter Neske and Emil Kettering *Martin Heidegger and National Socialism; Questions and Answers*, (New York: Paragon Books) 41–66.

10. Frankl, *The Will to Meaning*, 3–4.

11. Viktor Frankl, *Logos und Existenz* (Vienna: Amandus-Verlag, 1951), 4–5.

12. Viktor Frankl, *Der unbedingte Mensch* (Vienna: Franz Deuticke, 1949), vii.

13. Heidegger first presented these ideas in *Being and Time*. For an introduction, see Martin Heidegger, *Martin Heidegger: Basic Writings*, ed. and trans. David F. Krell (San Francisco: Harper, 1977). Also, Herbert Dreyfus, *Being-in-the-World: A Commentary on Heidegger's Being and Time, Division I* (Cambridge, Mass.: MIT Press, 1991). Finally, Charles Guignon, ed., *The Cambridge Companion to Heidegger* (Boston: Cambridge University Press, 1996).

14. See Frankl, *Der unbedingte Mensch*, 70, and Frankl, *Der unbewusste Gott* (Vienna: Amandus-Verlag, 1949), 31. Also, Martin Heidegger, *Being and Time*, trans. John Macquarrie and Edward Robinson (New York: Harper and Row, 1962), 427.

15. Frankl, *Der unbedingte Mensch*, 98. Also, Frankl, *Der unbewusste Gott*, 32.

16. Frankl, *The Unconscious God*, 31.

17. Ibid.

18. Heidegger attempted a "fundamental ontology" in Division I of *Being and Time*. But he abandoned this project on the grounds that it continued the Western metaphysical tradition. Heidegger then turned to a history of being. For his part, Frankl seemed unaware of Heidegger's turn from a fundamental ontology.

19. Izenberg, *The Existentialist Critique of Freud*, 259.

20. Ibid., 3–12.

21. Frankl, *Homo Patiens* (Vienna: Franz Deuticke, 1950), 101.

22. Ibid., 81.

23. Ibid., 35.

24. Ibid., 30–35.

25. Frankl, *Der unbedingte Mensch*, 39.

26. On Frankl's distinction between men and animals, see Frankl, *Der unbedingte Mensch*, 95, and Frankl, *Logos and Existence*, 63.

27. This is a title of a book by Frankl. See Frankl, *…trotzdem Ja zum Leben Sagen* (Vienna: Franz Deuticke, 1946). The book consisted of three lectures on psychological hygiene Frankl gave at the Volkshochschule in Vienna.

28. Frankl, *Der unbedingte Mensch*, 64–65.

29. Ibid., 41.

30. Ibid., 72.

31. See Frankl, "Zehn Thesen ueber die Person," in *Logos und Existenz*, 49–64.

32. Frankl, *The Unconscious God*, 13.

33. Ibid., 28.

34. Ibid., 31.

35. Viktor Frankl, "Concept of Man in Psychotherapy," *Pastoral Psychology* 6 (1955): 21.

36. Viktor Frankl, "Logos and Existence in Psychotherapy," *American Journal of Psychotherapy* 7 (1953): 8. Also see Frankl, *The Doctor and the Soul*, 40.

37. Ibid.

38. Frankl, *Homo Patiens*, 11.

39. Frankl, *Logos und Existenz*, 63–64.

40. Frankl, *Homo Patiens*, 8. In German: "'Seine' Wahrheit ist aber niemals 'eine' Wahrheit, sondern immer 'die' Wahrheit—jedoch die in seiner Perspektive gesehene Wahrheit. Ist es doch diese seine Perspektive, die ihm die Wahrheit ueberhaupt erst erschliesst.… So liegt die einzige Absolutheit, welche die Wahrheit dem Menschen verstattet, in der absoluten Einzigkeit der Perspektive, in der sich die Wahrheit jedem einzelnen Menschen offenbart. Und so braucht der Perspektivismus keinesweg in einen Relativismus auszumuenden."

41. Ibid., 60.

42. Frankl, *The Unconscious God*, 26.

43. Frankl, *Homo Patiens*, 23.

44. Frankl, *The Unconscious God*, 10.

45. Ibid., 61.

46. Frankl, *Der unbedingte Mensch*, 53–54.

47. Frankl, *The Doctor and the Soul*, 49.

48. Ibid., 48.

49. Marius G. Schneider, "The Existentialistic Concept of the Human Person in Viktor E. Frankl's Logotherapy," in *Heirs and Ancestors*, ed. John K. Ryan (Washington D.C.: Catholic University Press, 1973), 63.

50. Ibid., 63.

51. *Das Recht Auf Das Eigene Leben*, Document no. 14.385, Institute für Geschichte der Medezin (Vienna).

52. Proof he had knowledge comes from these comments by Frankl on the Steinhof hospital where he worked from 1933 to 1937, before the euthanasia practices of the late 1930s and early 1940s. "Let me cite the case of Dr. J. He was the only man I ever encountered in my whole life whom I would dare to call a Mephistophelean being, a satanic figure. At the time he was generally called 'the mass murderer of Steinhof'.… When the Nazis started their euthanasia program, he held all the strings in his hands and was so fanatic in the job assigned to him that he tried not to let one single psychotic individual escape the gas chamber." Frankl, *Man's Search for Meaning*, 208. This claim was first made in the 1963 edition. It is not clear why Frankl did not provide the full name; it was Dr. Erwin Jekeluis.

53. Frankl, *The Doctor and the Soul*, 34.

54. Ibid., 37.

55. Ibid.

56. Frankl, "Logos and Existence in Psychotherapy," 12.

57. Frankl, "Reductionism and Nihilism," in *Beyond Reductionism: New Perspectives in the Life Sciences*, ed. Arthur Koestler (New York: Macmillan, 1970), 407.

58. See Viktor Frankl, "Über Lehrbarkeit und Lernbarkeit der Psychotherapie," in Urban, *Festschrift*, 222–229.

59. Frankl, quoted in Donald Tweedie, *Logotherapy and the Christian Faith* (Grand Rapids, Mich.: Baker Book House, 1961), 79. This view must be common among theologians because Robert Schuller described Frankl as "beautiful," with a face "sculpted by the spirit within you." See Schuller's comments in "Dr. Robert Schuller Interviews Viktor Frankl," 12.

60. Frankl, "Concept of Man in Psychotherapy," 26.

61. For the more traditional view see George Mosse, *The Crisis of German Ideology* (New York: Grossett and Dunlap, 1964), and Fritz Stern, *The Politics of Cultural Despair* (New York: Doubleday, 1965).

62. For a thorough and excellent discussion of Heidegger's understanding of technology, see Michael Zimmerman, *Heidegger's Confrontation with Modernity: Technology, Politics, Art* (Bloomington: Indiana University Press, 1990).

63. Martin Heidegger, *Nietzsche I*, trans. David F. Krell (San Francisco: Harper, 1991), 157. Also see Krell's introductory comments, xii–xiv.

64. For an excellent discussion of this issue, see Herbert Dreyfus, "Heidegger on the Connection between Nihilism, Art, Technology, and Politics," in Guignon, *The Cambridge Companion to Heidegger*, 290–293. Also see Martin Heidegger, *The Question Concerning Technology and Other Essays*, trans. William Lovitt (New York: Harper and Row, 1977).

65. See Neske, G and Kettering E. *Martin Heidegger and National Socialism: Question and Answers*, especially Karsten Harries, "Introduction," xi–xl.

66. Ibid., xxx.

67. Ibid., 57.

Forgetting, Reconfiguring, and Vergangeheitsbewältigung

To be a Jewish citizen of Austria puts one in danger of being impaled on one horn of a dilemma or the other.
—Paul Grosz, "A Jewish View of the Anschluss"

A Western diplomat once quipped that postwar Austria was "an opera sung by the understudies." There is a great deal of truth in the claim since in 1919 Vienna had lost its status as an imperial capital, during the 1930s and early 1940s most of the city's Jews either fled or were deported, and many of the more celebrated cosmopolitan citizens had left by this time as well. Observers of postwar Austria also describe the onset of a crisis of national identity. The historical roots of this crisis are traced to construction of "Austria" by the resolutions and compromises among the great powers.[1] Subsequently, up until 1933, if not 1938, the majority of Austrians held a conviction about the unfeasibility of Austria as an independent nation. In the interwar years most Austrian politicians, Socialists included, clamored for an *Anschluss* with Germany.[2] But after the disastrous war, and the experience of Nazi "oppression" for seven years, the cultural relationship with Germany changed. Rather than a look of envy or sympathy, most Austrians felt disdain, if not outright disgust and hatred, toward Germany. Consequently, after 1945 any philo-Germanism was perceived as neo-Nazi.

The foundation stone in the construction of Austrian national identity was the victim clause of the 1943 Moscow Agreement. In this agreement, the three

Allied powers established that Austria was the first victim of Nazi Germany. The declaration also mentioned that Austria had to take responsibility for fighting the war at the side of Nazi Germany. But in the political climate of the Cold War, especially after the 1948 Communist coup in Czechoslovakia, Austria and the Allies had reasons to ignore the latter point.[3] The "myth" of Austrians as victims of the Nazis was necessary for the constitution of a westward and liberal leaning Austria.[4] In order to create a bulwark against the Soviets, Austria, Western Europe, and America all tacitly agreed to sustain the mendacious view of Austrian victimhood. But the truth that everyone knew was that Hitler, along with many of the leading Nazis, came from Austria, and there were over 600,000 Austrian Nazi Party members at the end of the war. The victim card also helped take the focus off the role Austrofascism as an abettor of Nazism and all parties were interested in capturing the votes of ex-Nazis. The point is that "Austria" was formed on rather tenuous foundations.[5]

Nevertheless, Austria's postwar economic success, along with the "invention of a tradition," led to the instilling of a national sentiment in the majority of the people, and the "myth" of Austrian victimization by the National Socialists has been widely accepted. Tony Judt argued that "in a curious way Austria resembled *East* Germany.... Both countries were arbitrary geographical expressions whose post-war public life rested on tacit agreement to fabricate for common consumption a flattering new identity – except that the exercise proved considerably more successful in the Austrian case."[6]

No doubt this "success" in contrast to East Germany was due to the fact that Austria was the only European country once occupied by Soviet troops to attain full independence after 1945. Once Austrian sovereignty was achieved, internal differences between political parties were glossed over, and the postwar political culture of Austria was characterized by a desire for stability. After experiencing the cultural trauma of civil war in the thirties, and "abuse" by the Nazi "occupation," Austria established a system of social peace. With the state treaty in 1955, and subsequent withdrawal of the Allied occupation forces, a more or less "corporate system" was constructed. In this system Parliament played little or no role in decision making. Instead, political party leaders controlled a system of patronage and ironed out differences between capital and the workers in backroom meetings. From 1955 until 1999 this form of political power was shared essentially between the People's Party (Christian Conservatives) and the Socialists. After 1999 the Freedom Party led by Haider came into shared governance with the People's Party.

The first crack in the stability of both the "social peace" and the tenuous Austrian national identity appeared with the Waldheim affair and the end of the Cold War. With the revelation that presidential aspirant Kurt Waldheim lied about his wartime activities, and that his resume "overlooked" his prewar membership in National Socialist clubs, the myth began to crumble.[7] Since

the Waldheim affair, Austria has been in a process of self-questioning that has led to a slow recovery of a buried and forgotten past. But discovering the malaise and ambiguity that lay behind the comfortable postwar political and cultural synthesis—a synthesis built on a collective amnesia—has had many ramifications.

Austria's problem with public memory was pan-European—existing in almost every country annexed or occupied by Nazi Germany. In these countries, and Austria is an extreme case, there was an "erection of an unnatural and unsustainable frontier between past and present" that has exonerated national histories from coresponsibility for Nazi crimes. For most Europeans National Socialism was a German problem. In the case of Austria, national identity became beholden to "a mendacious myth rooted in ambiguity."[8]

Given the amnesia and ambiguous past, it is not surprising that in the 1990s the Freedom Party (FPÖ) led by Jörg Haider attempted a renewed interest in trying to find a "usable" tradition.[9] Rather than denying the Nazi past, Haider attempted to recast the Waffen SS as "decent men" of spiritually superior character. Along with these and numerous other outrages, Haider described Nazi employment policies as "sound," and Nazi extermination camps as "punishment camps."

As a Jew, Holocaust survivor, and founder of the third school of Viennese psychology, Frankl had a peculiar role in postwar Austria. On the issue of the ambivalent past, Frankl chose the part of reconciler. This attitude of reconciliation eventually led to his success in a society placing a premium on "social peace." But to be honest, in postwar Austria Frankl had few other options, and in many ways his decisions mirror those of Bruno Kreisky, who was chancellor in the 1970s and also Jewish. For both Kreisky and Frankl it seems that professional success required downplaying the crimes of the Holocaust and supporting the myth of "Austrian-as-victims." No doubt the fact that the deeply imbedded Austrian anti-Semitism lingered on in society and culture even after the Holocaust impacted their attitudes. In postwar Austria there was also a tendency to deny or at least downplay the atrocities committed against the Jews, so neither Frankl nor Kreisky would ingratiate themselves to their fellow Austrians by reminding them of the crimes against the Jews.[10]

As a survivor of Auschwitz, Frankl spoke publically on the Holocaust and the Nazis with moral authority. And, in the postwar Austrian culture of denial and repression Frankl certainly was one of the few voices "describing" Auschwitz. Not surprisingly, Frankl was essentially overlooked by his fellow Austrians. Nevertheless, Frankl's chosen role of reconciler represented a peculiar example of how postwar Austria failed to come to terms "honestly" with the past. Frankl therefore had a role in downplaying the Nazi atrocities and the horrors of the Holocaust. He was also used to legitimize those with an ambiguous past. But to be fair, this engagement in white-washing of the past was the only possibility in the postwar Austrian culture of collective denial.

Forgetting and Forgiving

Upon his return to Vienna in 1945 Frankl expressed a strong desire to help his old friend Otto Pötzl. In addition to Frankl testifying on behalf of Pötzl in his denazification hearings, Frankl's 1946 genealogy of Viennese doctors designated Pötzl as the "leading brain surgeon."[11] Ironically, when Frankl made this claim Pötzl was being dismissed from his university position. As mentioned above, Frankl also contributed to his Festschrift. But exactly why he wanted to help Pötzl was never fully explicated. The sense of debt likely centered on their medical work and proclaimed sabotaging of euthanasia. Also, Pötzl might have played the role of Frankl's protector.[12]

We can therefore assume that in his play, *Synchronization in Buchenwald*, Frankl had protecting Pötzl in mind when he described feeling the "responsibility" to make up a "mercy list ... of people whose life will be in danger during the first waves of hate." He wanted to protect those who did "a lot of good, secretly ... including some who are wearing uniforms," because "here and there still beats a human heart."[13] Frankl apparently felt a "responsibility" to return to Vienna to protect those he described as "good" Nazis. For example he described hiding a "medical colleague in his apartment" in order to protect him from prosecution.[14] Frankl's urge toward reconciliation mirrored the postwar climate of social peace. Not surprisingly, in Austria de-Nazification of party members was curtailed, and as Frankl's comments revealed, there was a tendency to view ex-Nazis as victims.[15]

Frankl described how Emil Tuchman helped him upon his return to Vienna by connecting him with Bruno Pitterman. As mentioned, Pitterman was a long-standing Socialist whom Frankl knew from the 1920s when he was member of the Socialist student organization. Pitterman gave Frankl a Remington typewriter and also "had him sign a blank form" which was then used as an application for a position at the Vienna Policlinic Hospital.[16] In February of 1946 Frankl began work in the small city hospital and for the next twenty-five years Frankl was the head of the neurology department.

Frankl recognized that it was rather ironic that a man in his position should come out in 1946 against recognizing a collective guilt.[17] But as an Auschwitz survivor, Frankl felt he had the authority to pardon the perpetrators. In 1946, Frankl spoke against collective guilt in the French occupied zone. The next day a former SS officer came to him "with tears in his eyes." He asked Frankl "where he found the courage to take a stand against collective guilt." Frankl told him: "You can't do it, you would be speaking out of self-interest. But I am the former prisoner No. 119104, and so I can do it.... People will listen to me..."[18] According to Batthyány, Frankl's convictions were based in his belief that assigning guilt to a collective was impossible because guilt is particular and accusing the totality "contradicts what constitutes the nature of freedom and responsibility."[19]

Frankl was surely correct to claim there is no collective guilt. Only individuals, not nations, can be held guilty. National character is not universal. But there is individual guilt. And, as members of human communities, people have a collective responsibility.[20] But in 1946 Frankl began with the statement that there is no collective guilt, never asking whether we are responsible.

In a speech given at the Vienna Rathausplatz on 10 March 1988, on the fiftieth anniversary of "the occupation of Austria by the troops of Hitler's Germany," Frankl repeated his argument against collective guilt that he first made in 1946.[21] Once again, he claimed "there are only two races of men: those who are decent people, and those who are not." Frankl universalized this "distinction" as in "every nation, and within nations right through every political party…" He then extended this distinction to the "concentration camps" and the "more or less decent people who belonged to the S.S. And in the same way there were also scoundrels amongst the prisoners."[22]

Peter Gay has described this strategy of sidestepping responsibility as "comparative trivialization." That is, since there were some good SS and some bad prisoners we cannot make distinctions between them. Frankl's claims served to pacify guilt and avert focus from the point that some people chose to accommodate the Nazis while others took paths of resistance. Many others were indecent people, who decided to join the party and carry out its program fully aware it was an immoral, anti-democratic political agenda that worked by terrorizing certain people. Frankl knew these things. He also knew that a large portion of Austrians affirmed the *Anschluss*.

Nevertheless, Frankl did not attach his rejection of collective guilt to a condemnation of the Austrian Nazis. Nor did he condemn the role the anti-democratic, Christian, authoritarian state played in paving the way for Nazism. Instead, he affirmed the victim clause of the Moscow Agreement, and side-stepped Austrian responsibility by claiming "Ladies and Gentlemen, it was National Socialism which inflicted the scourge of racial persecution on us."[23] Frankl extended these apologetics and again side-stepped the issue of Austrian responsibility by blaming the "regime or system which brings the scoundrels to the top…. Therein lies the true peril." This distancing of responsibility excused everyone on the basis of the system. That is, everyone was just an insignificant cog, caught in the totalitarian system. This version served to deny responsibility and soothe the guilty conscience. Frankl also diffused responsibility for the Holocaust by claiming that "in principle any country is capable of perpetuating the Holocaust."[24]

Taking a different tack, Karl Jaspers argued that all Germans shared a "political liability" for the Nazi period. Writing in 1947, Jaspers was challenging the Germans to found their political outlook and new state by being honest about the crimes perpetuated in the name of Germans by the Nazi regime.[25] Unlike Jaspers, Frankl was unable to confront Austrian responsibility for taking an anti-democratic turn that led to the Fatherland Front and ultimately

Nazism. For Frankl the vacuous "system," not the people, was responsible for Nazism and the Holocaust.

Since he was helping commemorate the fiftieth anniversary of the Nazi occupation—which coincided with the Waldheim affair—Frankl also argued against making people "feel guilty or even ashamed ... unless they were determined to drive the young people today into the arms of the old-style Nazis or neo-Nazis."[26] Frankl's point is well taken. Burdensome guilt upon preceding generations could possibly lead to a neo-fascist reaction.[27] Even so, Jaspers pointed out that there is a type of metaphysical guilt that every human community has—a responsibility for what was done in the name of ancestors. In this limited sense, every generation of Austrians, and more broadly, the community of the West, has a responsibility for the legacy of fascism and the Holocaust. Not a responsibility for, but a responsibility to remember in order to guard against the reoccurrence.

But Frankl claimed the present generation should not be held responsible for "something their parents or grandparents had to answer for." The contradiction is that Frankl denied collective guilt in 1946, and to most observers Austrians never had to answer for their actions.

Frankl also argued against collective guilt in a memorial speech held upon request of the Society of Physicians in Vienna on 25 March 1949 for the members who died in the years 1938–1945. In this speech, he also "blamed the system that brought some men to guilt and which brought others to death." He then asserted an authoritative voice by articulating the experience of the victims. Frankl claimed "in their last words there was not a single word of hate—only words of longing came from their lips, and words of forgiveness..."[28] Given that he was a Holocaust survivor, Frankl's claims about the dying probably seemed believable. He therefore used his authority to place words of forgiveness on the lips of those who died. Clearly this version would soothe the guilty conscience regardless of whether the guilt was attributable to crimes committed, passivity, or perhaps simply survival.

Frankl's personal desire to reconcile—even with ex-Nazis—and resolve guilt dovetailed with Austrian needs. As a persecuted Jew he seemed the perfect spokesperson. One could argue that Frankl's "benevolent" forgiveness was a form of passive aggression that allowed him to humble his former oppressors. On some level this might be true. Nevertheless, by excusing the perpetrators, and by claiming to voice the dead's sentiments, he was stretching his authority by forgiving an offense that was done to someone else.

Frankl ended the speech, which was published in *The Jewish Echo*, with comments that could be read as autobiographical. Frankl described the "personal guilt of a man who has 'done nothing' wrong, but who has failed to do 'something' right." Frankl attributed this failure to "apprehension for himself or anxiety for his family." But he deflected the judgment of the gathered physicians by stating "whoever wishes to condemn such a man as a coward needs

first to prove that in the same situation he himself would have been a hero.... But it is prudent not to sit on judgment of others."[29] Frankl knew there were few heroes but everyone gathered knew he, as a Holocaust survivor, was a victim. Therefore, it was "prudent" not to judge him. But what did he exactly mean by the statement that no one can sit in judgment on those who have "done nothing right?" Obviously Frankl was deflecting coming to terms with guilt. But this was the guilt that Jaspers honestly faced when he stated "we are alive—that is our guilt ... we preferred to stay alive, on the feeble, though correct, ground that our death could not have helped anyone."[30]

Reconciling

An example of Frankl's role as reconciler and legitimizer was his (small) part in the Waldheim affair. On 9 September 1988 a picture of Frankl with Waldheim was printed in the *Neue Kronen Zeitung*.[31] "President Waldheim" handed Frankl, the former "concentration camp prisoner" who in the hell of National Socialism had lost his entire family, the Great Silver Badge of Honor with the Star. Frankl looked directly into the camera with his wife,[32] standing in the background with her eyes averted. Waldheim, smiling, towered over Frankl and appeared polished, genteel and happy. And why shouldn't he? Frankl was helping in the "domestic rehabilitation" of Waldheim. That Frankl took the medal from Waldheim in these circumstances, (post-affair Waldheim) shocked many Austrians.[33]

For the newly elected Waldheim, Frankl was useful for his "rehabilitation" on a number of levels. First because Frankl represented a survivor who apparently had no animosities toward "good" Nazis like Waldheim. Therefore his appearance with Waldheim had the effect of a de facto reduction of Waldheim's culpability for Nazi crimes, and represented a moral and political legitimation. More broadly, Frankl's conciliatory actions can be viewed as soothing Austria's wounded identity. And, by appearing with the ex-Nazi, he was also serving to reaffirm Austria's victimization myth. For his part, Frankl appeared heroic and gracious—big enough—to be capable of forgiveness.

There was also another layer to their relationship. Some of Waldheim's defenders resorted to a covert anti-Semitism by claiming he was being slandered by the World Jewish Congress (WJC). One example of a crude right-wing defense of Waldheim was Carl Hödl's attack on President Bronfman of the WJC. Hödl, the deputy mayor of Linz and member of the conservative, Christian-democratic Austrian People's Party (ÖVP), compared the attacks on Waldheim with the crucifixion of Jesus—and framed the debate in terms of Christians versus Jews. He also criticized the placing of Waldheim on the "Watch list" and Bronfman's description of Waldheim as "part of the [Nazi]

death machinery." Hödl cited Frankl's rejection of collective guilt to buttress his defense of Waldheim.[34] According to Hödl, Frankl's attitude of a reconciling, reasonable, good Jew was the correct attitude toward the Nazi past.[35]

Frankl had other uses for the political right in Vienna. His coronation as *Ehrenbürgerschaft*, (honorary citizen of Vienna) came surprisingly at the hand of Haider and the Freedom Party (FPÖ). Frankl's ties to the FPÖ apparently began in 1981. His philosophy of meaning, to be found in a "great idea" or in "giving to humanity," was cited by the party theorist, Fritz Wolfram.[36] But Frankl's reconciling spirit and subtle downplaying of Nazi atrocities was the center of his appeal for the FPÖ. As mentioned, the attempt to find a usable past was one of the main goals of Haider, who described himself as a "good friend" of Frankl. Frankl's claims that there is "no collective guilt," and that "there were good Nazis and bad Nazis," "good prisoners and bad prisoners," and "good SS and bad SS," fit nicely with the FPÖ agenda.[37]

The FPÖ did not have an easy time getting Frankl nominated. The Christian Conservatives thought the award should go to a Catholic university professor. The Socialist Party (SPÖ) was willing to go along with the nomination, although the leftist intellectuals were demanding a detailed resume from Frankl. For their part, the SPÖ tried to undermine the FPÖ's efforts by offering Frankl another, although less esteemed, citizenship award. Frankl declined, and at this point the FPÖ forced the issue by going public with the nomination and starting a petition campaign. In these circumstances the other parties ended up bequeathing the *Ehrenbürgerschaft* on Frankl.[38] The vote was a unanimous 99–0.

The famed Nazi hunter Simon Wiesenthal was also nominated for the award exactly at the same time as Frankl. But the FPÖ voted against the nomination because the Wiesenthal Center had hung Haider's photo next to the right-wing extremists, Jean Le Pen and David Duke, at the museum of tolerance. For his part Wiesenthal viewed the FPÖ "no votes as a badge of honor, and said that his name and the prize would have no meaning if extremists voted for him."[39]

Frankl eventually "distanced" himself from Haider, and had "little understanding" for Haider's speaking to the Waffen SS.[40] But Rüdiger Stix, a leading member of the FPÖ and supporter of Frankl's nomination, bitterly pointed out that this remark by Frankl seemed disingenuous, because Frankl, like Haider, often claimed there were good SS. Frankl's daughter, Gabriele Vesely-Frankl, also reiterated the claim of "distance" from Haider. She described the accidental grounds of Haider's and Frankl's "friendship" and defended her father with the claim that he is "no politician."[41] Nevertheless, Frankl made his political positions public. For example, in January 1993 Frankl was interviewed on television by Johannes Kunz. Frankl claimed there was a necessity "for a dialog with the right extremists," because the cultural crisis was attributable to a sense of meaninglessness and a lack of a rewarding life. Therefore, dialog and democratic tolerance was the best way to avoid "terrorist actions."[42]

In the postwar political culture of reconciliation, Viktor Frankl came to be recognized as a 'leading citizen' of Vienna.[43] After the war Frankl assumed the moral high ground for himself and the Austrian people. His claims about collective guilt seemed legitimate because the call came from a person "morally purified" by the oppression of Auschwitz. And like Austria, Frankl will first and foremost be a *victim* of the Nazis. Life under the Nazis was treacherous and besieged with extenuating circumstances. Also, Austria's occupation until 1955 by the Allies, along with the myth that it was the first victim of the Nazis, conveniently ruled out a self-induced moral purge. But with Waldheim and in some sense culminating with the Schüssel Era, Austria achieved the long overdue process of introspection. Tony Judt argued, "Today the pertinent European reference is not baptism. It is extermination.... Holocaust recognition is our contemporary European entry ticket."[44] Based on Judt's contention it appears Austria has earned its European entry ticket by successfully creating "a dense landscape of World War II memorials" and is no longer "the black sheep of Europe."[45] Frankl didn't live to see Austria come to terms with its past. And it is doubtful whether the "good humanist" Frankl was even fully conscious of his role in the burial of the past. Frankl's argument against collective guilt, which served to foreclose notions of collective responsibility, fit the Austrian milieu after the war. It was also likely key to his success on both a professional and psychological level, to help his fellow Austrians bury the past. This became his "use" of his survival. By 1988 Frankl could claim "that the only people who are justified" in saying "people should have preferred imprisonment to compromise or coming to terms with the Nazis ... are people who ... did indeed allow themselves to be incarcerated in a concentration camp rather than betray themselves or their convictions."[46] Frankl overlooked the fact that some people compromised with the Nazis and were still sent to the camps. By 1988, Frankl's survival of Auschwitz had placed him beyond reproach. After pardoning individual ambiguous actions, he could use his badge of survival to pardon Austria.

Not surprisingly, some Austrians and Jews in particular were disappointed by Frankl's cultural role. For example Klingberg describes how Frankl's reconciling attitude and stance on collective guilt ultimately led to a frayed relationship with other Viennese Jews.[47] Frankl's attitude of reconciliation was also not well received by the American Jewish community. Klingberg describes how in 1978, Frankl gave a lecture at the Institute of Adult Jewish Studies at Congregation B'nai Jeshurun on the Upper East Side of New York City where he rejected collective guilt and also mentioned the Bruno Kreisky (the Austrian chancellor who was Jewish and shared similar views as Frankl) that led to an outburst of boos from the audience and how Frankl was called a "Nazi Pig."[48] It appears although Austria eventually mastered the horrendous past, Frankl's personal history that included a connection to the Nazi Psychotherapy movement, involved working with Pötzl, and culminated with his interaction with

Waldheim and Haider in the last decade of his life left his own past a multi-dimensional all-too–Austrian Jewish tragedy—unmastered.

Finally there is a need to understand and analyze Frankl's role in America. With the badge of Auschwitz as his legitimation, in September 1957, Frankl gave a lecture at Princeton. He claimed, "I am hypersensitive to the slightest suggestion of nihilism....because I have had to overcome nihilism within myself." He then connected his self-purge with his "existential self-analysis," claiming that "I can see the mote—the mote!—in the other's eyes so well because I have had to tear the beam out of my own."[49] Purged and confident, Frankl offered America his solution for the dilemma of the twentieth century.

Notes

The German term *Vergangenheitsbewältigung* is a compound noun that translates as mastering or conquering the past. The term is used to describe how the uncomfortable reality of the Austrian past is conquered through a process of forgetting and reconfiguring.

1. In 1918, with the treaty of St. Germain, and in 1943, with the Moscow Agreement (the latter claimed Austria was the first victim of Nazism), the "state" of Austria was determined by diplomatic resolutions among the victorious powers.

2. In May 1933, after Hitler's seizure of power in Germany, the Socialists removed the clause for a union with Germany from their platform. But as the archive footage reveals, there was little or no resistance to the 1938 *Anschluss* by the Austrian people. For an excellent discussion of these issues, see Richard Mitten, *The Politics of Anti-Semitic Prejudice* (Boulder, Co.: Westview, 1992), 12–17.

3. For an excellent discussion of these issues, see Fritz Fellner, "The Problem of the Austrian Nation after 1945," *Journal of Modern History* 60 (June 1988): 264–289.

4. On why Stalin failed to gain control of Austria, the political motivations behind America's accepting the "myth" of Austria's victimization, and the subsequent abandoning of the de-Nazification of Austria, see Harry Piotrowski, "The Soviet Union and the Renner Government of Austria, April–November 1945," *Central European History* (1988): 246–277.

5. The long-standing political conservatism in Austria is exemplified by Dolfuss's subduing of the workers in February 1934 and the defeat of the Nazi coup by the Austrian state after Dolfuss's assassination in July of 1934. In both events the forces for an "Austrian order" defeated the political aspirations of both the left and right. In sum, the absence of a positive democratic tradition makes the political foundations of the second republic very shaky. For a useful overview see Melanie Sully, *A Contemporary History of Austria* (New York: Routledge, 1990), 110–115.

6. Tony Judt, *Postwar: A History of Europe Since 1945* (New York: Penguin Books, 2005), 263.

7. For an excellent discussion of these issues, see Mitten, *The Politics of Antisemitic Prejudice*, especially "When 'the Past' Catches Up," 246–261.

8. Tony Judt, "The Past is Another Country: Myth and Memory in Postwar Europe," *Daedalus* (1992–1994): 83–118. Also, Tony Judt, "Austria and the Ghost of the New Europe," *New York Review* (15 February 1996): 22–25.

9. The FPÖ was originally the League of Independents formed in 1949. The League was made up of ex-Nazis, Monarchists, and other right-leaning figures. Most commentators considered Haider a political opportunist and not a neo-Nazi. But there was a political philosophy that was anti-democratic, anti-capitalist, and authoritarian behind his opportunism. This was evidenced, for example, by his disdain for "foreigners," his hatred of "corrupt" government, his proclaimed desire to remain isolated from the European Union, and his call for a third republic. See Jörg Haider, *Die Freiheit die ich meine* (Vienna: Ulstein, 1993). For a discussion of these issues and a

history of the party, see Max Riedlsperger, "FPO: Liberal or Nazi?," in *Conquering the Past: Austrian Nazism, Yesterday and Today*, ed. F. Parkinson (Indiana: Wayne State University, 1989), 257–275. Also see Tony Judt, "Austria and the Ghost of the New Europe."

10. On these issues, see Robert Wistrich, *Austrians and Jews in the Twentieth Century: From Franz Joseph to Waldheim* (New York: St. Martin's Press, 1992), especially Robert Knight, "'Neutrality,' not Sympathy: Jews in Post-War Austria," 220–233, and, in the same volume, Robert Wistrich, "The Kreisky Phenomenon: A Reassessment," 234–251.

11. Viktor Frankl, "Wien und die Seelenheilkunde," *Wiener Kurier* (23 March 1946): 11.

12. However, Else Pappenheim, who worked at the university clinic under Pötzl until the *Anschluss*, recalled no special relationship between Frankl and Pötzl. (Pappenheim Interview.)

13. Frankl, *Synchronization in Buchenwald*, 25.

14. Frankl, *Was nicht in meinen*, 81.

15. On these issues, see Knight, "'Neutrality' not Sympathy: Jews in Post-War Austria," 224–227.

16. Frankl, *Was nicht in meinen*, 82. Also see Klingberg, *When Life Calls Out to Us*, 156.

17. Ibid., 80–81.

18. Ibid.

19. A. Batthyány, *Mythos Frankl?*, 10.

20. Recognizing "collective responsibility" is arguably a constituent feature of democratic society.

21. See Frankl, *Logos und Existenz* (Vienna: Amandus-Verlag, 1951), specifically, "Die Existenzanalyse und die Probleme der Zeit (1946)," 24–31.

22. Frankl, "There Is No Collective Guilt," 5.

23. Ibid.

24. Ibid.

25. See Karl Jaspers, "The Question of German Guilt," in *Karl Jaspers: Basic Philosophical Writings*, trans. and ed. Edith Ehrlich, Leonard H. Ehrlich, and George B. Pepper (New Jersey: Humanities Press, 1986), 396–408.

26. Frankl, "There is no Collective Guilt," 5.

27. This claim for an unburdened past is similar to Hannah Arendt's notion of "natality," in which each generation has the opportunity to start anew. For an interesting insight into the psychology of guilt, contemporary Germans, and the Nazi past, see Peter Sichrovsky, *Born Guilty* (New York: Basic Books, 1993).

28. Frankl, "In Memorium," *The Jewish Echo: Periodical of Jewish Intellectuals* 5, no. 6, (1949): 1.

29. Ibid.

30. Jaspers, *The Question of German Guilt*, 400.

31. The *Neue Kronen Zeitung* was the largest selling daily paper, and has a strong rightist orientation.

32. Frankl remarried shortly after the war.

33. According to Klingberg, the Frankls and Waldheims were "social acquaintances." Klingberg, *When Life Calls Out to Us*, 301.

34. See Carl Hödl, *Leben ist nicht Zufall* (Vienna: n.p., 1990), 141–177.

35. On the WJC and Waldheim, see Mitten, *The Politics of Antisemitic Prejudice*, 119–137.

36. Fritz Wolfram, "Die Problematik einer weiteren Arbeitszeitverkuerzung und Freizeitvermehrung," *freie argumente* no. 2 (January 1981): 29.

37. Frankl made this last claim first in his 1963 edition of *Man's Search for Meaning*, 136 (ftn), and repeated it in *Was nicht in meinen*, 80, and once again on a nationally broadcast television interview in 1994, Wolf Interview (FPÖ). Dr. Rüdiger Stix, FPÖ member in the Defense Ministry, claimed they nominated Frankl based on the 1993 interview. Significantly, in 1993 the more liberal "leftist" members of the FPÖ left the party to form the Liberal Forum. Frankl seemed to be useful in the attempt to legitimize and rehabilitate a rightist group.

38. The information on the politics behind Frankl's nomination comes from my interview with Dr. Rüdiger Stix of the FPÖ, 15 June 1996.

39. See *Simon Wiesenthal Center News Release*, 29 June 1995.

40. See "Viktor Frankl distanziert sich von F-Chef Haider," *Der Standard* (13 January 1996), and "Frankl an Haider: Verägerung über den 'Freund,'" *News* (March 1996). However, Haider apparently visited Frankl on his deathbed.

41. Gabriella Vesely-Frankl, "Lasst Frankl aus dem Spiel!" *profil* no. 4 (22 January 1996): 70–71.

42. See "Viktor Frankl für echten Dialog mit den Rechtsextremisten," *Politik* no. 6 (26 January 1993).

43. Frankl's worldwide renown was also exemplified by the fact he gave the keynote address to the first World Congress of Psychotherapy, held in Vienna in July 1996.

44. Tony Judt, *Postwar*, 803.

45. See Günter Bischof, "Victims? Perpetrators? 'Punching Bags' of European Historical Memory? The Austrians and Their World War II Legacies" *German Studies Review* 27 (Feb. 2004): 24.

46. Frankl, "There is No Collective Guilt," 5.

47. Klingberg, *When Life Calls Out to Us*, 229.

48. Ibid., 230

49. Frankl, "Collective Neuroses of the Present Day," *International Journal für prophylaktische Medizin und Socialhygiene* 2 (3 June 1958): 5.

Frankl in America

Transcending the Angel Beast

———————

More than a third of American adults claim that God speaks to them directly. Am I alone in finding this a scary statistic? What in the world do they mean?
— Arthur Schlesinger, "The Worst Corruption"

The trend moves toward a profoundly personalized religion, so that every man will arrive at a language of his own, find the words of his own, when addressing himself to the ultimate being.
— Viktor Frankl, *The Will to Meaning*

Throughout the 1960s and early 1970s Frankl lectured and taught in America. When he arrived in America in 1959 he presented himself as having solved the problem of nihilism. This assertion, combined with his survival of Auschwitz, provided Frankl with an immediate intellectual legitimacy and moral authority in America. Even without these attributes, Frankl would have likely been well received for two reasons. First, in the early 1950s the groundwork had been laid by a series of articles in American journals including the spread "A Psychiatrist Discovers God: We are Born to Believe" in the *Women's Home Companion* in April 1954. Second, there was the precedence of the intellectual migration from Europe to America that had been produced by Hitler's regime. Although only a small number of the migrants made it to America, those that did were some of the leading figures in their respective fields.[1] America's absorption of refugee intellectuals was fraught with difficulties, but the overall effects were

———————

positive.[2] In summing up the intellectual migration, H. Stuart Hughes described the effect as the "deprovincialization" of the American mind.[3] Given these circumstances Frankl, as a late arrival with established connections, could expect a warm welcome. Why Frankl "migrated" is not exactly clear. He often remarked that his work was not well received in postwar Austria.[4] Also, despite his reconciling attitude, as a survivor of the Holocaust, Frankl was a painful reminder of Nazism and Austrian anti-Semitism. It is likely, then, that Frankl hoped to find a more receptive audience for his ideas in America.

New Start?

Frankl's introduction to America came through his good friend Paul Polak. Polak was the physician in charge at the sanitarium "Maria Theresia Schlössel," which before the war was the Rothschild hospital. There was a strong mutual respect between the two because Frankl dedicated his book *Logos und Existenz* (1951) to Polak. In 1949, Polak wrote a short introductory article on "Frankl's Existential Analysis" for the *American Journal of Psychotherapy*. Polak began his article with the claim that the "advanced methods" of the Viennese "depth psychology … became completely discarded during the Nazi regime." Therefore, psychology had to be renewed, because "no ideology would have any validity for the present European generation," unless "it integrated the … mental suffering this generation had to endure during the last decade."[5] Polak then described how Frankl's "new start" represented "a new trend in thinking and a 'third school' to originate in Vienna." This declaration of a "new start" made no mention of the fact that Frankl developed the foundation for his therapy in the 1930s. In addition, Polak presented Frankl's intellectual heritage as stemming from Karl Jaspers and Max Scheler and as a rejection of the "nihilistic and atheistic beliefs of Jean Paul Sartre."

Polak also highlighted the central role of suffering in the thought of Frankl. He described how Frankl saw "human existence from the perspective of suffering" and maintained that for the "realization of the highest purpose of human existence, suffering becomes endowed with an individual and inalienable meaning in every specific case."[6] Despite Polak's promotion, the "new" paradigm of higher meaning through suffering was somewhat slow to catch on in America.

The First Disciple

Eventually the torch was picked up by Edith Weisskopf-Joelson. Weisskopf-Joelson was quite an interesting figure. Jewish, she immigrated to America from Vienna in 1939, two years after she received her doctorate in psychology from

the University of Vienna. In 1955, in an apparent response to Frankl's arti-
cles introducing his work in the United States,[7] Weisskopf-Joelson presented
"some comments on a Viennese school of psychiatry." Her initial comments
were hedgingly critical. She claimed "some parts of Frankl's teaching are so
mystical and confused that it would be without value to report them here," and
that "his teachings have become a philosophy of life, or perhaps a religion for
many people."[8]

In her first article, Weisskopf-Joelson attempted to explain the religious
thrust of Frankl's work in relationship to the demise of fascism. Accordingly,
"one gets the impression that Frankl's spiritual attitudes aim to counteract some
of the demoralization due to the breakdown of National Socialism and the
lack of any supporting faith to take its place."[9] Weisskopf-Joelson's presentation
of logotherapy as a replacement for the cultural void left by the fascist failure
neglected the fact that logotherapy was more aptly conceived as a continuation,
rather than a replacement, of certain existential and spiritualistic trends within
psychotherapy. It is not clear why, but despite her initial reservations, Weiss-
kopf-Joelson became an admirer and ardent supporter of Viktor Frankl from
1958 on.[10]

As she was an early promoter of Frankl in America, Weisskopf-Joelson's
biography provides an interesting perspective on his influence. After a diffi-
cult immigration and adjustment, throughout the 1960s she was in and out of
psychiatric hospitals. In her memoirs, entitled *Father, Have I kept my Promise?:
Madness as Seen from Within*, with an afterward by Frankl, Weisskopf-Joelson
described her madness and how Frankl's ideas helped her find meaning in it.
In the afterward, Frankl described Edith's struggles in terms of a fallen disciple
who turned from the master's teaching. He framed her madness as the "abys-
mal despair that accompanies anyone who chooses to return from the spiritual
heights and peaks to the depths of the valleys."[11]

Weisskopf-Joelson also revealed that throughout her life she had ambiva-
lence about Jews and her own Jewish heritage. In her memoir she described the
promise she made to her father on his deathbed in these terms.

> But before you died I sat at your bedside in the hospital, and you said, "You must
> promise me …" And I promised.
> 'For most of my life I forgot what I promised.'
> Forgive me, Father.
> Forgive me for having looked down upon the Jews with caftans, beards and
> sideburns. Those Jews with their sad eyes who are a part of me, a part which I
> could not accept.[12]

Although the exact words of her father's request remained unwritten,
Weisskopf-Joelson's honesty is admirable. But the confession of a type of self-
hatred, along with the suggestion that logotherapy was to counteract the "de-
moralization" due to the breakdown of National Socialism, suggests that she
had some deep-seated, unresolved psychic issues.

Weisskopf-Joelson's reflections teach us a number of things about her as one of Frankl's key disciples. Her autobiography revealed she experienced traumatic social dislocation in her transition to America. Although she acquired employment, married, and discovered Frankl, nothing seemed to stop her encroaching madness. Her autobiography suggested that a key element in her psychic turmoil was her inability to fulfill her promise to her father and accept her ancestors.[13] Still, we can only surmise what Weisskopf-Joelson found so appealing in Frankl's logotherapy. Significantly, a central premise that Weisskopf-Joelson took from Frankl's thinking was a denial of the traditional therapeutic strategy for overcoming neurosis. Weisskopf-Joelson argued that "it is quite possible that certain factors might cause neuroses during early childhood and that entirely different factors might relieve neuroses during adulthood."[14] Frankl often quoted this comment in a positive light because it affirmed his therapeutic techniques. Apparently, Weisskopf-Joelson found something in Frankl's ideas to help her come to terms with her past and social dislocation. But these therapeutic strategies were not focused on relieving repression to overcome neurosis. Instead, Frankl represented a solid intellectual ground or a "secular religion," as she would become fond of describing it, to quell her tensions. But as her mental breakdown in 1962 suggested, Frankl's vision failed to prevent an encroaching crisis. From the "confession" in her autobiography she was apparently finally resolving her "issues" just before she died. But her struggles are just a backdrop to our central concern—Frankl and his subsequent influence in the United States.

Promoting

In her promotion of Frankl, Weisskopf-Joelson suggested that logotherapy had attracted many followers in Austria. Then she questioned whether Frankl's "ideology" would be "equally effective on other cultural soil" According to Weisskopf-Joelson, there was a need to investigate one of the central problems of our time: "From what kinds of ideologies can different types of individuals benefit? What kind of 'religion' do different personalities need?"[15] Again, Weisskopf-Joelson recognized logotherapy as an ideology and surrogate religion, but instead of expressing reservation, she seemed to think this quality was positive. She also claimed that by giving "unavoidable suffering the status of a positive value logotherapy borrows from the wisdom of religion." Weisskopf-Joelson thought this would be especially helpful in counteracting "certain unhealthy trends" in the United States, where the "sufferer is given very little opportunity to be proud of his suffering." According to Weisskopf-Joelson, America is "pervaded by ... fun morality," where it is "ethically desirable to be happy and have fun." This morality only served to increase "the burden of the unhappy" because "he is not only unhappy, but also ashamed of being unhappy."[16]

Weisskopf-Joelson proscription was to advocate the "improvement of mental health through popular mass-media such as lectures, books, radio, and television programs." She claimed that "logotherapy lends itself well to this kind of application and its proponents have been active in this direction."[17]

Weisskopf-Joelson sensed that Frankl's vision also met American political needs in the 1960s. She prescribed Frankl's heroic suffering as the right ideology for fighting the Cold War, because "totalitarian systems" attempt to compensate for "existential frustrations," and logotherapy offered a "defense system" against such ideologies.[18] In order to create this defense system Weisskopf-Joelson described logotherapy as a "pedagogic tool," through which "the value system which logotherapy calls 'the meaning of life' is 'learned' by the patient during therapy rather than brought to consciousness."[19]

Other Disciples

The key elements of Frankl's support in America came from the religiously oriented. This is because in the mid 1950s Frankl began to recruit Methodist ministers and pastoral psychologists to study with him. Among those who went to Vienna were Haddon Klingberg (his official biographer), Paul E. Johnson, from Boston University School of Theology, Melvin Kimble, from Lutheran-Northwestern Seminaries, and Robert Leslie, from the Pacific School of Religion. The latter published a book entitled *Jesus and Logotherapy*, which discussed the similarities between logotherapy and the teachings of the New Testament. Leslie was also the curator of the Frankl Library and Memorabilia at the Graduate Theological Union Library in Berkeley, California. Paul Johnson, although never a full-fledged disciple, did write a favorable review of logotherapy, entitled "The Challenge of Logotherapy," for the *Journal of Religion and Health* in 1968.[20]

Other disciples of Frankl attempted to paste Christianity onto logotherapy. The pastoral psychologist Donald Tweedie was another early disciple who studied in Vienna. Tweedie wrote two books on Frankl. The first one, *Logotherapy and the Christian Faith: An Evaluation of Frankl's Existential Approach to Psychotherapy*, was an overview of Frankl's postwar work. Tweedie described how Frankl's conception of humanity was a mirror of the Christian view. He also argued that logotherapeutic notion of "spirit" was similar to the biblical conception of the "heart." Tweedie's uncritical acclaim was the first synopsis of Frankl's ideas for the American audience. His second book, *The Christian and the Couch: An Introduction to Christian Logotherapy* is a much lighter fare, and attempted to develop a "Christian Logotherapy" that considered "in some detail the relevance of the person and work of Jesus Christ to the theory and practice of psychotherapy."[21]

Another work with a Christian orientation by one of Frankl's disciples was A.J. Ungersma's *The Search for Meaning: A New Approach in Psychotherapy*

and Pastoral Psychology. Ungersma relied on Frankl's logotherapy to address the question of the relationship between psychotherapy and religion. Not surprisingly, Ungersma found the answer in logotherapy, and he became an uncritical promoter, claiming: "Frankl's work is still in the formative stage, still developing, and thus it is too early to sharpen the knives of dissection."[22]

From this brief overview of Frankl's disciples we can draw a few conclusions. First, all of them were interested in using Frankl's logotherapy to buttress Christianity. Second, the uncritical praise reflected the solace Frankl's logotherapy provided for the religiously oriented. To them, Frankl probably seemed like a breath of fresh air—here was a therapy that could be used to promote a Christian world view.

Jewish Disciples

Frankl's psychology found little resonance among religiously oriented Jews. Apparently mainly Christian thinkers were drawn to study with him, and his ideas about guilt, death, and suffering were very compatible with a Christian world view.

In 1965, however, a former student of Frankl, Rabbi Earl Grollman, claimed that Frankl's "works breathe the very spirit of Judaism." Although Frankl apparently "reviewed the article and authenticated its contents," Grollman claimed Frankl's criticisms of Freud and Adler were "too pat and often fatuous." This led Frankl to give a reprint of the article to Swan Hayworth, a Professor of Psychology of Religion at the Southern Baptist Theological Seminary who was studying with Frankl at the time. Hayworth defended Frankl by claiming he had "not heard him criticize his former teachers." He also claimed that Grollman's article suggested Frankl was a "good Jew" but a "poor psychiatrist," and therefore played into the hands of Frankl's enemies. Grollman responded by claiming, "in truth, I am neither his friend nor his enemy, his apologist nor his defamer."[23]

Eventually, the torch was picked up by Rabbi Reuven Bulka in the 1970s. Bulka received his Ph.D. from the University of Ottawa in 1971. His dissertation was on logotherapy, and throughout the 1970s and 1980s Bulka promoted logotherapy as "most akin" with "the faith system … Judaism."[24] In the forward to Bulka's book on logotherapy, Frankl remarked how "Jewish responses" to logotherapy "were relatively rare … until Dr. Reuven P. Bulka."[25]

Frankl's response to Bulka's efforts is rather interesting. Frankl framed Bulka's attempt to connect logotherapy and Judaism as

> a mosaic … single pieces each of which forms part of the whole picture. And it is precisely the fragmentary quality—or should I say, the humility?—which makes for the beauty of a mosaic.
>
> This feature corresponds, on the part of Dr. Bulka, to the modesty with which he explicates his comparative studies in this "mosaic-esque" book. Dealing with

logotherapy as evaluated from the viewpoint of Judaism, it may aptly be defined as a 'mosaic' mosaic.[26]

What Frankl meant by logotherapy and Judaism as of a "fragmentary quality" or "the humility?" is not clear. Frankl used the metaphor of the mosaic in his 1937 article in the *Zentralblatt*. There he stated: "like in a mosaic where each little part is indispensable … the individual in the community becomes an absolute member in the higher whole."[27] His "apt" definition of Bulka's work as a "mosaic" mosaic is peculiar. Is Judaism the indispensable part in the higher whole of Christianity for Frankl? In prefacing this passage, Frankl described how he had to part with a small piece of a mosaic that came from an ancient synagogue in Jerusalem at Auschwitz. Is Frankl then suggesting that Bulka is the mosaic recovered? What seems clear is that Frankl had come to accept that Bulka could only make a "fragmentary and humble" contribution to logotherapy.

Humanistic Psychology

Frankl was introduced to the major figures of humanistic psychology by the renowned Harvard psychologist Gordon Allport. The relationship with Allport stemmed from Frankl's lecture tour of American universities in 1957. The tour was sponsored by the Religion in Education Foundation (RIE) and arranged by the director, Randolph Sasnett. For his part, Sasnett had gained Allport's recognition for his book, *The Mind of Jesus and the Future Mind*. When Frankl lectured at Harvard University he was hosted by Allport. Allport was quite impressed with Frankl's lecture on his concentration camp experience. Therefore, Allport requested an English translation of his … *Trotzdem Ja zum Leben Sagen (Ein Psycholog erlebt das Konzentrationslager)*. Allport read the manuscript in one sitting, and was so awed he agreed to write a preface for the English translation. Then Sasnett, with Allport's blessing, convinced Beacon Press to publish Frankl's eventual best seller in 1959. The relationship with Allport and the RIE was solidified, and Frankl was promoted by them on five more American lecture tours in the 1960s.[28]

With Allport's support, Frankl's testimony became exceptionally successful. The Library of Congress listed this "best seller" as one of the "ten most influential books in America." Originally the title was *From Death-Camp to Existentialism: A Psychiatrist's Path to a New Therapy*. In 1961 the title was changed to *Man's Search for Meaning* because it was "more appropriate for the long run." Apparently, Frankl's message of hope, assurance of the existence of God, and downplaying of the horrors of the Holocaust fit the spiritual and psychological needs of many Americans. In the American marketplace of consumer capitalism, Frankl was a forerunner of self-help and "retail spirituality."

Gordon Allport's support of Frankl was also significant because he was recognized as an influential forerunner of the humanistic turn in American psychology. In the simplest terms, American humanistic psychology involved incorporating the intellectual insights of phenomenology and existentialism in order to overcome what was considered the fragmentary and one-sided portrayals of human experience in the traditional psychoanalysis of Freud, and the behavioristic approach of B. F. Skinner.[29] However, the first policy statements of the humanistic psychology movement argued that the goal was "not to deny the psychoanalytic and behavioristic orientations, but rather to incorporate these views within a broader phenomenological orientation."[30] In essence, humanistic psychology aimed to uncover what was considered essentially human by conceiving and propagating a holistic conception of the self. Eventually, the humanistic psychology movement of the 1960s found solace in a religiously oriented world view or eastern mysticism.[31] Notably, introducing religion as a "legitimate" issue for psychology was something both Frankl and Allport shared from the very beginning.[32]

The initial politics of humanist psychology in America ran from the liberal and moderate left to the utopian cultural aspirations of radical left and the human potential movement.[33] Since the 1970s the leftist energies have dissipated, and many of the techniques developed by the humanist psychologists have been implemented in corporate America.

Dimensional Ontology

In terms of his contribution to humanistic psychology, Frankl tried to assume a leadership role in the movement based on his theory of dimensional ontology. Dimensional ontology was outlined in *The Unconscious God* (1946) when he was "proving" the existence of a spiritual unconscious. In 1956 he published *On the Theory and Therapy of Mental Disorders* that blended the worlds of medical and psychiatric practice with psychological counseling. In his English translation of *On the Theory and Therapy of Mental Disorders* James DuBois provides an excellent introduction and overview of Frankl's therapeutic vision. DuBois concludes "logotherapy not only has, but is a worldview. At the center of the worldview is Frankl's dimensional ontology…"[34] The initial ideas of dimensional ontology were presented to the American audience in "The Spiritual Dimension in Existential Analysis and Logotherapy" published in the *Journal of Individual Psychology* in 1959.[35]

Frankl declared that dimensional ontology overcame existential subjectivism by depicting the "wholeness" of the individual. But the picture of humanity that emerged in dimensional ontology was actually a triad, composed of the somatic, psychic, and noological dimensions. Nevertheless, dimensional ontology

was Frankl's attempt to reconcile the mind/body dualism and maintain with
Heidegger that there is wholeness to being.

> ... I am speaking of dimensions and not, as has formally and generally been done,
> of layers of being....This means that we no longer speak of physical, psychical, and
> spiritual layers, because as long as we do so it would appear that the layers could
> be separated from one another. On the other hand, if we try to understand body,
> psyche, and mind as different dimensions of one and the same being, its wholeness
> is not in the least destroyed. Such a dimensional interpretation refrains from seeing
> the whole phenomenon as though it were composed of many elements.[36]

Frankl often used figurative representations, cones, cylinders, squares, and
the shadows these images produce to make the claim that viewing humans in
terms of dimensions avoids the problem of layers. For instance, a cone's shadow
may be either a triangle or circle depending on which "dimension it is reduced
to."[37] Despite the assertion of wholeness it appears that dimensional ontology
crystallized mind/body dualism. This is because Frankl's "wholeness," located
in the higher noological dimension, depended on recognition of a tripartite
division of human experience. Despite these contradictions, Frankl used the
theory to present himself as the leader of existential psychology.

Frankl's goal of leading the humanist psychology movement was reflected
in his article, "The Spiritual Dimension in Existential Analysis and Logother-
apy." The thrust of Frankl's aims was to distinguish himself from the Daseins-
analysis of Ludwig Binswanger and Medard Boss. He cited his friend Paul
Polak, who differentiated between the illumination of existence by Binswanger
and the illumination of meaning by Frankl. Frankl envisioned himself as sur-
passing Binswanger in his articulation of the dimension of meaning. Frankl
claimed Ludwig Binswanger's Daseinsanalysis amounted "to an ontologizing
of Alfred Adler's tenet of tendentious apperception." According to Frankl, Da-
seinsanalysis uncovers "the a priori structure of Daseinsgestalten," which "cor-
responds to a specific subjective mode of experiencing the world. What Adler
called the person's style of life."[38] Frankl's claims were certainly an oversimplifi-
cation, but dismissing the originality of Daseinsanalysis by reducing it to a form
of Adlerianism served Frankl's purpose of leading the humanistic psychology
movement in two ways. Since he claimed to have overcome Adler and repre-
sented a "third school," Daseinsanalysis (as essentially Adlerian) was now also
surpassed. Second, it served Frankl's intention of occupying the grounds of the
"true" existential analysis in America.

Dimensional ontology not only allowed Frankl to dismiss Daseinsanalysis
as nothing but a derivation of Adlerianism, it also *necessitated* his rejection of
the Heideggerian vision of "the unity of the being-in-the-world." Therefore,
"existential analysis emphasizes the manifold character of body-mind-spirit
within the unity of human existence, ... in order to be able to appeal to what
is called in logotherapy the defiant power of man's spirit."[39]

The "manifold character" of Frankl's dimensional ontology is understood as his varied strategies for dealing with human malady. As a medical doctor and a professor of neurology and psychiatry, Frankl recognized that the unity of being, proposed by pure Heideggerian existentialism, was of no therapeutic use when confronting diseases that were either somatic or psychic in origin. Therefore, if Frankl examined a patient "neurologically" because he was "suspected of having a brain tumor," he must "act 'as if' he existed only in this dimension." According to Frankl, "science must methodically disregard the full dimensionality of reality and be based upon the indispensable fiction of a unidimensional world."[40] Essentially then, dimensional ontology crystallized mind/body dualism, because as he points out if he approached a patient from the standpoint of pure Heideggerian existentialism it would be impossible for Frankl to practice traditional medicine.

Techniques

Frankl also used the theory of dimensional ontology to develop practical psychotherapeutic techniques. These techniques were dependent on the noological dimension where "man becomes able to detach himself from his psychological condition." The "specifically human" capability for "self-detachment is mobilized ... against pathological events within the psychological dimension."[41] Frankl's most influential therapeutic technique was paradoxical intention. This therapy depended on the noological dimension and what might be playfully described as healthy schizophrenia. Essentially, paradoxical intention is laughing at your fears. Thus, the "capacity of self-detachment is mobilized ... in the special logotherapeutic technique of paradoxical intention."[42]

Frankl claimed the key to understanding why paradoxical intention is effective is what he calls "anticipatory anxiety" or "anxiety about anxiety." That is, "a given symptom evokes, on the part of the patient, a response in terms of the fearful expectation that it might recur; fear, however, always tends to make true precisely that which one is afraid of, and by the same token, anticipatory anxiety is liable to trigger off what the patient so fearfully expects to happen. Thus, a self-sustaining vicious circle is established: A symptom evokes a phobia; the phobia provokes the symptom; and the reoccurrence of the symptom reinforces the phobia."[43]

Frankl argued that this "vicious circle" and "fear of fear" along with "flight from fear" were the key components of phobias and obsessive compulsive patterns. "While 'flight from fear' is characteristic of the phobic pattern, the obsessive-compulsive patient is characterized by his 'fight against obsessions and compulsions.' But alas, the more he fights them the stronger they become: Pressure induces counterpressure, and counterpressure, in turn, increases pressure."[44]

Frankl claimed that the therapeutic technique of paradoxical intention could break this vicious circle when "the patient is encouraged to do, or wish to happen, the very things he fears." "In this way, we help the phobic patient stop fleeing from his fears, and the obsessive compulsive patient stop fighting his obsessions and compulsions.... the pathogenic fear is now replaced by a paradoxical wish. Now, 'the bull is taken by the horns,'.... The vicious circle of anticipatory anxiety is unhinged."[45]

The broad influence of paradoxical intention, especially among behavior therapists and social workers, suggests it is an effective therapeutic technique. Frankl exemplified the success of the therapy when it kept him from performing a leuctomy on a woman who was suffering from a hand washing and cleanliness compulsion. After logotherapy "the improvement in her condition persisted, and thus the leuctomy, which previously had seemed unavoidable, had now become unnecessary."[46]

On the other hand, the criticisms of this technique are readily apparent. A depth psychologist would most likely dismiss paradoxical intention as mere suggestion. Also, although the "vicious circle" might for a moment become unhinged, the underlying cause of the compulsion or obsession is not resolved. Finally, as Frankl surely recognized, common sense suggests that if the compulsion is toward self-destructive or socially destructive behavior such a prescription would have negative consequences.

Frankl also developed a similar technique called dereflection, which was especially useful for sex therapy. He framed male impotence and the inorgasmic female as problems of "fighting for pleasure." The therapy of dereflection was to avoid the "hyper-attention" and "hyper-reflection ... and instead of watching and observing himself, he should forget himself."[47] Frankl claimed that dereflection or avoidance of the anxiety of striving allowed for the pleasure to occur almost unconsciously. According to Frankl, the problem occurred when "the feeling of pleasure of the orgasm was made the goal, while under normal circumstances it arises as an automatic consequence."[48] But Frankl was not a "free love" sexual revolutionary because he correlated striving for pleasure to the phenomenological experience of shame. Therefore, shame was positive when it led "to the most intense devotion to an object of love."[49]

Frankl in the Movement

In 1958, Rollo May introduced existential psychotherapy to America.[50] May argued for the necessity of existentialism to counteract the subject/object dualism that was inherent in traditional therapies. He claimed this dualism was a false dichotomy because there were no objective meanings outside a subject that originates and projects meanings.[51] This work made Rollo May the forerunner of the existential psychotherapy movement in the United States.

In 1961, May continued his role as a "cultural guide" in existential psychotherapy by editing *Existential Psychology*. In this book he provided a short, but complimentary, overview of logotherapy. May compared Frankl to Bettelheim, and related Frankl's survival of the concentration camps to his conception of meaning, will, and freedom. However, he concluded on a slightly critical note, claiming that "logotherapy hovers close to authoritarianism," because "there seem to be clear solutions to all problems, which belies the complexity of actual life. It seems that if the patient cannot find his goal, Frankl supplies him with one. This would seem to take over the patients' responsibility and ... diminish the patient as a person."[52]

May recognized the pedagogical side of logotherapy. Apparently, May was sensitive to such an issue given his existentialist and thus individualistic perspective. Frankl's response to May came fourteen years later, in the postscript to the English translation of *The Unconscious God*.

In this book Frankl claimed not that God has been repressed but rather that God is a component of the unconscious (will to meaning). Based on the thesis of the book, Frankl's suggestion that it is up to the patient to "answer the question of how to interpret his life, that is to say, whether along the lines of theism or atheism," seems slightly misleading.[53] Overlooking this issue, Frankl continued the disclaimer about religion, logotherapy, and the "authoritarian element." He directly cited May's criticism and claimed "logotherapy does not at all 'hover close to authoritarianism,' and least of all does it amount to 'taking over the patient's responsibility and diminishing him as a person' (Rollo May, *Existential Psychology*.)"[54]

Nevertheless, May's criticism apparently had an effect on Frankl. Although Frankl didn't directly confront May's criticisms until 1975, in the mid 1960s he began claiming that logotherapy could be used in a secular fashion. For example, in 1969 Frankl stated "logotherapy must be available for every patient and usable in the hands of every doctor, whether his 'Weltanschauung' is theistic or agnostic."[55] Toward the end of his life, however, Frankl returned to the overt promotion of religion because he published a new edition (although essentially unrevised) of *The Unconscious God* under the title *Man's Search for Ultimate Meaning*, and added the claim that "religion, we may say, revealed itself as the fulfillment of what we now call the 'will to ultimate meaning.'"[56] Frankl's response in 1975 to May, although delayed, did spark a debate over the authoritarian nature of logotherapy. The defense of Frankl was initiated by the Rabbi Reuven Bulka in an article entitled, "Is Logotherapy Authoritarian?"[57] Bulka's article was followed by a reply from both May and Frankl.[58] May sustained his assertion that logotherapy was authoritarian. He also cut to the central point when he argued that Bulka's representative case study of a schizophrenic cured by Frankl had the "same authoritarian character as fundamentalistic religion" and: "... in this therapeutic encounter there are three interchanges between the patient and Frankl. Frankl begins each one of them with a clear and unmistak-

able 'Don't.' The first 'don't' he emphasizes by adding another a little later in the sentence. Such categorical instruction illustrates the authoritarian character of logotherapy as practiced by Frankl to which I referred."[59]

Frankl's response was highly defensive, flippant, slightly arrogant and eluded the issues raised by May. He began by claiming that his attitude toward the patient was one where he "wanted to say something to her, not as the Head of the Neuropsychiatric Hospital of Vienna, but rather as a human being to another human being." But after this disclaimer, Frankl, repositioned himself as a medical authority to justify his use of "don't."

> Now, if anyone labels as authoritarian the fact that a medical doctor recommends to his patients to the best of his knowledge and for the sake of their recovery what they should do or should not do, I gladly take the blame. And if anyone labels it 'authoritarian' if a medical doctor truthfully tells the patient the prognosis is good, I gladly take the blame. But if the patient says that she 'believes' in the good prognosis and anyone compares this 'faith' with 'fundamentalistic religion,' as a member of a medical faculty I must leave such a comparison to the judgment of members of theological faculties.[60]

Disregarding the sarcasm, Frankl's reliance on medical credentials to justify his "human response" failed to fully address May's criticisms of his authoritarian attitude and the religious aspects of logotherapy.

This debate, and Frankl's remarks, served only to create more ambiguity over the exact relationship between religion and logotherapy. This left some of his followers uneasy, making them question whether the master was a true believer. Reuven Bulka exemplified this tension when he stated: "... with logotherapy avowing a secular stance, and with the pulls exerted upon it by those who see theology in it, as well as by those who see more specific religious connotation in it, there appears to be an essential dilemma in coming to grips with what logotherapy is all about."[61]

Despite Frankl's disclaimers, for his followers logotherapy was a surrogate religion. For example, in 1975 Weisskopf-Joelson stated, "by proposing a secular equivalent to the concept 'God'.... Logotherapy reveals itself as ... a faith more than a scientific therapeutic school."[62] In this regard Frankl's role is somewhere between high priest, "prophet, guru, and preacher disguised as a psychiatrist."[63] The centrality of the master—Frankl—for sustaining his follower's religious belief was apparent in Bulka's description of the relationship between logotherapy and religion.

> While being admittedly a man of faith, Frankl refuses to let that faith spill over into logotherapy. Frankl even acknowledges that his system ultimately leads to faith. In the final analysis it must certainly appear questionable whether humans could really be responsible before something—or whether responsibility is only possible when it is before someone. A more assertive statement is that 'the true discovery of man, the inventio hominis, occurs in the imitatio Dei.' Beyond this, Frankl even shows some clinical implications for the condition which he calls repressed religiousness.[64]

Frankl's assurance that God existed was profound comfort for many of his followers. He claimed that "God is not dead because he remains silent" because "the 'living' God has been a 'hidden' God all along. You must not expect him to answer your call.... The fact that no answer comes back to you is proof that your call has reached the addressee, the infinite."[65] In the end Frankl resorted to such platitudes to assure the existence of God. For his followers, Frankl provided solace in a world they considered overrun by a combination of science, secularization, and relativism. Thus Frankl, the self-proclaimed conqueror of nihilism, offered the way out of what for many is an existential morass. But the key is Frankl, he is the: "live personality ... that has transcended the dictates of science and, in the process, has afforded all persons the real possibility of meaningful fulfillment, and for those who still refuse to believe he offers in a very definite way, 'a religion for the non-religious.'"[66]

Frankl's grandiosity and religious impulse was rejected by May as authoritarian, and yet, these were also some of the very reasons Frankl became so popular in America.

Meaning

The debate between May and Frankl extended into differences over theoretical conceptions of existential authenticity. In America, Frankl presented himself as offering a neo-Heideggerian existentialism that he claimed did not fall into the subjectivist valuations of Sartre.[67] Frankl's anti-subjectivist, and as we have seen, quasi-religious response to the question of meaning differentiated him from the mainstream of humanist psychology. At the heart of the tension between May and Frankl was the conflict between subjective versus objective meaning. Bulka described their dispute as "rooted in their differences over the issue of self-expression versus self-transcendence and the ethics of inwardness versus the objective value world."[68] Bulka claimed that Frankl's spiritual dimension was the realm of self-transcendence where the individual can access the objective value world. According to Bulka, Frankl offered a way to overcome the subjective and thus limited values of May's "self-expression" and "ethics of inwardness." But even Bulka recognized that from May's position of existential subjectivity, Frankl's claim of objective value may seem authoritarian:

> May's system focuses on self-perceived truth and the aware person searching consciously within the self, in freedom, to find these verities. From this perspective, it 'seems' as if a world view which places values outside the person, in a trans-subjective or objective setting, is authoritarian. [Here Bulka footnotes] (In a personal conversation, Frankl related to me a conversation he had with Heidegger, in which he confronted Heidegger with the fact that in America he is interpreted along the lines of subjectivism. Enraged, Heidegger exclaimed, "I am in no way a subjectivist").[69]

Bulka's revelation is interesting. Since he understood the substance of May's critique, he turned to present Frankl's existential authority as originating in the "higher" authority of Heidegger. It seems the "priesthood" was intact.[70] In May's defense, it is clear he at least saw the contradictions (but perhaps not the solution) in the subjectivism of Sartre.[71]

The tension between subjective versus objective meaning had been apparent in the work of Frankl since the 1930s. Frankl once again framed the issue in terms of the role of the therapist. In an early article in America Frankl protected himself from charges of therapeutic authoritarianism by claiming: "Of course it is never the task of the therapist to 'give' a meaning to the life of a patient. It is up to the patient himself to 'find' the concrete Meaning of his existence. The therapist merely assists him in this endeavor. That he must 'find' the meaning implies that this meaning is to be discovered and not invented. It implies that the meaning of one's life is in a certain sense objective."[72]

But May would have likely responded that it is just this assertion of the objectivity of Meaning, with a big M, that contained the authoritarianism.

Rogers

Frankl's confidence in Meaning led him to criticize the encounter group movement led by Carl Rogers. A short history is in order. The predecessor to the encounter group movement was Kurt Lewin's T-group. These training groups were developed after the war at the Massachusetts Institute of Technology. Rogers described how "the encounter group tends to emphasize personal growth and the development and improvement of interpersonal communication and relationships through an experiential process."[73] This conception of encounter groups sounds decent and innocuous. Although Frankl didn't mention him by name, clearly he had Rogers and his encounter groups in mind when he wrote "Encounter: The Concept and its Vulgarization." This article was published in the *Journal of the American Academy of Psychoanalysis*.[74] Frankl's criticism of the encounter group movement centered on his claim that there is an absence of the self-transcendent element in the groups. Instead, he suggested the groups were really only about self-expression. Apparently Rogers never dignified Frankl's criticisms with a response.

It seems the real intention of the article was Frankl's desire to claim independence from the humanistic psychology movement—"in order to take a critical stand toward it."[75] Apparently he not only wanted his autonomy, but he also wanted logotherapy to surpass the humanist psychology movement. Once again the grandiosity of Frankl was revealed. But this raised the question, what would be the proper encounter group—according to logotherapy?

In his book *The Unheard Cry for Meaning* Frankl began to answer this question. Citing Charlotte Bühler[76] on the "beneficial" aspects of encounter groups,

Frankl claimed: "... a properly conceived encounter group can surely provide a context of mutual assistance in which to discuss life's meaning. The properly conceived encounter group not only indulges in the self-expression of the members but also promotes their self-transcendence."[77]

If we read "self-transcendence" as a code word for religious sentiment, "the properly conceived" logotherapy group appears to be quasi-religious. As May said logotherapy appears as a "fundamental religion."

Maslow

Frankl also became engaged in a debate with another founder of the humanistic psychology movement, Abraham Maslow. Maslow made significant intellectual contributions to humanistic psychology. For example, he conceptualized a hierarchy of human needs, characterized people who were self-actualizers, and defined peak experiences. The latter two ideas, which attempted to both articulate and invest human experience with immanent meaning, were influential ideas for the radical left in the 1960s.[78] The debate between Frankl and Maslow was initiated by Frankl in 1960, in an article "Beyond Self-actualization and Self-expression" published in the *Journal of Existential Psychology*. This led to a highly revised version of Frankl's critique of Maslow in the *Journal of Humanistic Psychology* in 1966, with a response by Maslow.[79]

The controversy between Frankl and Maslow recapitulated the philosophical issue of the subjective versus objective source of meaning. Frankl initially aligned himself with the emerging vision of the humanist psychology movement by criticizing both behaviorism and Freud. He claimed that these therapies were homeostatic interpretations of human experience and overlooked "the nature of propriate striving." He cited both Allport and Maslow as sharing his insight into the dynamic quality of human experience and criticism of the homeostatic model. But according to him, their "criticisms do not go far enough" because for Allport and Maslow self-realization remains the main motive of human experience. Also, "appointing self-realization as 'the ultimate motive'" served to devalue the world, by making "its objects a mere means to an end." Then Frankl pointed out this devaluation in the contention of "A. H. Maslow ... that 'the environment is no more than means to the person's self-actualizing ends.'"[80]

Frankl defined self-actualizing as "the fulfillment of the available possibilities, or potentialities, within the subject, one might well call it potentialism." But this potentialism or self-actualization cannot circumscribe "man's 'primary intention,' or even his 'ultimate destination.'" The self-actualization, or the potentialism, of Maslow (and we might add the subjectvism of Rollo May), Frankl criticized for lacking "self-transcendence," and thus remained subjectivist and relativistic. In so doing, Frankl restated the vision he had expounded since the 1930s:

The potentialities of life are not indifferent possibilities, but must be seen in light of meaning and values. At any given time only one of the possible choices of the individual fulfills the necessity of his life task. Herein is involved the challenge of each life situation—the challenge to responsibility. Man must make his choice concerning the mass of present potentials: which will be condemned to non-being and which one shall be actualized, and thus rescued for eternity. Decisions are final for the only really transitory aspects of life are potentialities. When one is actualized, it is actualized forever and can never be destroyed. Man, therefore, must face the responsibility for these immortal 'footprints in the sands of time.' He must decide, for weal or for woe, what will be the monument of his existence.[81]

In 1966, Frankl extended these ideas in an article for the *Journal of Humanistic Psychology*. He titled this piece "Self-transcendence as a Human Phenomenon." Frankl maintained his criticisms of Maslow's self-actualization and stated them even more forcefully: "self-actualization is not man's ultimate destination, not even his primary intention. Self-actualization, if made an end in itself, contradicts the self-transcending quality of human existence."[82] But Frankl was also much more conciliatory, especially toward Maslow. He claimed that the will to meaning was "perfectly in accordance with Maslow's own view since he admits himself, e.g., that the 'business of self-actualization' can best be carried out via a commitment to an important job."[83] From Frankl's tone, it seems Maslow had come to see things from Frankl's point of view.

Frankl continued his criticisms of Maslow by turning to the issue of peak experiences.[84] According to Frankl, "will cannot be demanded, commanded, or ordered. One cannot will to will." Thus "peak experiences … are, and must remain effects.… They, too, ensue and cannot be pursued." Frankl then claimed that the whole concept of peak experiences is "more than a generalization; … it is even an oversimplification." What Frankl meant by oversimplification is that all peak experiences were perceived as "uniform" even though (and here he quotes Maslow): "the stimuli are very different: we get them from rock-and-roll, drug addiction, and alcohol," yet, "the subjective experience tends to be similar." This reduction of peak experience to uniformity was wrong according to Frankl because it "shuts out" and fails to recognize the "self-transcendent quality of human existence."[85]

Sustained by his belief in the transcendent realm, Frankl articulated a direct attack on Maslow's notion "that in peak experiences the 'is' and the 'ought' merge with each other." Against Maslow, Frankl claimed that "meaning has to be prevented from coinciding with being. I should say that it is the meaning of meaning to set the pace of being …" Then Frankl, gave this definition of authenticity: "Human existence is not authentic unless it is to live in terms of self-transcendence. Self-actualization is an unintentional effect of the intentionality of life."[86]

Maslow's reply to Frankl was deferential and conciliatory. Clearly he respected the intellectual and moral authority of Frankl. Also, it appears they had a personal correspondence (that may have been prompted by Frankl's initial

criticism) where they ironed out some of their differences. Maslow's response also revealed that his admiration of Frankl was in a large part attributable to Frankl's survival of Auschwitz.

Maslow attempted to reconcile differences by suggesting the tensions were mostly attributable to linguistics. He therefore agreed "with Frankl that man's primary concern ... 'highest concern' is his will to meaning."[87] Maslow also remarked that they ultimately shared the same conception of self-actualization. He agreed with Frankl that those: "who are selected out as self-actualizing practically always have a mission in life ... this ... can be called self-actualization, authenticity, fulfillment, the achievement of meaning, self-transcendence, finding oneself..."[88]

On Frankl's critique of the origins, nature, and possibility of peak experiences, Maslow was also conciliatory. He agreed "hunting peak experiences directly doesn't ordinarily work." Then Maslow described how he had revised and nuanced his concept of peak experience in light of Frankl's critique.

> It is clearer to me now that peak emotions may come without obvious insight or growth or benefit of any kind beyond the effects of pleasure itself. Such raptures may be very profound and yet be almost contentless. The prime examples are sex and LSD, but there are others as well. Sex, Lsd, etc., may bring illumination, or they may not. Furthermore, insight (B-cognition) can come without emotional ecstacies. Indeed, B-cognition can come from pain suffering, and tragedy, as Dr. Frankl has helped to teach us.[89]

After Frankl's criticisms, Maslow seemed pessimistic and almost guilty about feeling good. He also made the strange claim that "rapture" may be almost contentless. Apparently, Maslow had begun to internalize Frankl's claim that the highest truth of human experience was to be found in the "tragic triad of death, guilt and suffering."[90] Now B-cognition, or self-growth with "content," could be realized through pain and suffering. It seems Maslow had lost conviction in the primacy of pleasure in human experience, rapture had become contentless, and suffering offered fulfillment. But Maslow didn't completely give in. After attempting to reconstruct a hierarchy of pleasure from "the cessation of pain, ... the pleasure of a hot bath ... on up through the happiness of being with loved friends," he took a stand against Frankl's claims about meaning and suffering by stating: "And yet once we have agreed with Dr. Frankl on the intellectual dangers of making pleasure into a deity, we can then feel quite free to enjoy the small harmless pleasures of life. Even if they teach us nothing, they are still a blessing. Pleasure itself is not a danger; it is only man-made theories about pleasure that are a danger."[91]

If we take the exchange at face value it seems Frankl's impact was to undermine the celebration of pleasure and immanent meaning in the humanist psychology of Maslow. Pleasures were no longer "Meaningful," only accepted as harmless. The reversal was complete. The "highest" meaning was to be achieved through suffering.

In the end, Maslow turned toward spiritual values and a type of puritan asceticism. He thus claimed that self-actualizing people were "devoted to a cause or calling beyond themselves." The calling is an "incarnation of the ultimate values of truth, goodness, beauty, justice, oneness, order, comprehensiveness, perfection, etc."[92] But in order to place this "higher meaning" within an immanent understanding of human experience, Maslow turned to an idealization of human nature, where this "higher life or the spiritual life … is founded solidly in the biological nature of the human species." With this idea Maslow began to turn toward the "farthest reaches of human nature."

After absorbing Frankl's criticisms, Maslow accepted a transcendent realm, but wanted to give it a more "detailed meaning." Maslow being a humanist, in the tradition of the Enlightenment, this detailed meaning became an attempt to maintain an immanent understanding of human experience. Therefore, Maslow counteracted Frankl's claim that the subject/object dualism was inescapable. Instead, Maslow argued that once basic species needs had been met, the subject/object split could be overcome by realizing higher values—by finding a calling. In his words: "While there is still a useful conceptual difference between drives and yearnings, pushes and pulls at most levels, the difference becomes shadowy and may even be transcended at this highest level in which the highest values of the world and of the person become the same."[93]

In a sense Maslow had met Frankl halfway. In order to counteract Frankl's spiritual dimension and the value of suffering, he idealized human nature and accepted a realm of transcendent values. But Maslow's ideals were not "silent" as God was for Frankl. Therefore, Maslow could still experience ideals and maintained an immanent conception of fulfilled human meaning where the subject/object split was overcome. Maslow also stopped short of Frankl's rejection of the humanistic aspirations of fulfilled meaning in this world. Late in life though, Maslow (and most of the humanistic psychology movement) followed Frankl's trajectory and took flight into "the farther reaches of human nature." Maslow however did make an impact on the counterculture because both Abbie Hoffman and Richard Flacks (radicals in the sixties; the latter was a member of the Students for a Democratic Society) claimed Maslow as an influence.[94]

From his redeemed perspective of self-transcendence, and legitimized by his survival of the Holocaust, Frankl was able to level criticism at Maslow and the humanist psychology movement. From the perspective of his transcendent realm, he directed his attack at the subjectivist and "pleasurable" side of humanist psychology. This was the radical side of the movement that was focused on making meaning immanent within experience. But for Frankl, "meaning could not coincide with being." It seems that because Frankl could not find "ultimate Meaning" in an immanent sense he instilled as permanent, "the polar field of tension between the subject-object."

Therefore, the world view that had been generated by Frankl's experiences was now offered as a more adequate vision of humanity than that of the hu-

manistic psychology movement. From this perspective, Frankl summed up his prescription for the proper psychotherapeutic approach to human fulfillment in America:

> It appears ... that those theories of man which are circumscribed by the individual himself, whether based upon the reduction of his tension as in homeostasis theory, or the fulfillment of the greatest number of immanent possibilities as in self-actualization, when weighed, are found wanting. It is the contention of the author that an adequate view of man can only be properly formulated when it goes beyond homeostasis, beyond self-actualization—even beyond man himself!—to that transcendent sphere of human existence in which man chooses what he will do and what he will be in the midst of an objective world of meanings and values.[95]

In this quasi-religious world Frankl found his Meaning. Frankl's turn toward the spiritual dimension, and in particular his debate with Maslow, undermined the radical aspirations of humanistic psychology that wanted fulfillment in the here and now.

In sum, the humanistic psychology movement contained revolutionary possibilities for human experience and consciousness. But Frankl had a reactionary, authoritarian, and quasi-religious influence on the movement. Frankl's goal was to introduce Americans to his existential insights that originated in his critique of Freud and Adler, developed in the light of Nazism, and crystallized in the working through of his wartime experience.

In the end Frankl inspired millions with his "nevertheless say yes to life" that attempted to close the open-ended fractured culture of Western modernity. But the vision of meaning, and life, he said yes to was focused on finding ultimate Meaning in the "tragic triad of guilt, suffering and death." Frankl therefore rejected Freud and Adler and claimed independence from the American humanist psychology movement. He affirmed a revolutionary "third path" in a spiritualistic vision of psychotherapy that he felt would have appeal for the central figures involved in the Nazi psychotherapy movement. In his efforts to practice innovative medicine and survive the Nazi occupation he conducted medical experiments on his fellow Jewish victims. When working through the trauma of his wartime experience he relied on his spiritualistic perspective to find Meaning in the Holocaust. In Austria his reconciling attitude led him to publicly legitimize Haider and Waldheim, and in America he inspired a generation of religious leaders. His life was fascinating and inspiring, but also profoundly tragic—an emblematic twentieth-century tragedy.

When Frankl first came to America a key lesson he wanted to impart to the American people is that "Freedom is in danger of degenerating into mere arbitrariness unless it is lived in terms of responsibleness. That is why I recommend that the Statue of Liberty on the East Coast be supplemented by a Statue of Responsibility on the West Coast."[96] Currently there is a groundswell of support for such a project and a prototype has been sculpted.[97] After reflecting on this detailed story of Viktor Frankl's Search for Meaning we need to ask

ourselves, is Frankl a hero? Is his prescription correct; should Americans update the values of "life, liberty and the pursuit of happiness" to "life, liberty and the pursuit of responsibility"?

Notes

1. For list of notable émigrés, see Donald Fleming, ed., *The Intellectual Migration* (Cambridge, Mass.: Harvard University Press, 1969): 375.

2. On the difficult transition for the émigrés and the defensiveness and territoriality of many Americans, see Lewis Coser, *Refugee Scholars in America* (New Haven: Yale University Press, 1984), 3–18.

3. H. Stuart Hughes, "Social Theory in a New Context," in *The Muses Flee Hitler: Cultural Transfer and Adaptation, 1930-1945*, ed. Jarrel Jackman (Washington, D.C.: Smithsonian Institution Press, 1983), 111–122.

4. See Corrigan Interview (GTU). Also, Guttmann Interview (WCP).

5. Polak, "Frankl's Existential Analysis," 518.

6. Ibid.

7. The first, Viktor Frankl, "The Pleasure Principle and Sexual Neurosis," *International Journal of Sexology* 5 (1952), contained Frankl's criticisms of Freud along with a discussion of Frankl's therapeutic techniques. The second article was Viktor Frankl, "Logos and Existence in Psychotherapy," *American Journal of Psychotherapy* 7 (1953).

8. Edith Weisskopf-Joelson, "Some Comments on a Viennese School of Psychiatry," *The Journal of Abnormal and Social Psychology* 51, no. 3 (November 1955): 701–702.

9. Ibid., 702.

10. In the 1963 edition of *Man's Search for Meaning*, Frankl cited Weisskopf-Joelson favorably and presented her as a disciple of logotherapy, 180–181.

11. Frankl, afterword to Edith Weisskopf-Joelson, *Father, Have I kept My Promise? Madness as Seen from Within* (Indiana: Purdue University Press, 1988), 137.

12. Weisskopf-Joelson, *Father, Have I kept my Promise?*, 23.

13. The obvious critique to my assertion is that her madness was from physiological sources. This is possible, but she did recover. Therefore there is arguably a strong psychological component.

14. Weisskopf-Joelson, "Comments," 702.

15. Ibid., 703.

16. Edith Weisskopf-Joelson, "Logotherapy and Existential Analysis," *Acta Psychotherapeutica: International Journal for Psychotherapy, Psychosomatics, Special Education* 4 no. 3 (1958): 195.

17. Ibid., 202. In the 1992 edition of *Man's Search for Meaning*, the "English language bibliography" contains eight pages of films, records, and tapes.

18. Weisskopf-Joelson, "Logotherapy and Existential Analysis," 203.

19. Ibid., 194.

20. Also see Paul Johnson, "Logotherapy: A Corrective for Determinism," *Christian Advocate* 5 (23 November 1961).

21. Donald Tweedie, *The Christian and the Couch* (Michigan: Baker Book House, 1963), 5.

22. Aron J. Ungersma, *The Search for Meaning: A New Approach in Psychotherapy and Pastoral Psychology* (Philadelphia: Westminster Press, 1961), 9.

23. See Earl Grollman, "The Logotherapy of Viktor Frankl," *Judaism* 8 (1965): 22–38. For the response by Hayworth and Grollman, see *Judaism* 14 (1965): 351–353.

24. Reuven Bulka, *The Quest for Ultimate Meaning* (New York: Philosophical Library, 1978), 61. Also see Reuven Bulka, "From Confusion to Fusion," *The Other Side of the Couch*, ed. Mark Stern (New York: Pilgrim Press, 1981), 170–179.

25. Frankl, forward to *The Quest for Ultimate Meaning*, by Reuven Bulka, vii.

26. Ibid., viii.

27. Viktor Frankl, "Zur geistigen Problematik der Psychotherapie," 41.

28. By way of contextualizing Allport's strong promotion of Frankl we should mention that he was aware that the American Psychological Association's efforts to help refugee psychologists between 1938 and 1943 were "modest" and had few successes. Allport's support might have been recompense—although he was quite taken with Frankl's Holocaust testimony. See Jean Mandler, "The Diaspora of Experimental Psychology," in Fleming, *The Intellectual Migration*, 383.

29. The tension between the objective positivism of experimental psychology and subjective experiential psychology has been described as the intellectual dynamic of American humanist psychology. See Roy Jose DeCarvalho, *The Founders of Humanist Psychology* (New York: Praeger, 1991), 1–7.

30. DeCarvalho, *The Founders of Humanistic Psychology*, 11.

31. Although the religious element was not an initial concern in the 1960s, as the movement developed it turned toward these issues. For an example, see the last work of Abraham Maslow, *Farther Reaches of Human Nature* (New York: Viking, 1971).

32. For example, Gordon Allport, *The Individual and His Religion* (New York: Macmillan, 1960), described the intellectual grounds of the religious sentiment within a Christian perspective.

33. The central humanist psychologists, Carl Rogers, Rollo May, and Abraham Maslow, were liberal in outlook. Maslow's ideas on "self-actualization" were taken over and used by "hippies" who celebrated free-love and drugs. Similarly, Roger's ideas on "Encounters" became "happenings" for the radicals. The more radical and utopian energies were "institutionalized" in the human potential movement exemplified by the Esalen Institute in Big Sur, California. On the liberal politics, see the collection of essays, Rollo May, *Politics and Innocence* (Dallas, Tex.: Saybrook, 1986), especially Allan Buss, "Humanistic Psychology as Liberal Ideology." On the radical politics, see J. Shaffer, *Humanistic Psychology* (New Jersey: Prentice Hall, 1978), chap. 6.

34. Frankl, *On the Theory and Therapy of Mental Disorders: An Introduction to Logotherapy and Existential Analysis*, trans. James M. Dubois (New York: Brunner-Routledge, 2004), xxxix.

35. Frankl revised this paper, published it as "Existential Analysis and Dimensional Ontology," and included it in one of "the selected papers on Logotherapy" in *Psychotherapy and Existentialism*, published in 1967. Also, a simpler theoretical summation of Frankl's dimensional ontology can be found in Frankl, *The Unheard Cry for Meaning: Psychotherapy and Humanism* (New York: Simon and Schuster, 1978), in the chapter, "Determinism and Humanism: Critique of Pan-Determinism."

36. Frankl, "Existential Analysis and Dimensional Ontology," *Psychotherapy and Existentialism*, 135.

37. For his full description of images and shadows as an analogy for dimensional ontology, see Frankl, *The Unheard Cry for Meaning*, 44–64.

38. Frankl, "Existential Analysis and Dimensional Ontology," 132.

39. Ibid., 133.

40. Ibid., 139.

41. Frankl, "Psychiatry and Man's Quest for Meaning," *Journal of Religion and Health* 1, no. 2 (January 1962): 95.

42. Frankl, "Philosophical Foundations of Logotherapy," in *Phenomenology: Pure and Applied*, ed. Erwin Strauss (Pittsburgh: Duquesne University Press, 1964), 5.

43. Frankl, "Paradoxical Intention and Dereflection," *Psychotherapy: Theory, Research and Practice* 12, no. 3 (1975): 226.

44. Ibid., 227.

45. Ibid.

46. Frankl, "Paradoxical Intention," *American Journal of Psychotherapy* 14, no. 3 (July 1960): 528.

47. Frankl, "Paradoxical Intention and Dereflection," 234.

48. Frankl, "The Pleasure Principle and Sexual Neurosis," 129.

49. Ibid., 130.

50. See May, *Existence*.

51. See Rollo May, *Existence*, especially "The Origins and Significance of the Existential Movement in Psychology."

52. Rollo May, *Existential Psychology* (New York: Random House, 1961), 42.

53. Frankl, *The Unconscious God*, 121.

54. Ibid.

55. Frankl, *The Will to Meaning*, 143. In terms of the Austrian scene, the religious character of logotherapy was critically pointed out in 1947 by the Adlerian Ferdinand Birnbaum. This article was translated and reprinted. See Ferdinand Birnbaum, "Frankl's Existential Psychology from the Viewpoint of Individual Psychology," *Journal of Individual Psychology* 17 (1961): 162–166.

56. Frankl, *Man's Search for Ultimate Meaning* (New York: Insight Books, 1997), 153. The new title was the same as the title of Frankl's Oskar Pfister Award Lecture, given before the American Psychiatric Association in 1985. The lecture was included in the book as the final chapter.

57. Reuven Bulka, "Is Logotherapy Authoritarian?," *Journal of Humanistic Psychology* 18, no. 4 (Fall 1978): 46–54.

58. This exchange between May and Frankl in the *Journal of Humanistic Psychology* 18, no. 4 (Fall 1978) was reprinted in Bulka, *The Quest For Ultimate Meaning*, 5–19.

59. Rollo May, "Response to Bulka's Article," *Journal of Humanistic Psychology* 18, no. 4 (Fall 1978): 55.

60. Frankl, "Response to May," *Journal of Humanistic Psychology* 18, no. 4 (Fall 1978): 57–58.

61. Bulka, *The Quest for Ultimate Meaning*, 41.

62. Edith Weisskopf-Joelson, "Logotherapy: Science or Faith," *Psychotherapy: Theory, Research and Practice* 12, no. 3 (Fall 1975): 238.

63. Ibid., 240.

64. Bulka, *The Quest for Ultimate Meaning*, 38–39.

65. Frankl, *The Will to Meaning*, 154.

66. Bulka, *The Quest for Ultimate Meaning*, 44.

67. See Frankl, *The Will to Meaning*, 3–4, 60.

68. Bulka, "Is Logotherapy Authoritarian?," 50.

69. Bulka, *The Quest for Ultimate Meaning*, 50.

70. Frankl was subtle, but by his "personal relationship" with Heidegger, and by "analogy," he did try to suggest they shared a religious conviction. On this issue see Frankl, *The Will to Meaning*, 151–152.

71. For May's critique of Sartre's ideas on psychoanalysis, see his introduction to *Existential Psychoanalysis* by Jean Paul Sartre (Chicago: Gateway edition, 1962). May argued that despite Sartre's criticism of humanism, he relied on humanism to sustain his critique.

72. Frankl, "Beyond Self-actualization and Self-expression," *Journal of Existential Psychology* 1, no. 1 (1960): 11.

73. Carl Rogers, *Carl Rogers on Encounter Groups* (New York: Harrow, 1970), 5.

74. In 1978, the article was slightly revised and published in Frankl, *The Unheard Cry for Meaning*.

75. Viktor Frankl, "Encounter: The Concept and Its Vulgarization," *Journal of the American Academy of Psychoanalysis* 1, no. 1 (1973): 73.

76. Charlotte Bühler followed her husband in immigrating to America, and, unlike her husband, was well received and successful. In 1965 she became the president of the American Association for Humanistic Psychology.

77. Frankl, *The Unheard Cry for Meaning*, 77.

78. For an excellent discussion of the leftward sway of American culture and politics in the 1960s, see Morris Dickstein, *The Gates of Eden* (New York: Penguin, 1989).

79. These two papers were republished in *Readings in Humanistic Psychology*, ed. Anthony Sutich and Miles Vich (New York: The Free Press, 1969).

80. Frankl, "Beyond Self-actualization and Self-expression," 12.

81. Ibid., 13–14

82. Frankl, "Self-transcendence as a Human Phenomenon," *Journal of Humanistic Psychology* 6 (1966): 100.

83. Ibid.

84. Simply stated, peak experiences are those rare moments in life when subject/object dualism is overcome. Radicals found these moments in drugs and sex, while others turned to commune with nature or "God."

85. Frankl, "Self-transcendence as a Human Phenomenon," 101.

86. Ibid. From an existentialist point of view, the claim that meaning transcends (or sets the pace of) being is more aptly considered a form of alienation, not authenticity.

87. Abraham Maslow, "Comments on Dr. Frankl's Paper," *Journal of Humanistic Psychology* 6 (1966): 108.

88. Ibid., 109.

89. Ibid., 110.

90. Frankl, "Philosophical Foundations of Logotherapy," in Strauss, *Phenomenology*, 16.

91. Maslow, "Comments on Dr. Frankl's Paper," 110–111.

92. Ibid., 111.

93. Ibid., 121.

94. The relationship between Maslow and the sixties counterculture is discussed in Rollo May, *Politics and Innocence*, 71–111.

95. Ibid.

96. See *Responsibility Foundation*, http://www.statueofresponsibility.com/history.html, accessed 10 August 2014.

97. Ibid.

Holocaust Survival and History

*I was once more Edward Hyde. A moment before I had been safe of
all men's respect, wealthy and beloved.*
 —Robert Louis Stevenson *Dr. Jekyll and Mr. Hyde*

Seventy years since the end of the Second World War the cultural implications
of the Holocaust continue to reverberate. Among historians and cultural theo-
rists the Holocaust remains a touchstone, albeit an often contested touchstone,
in terms of historical significance. As the traditional conceptions of the Holo-
caust as *unique* or *unprecedented* become eclipsed by interpretations that connect
the Holocaust to genocidal processes unleashed by the combined enlightened
and atavistic human energies of modernity—where nineteenth-century colo-
nial genocides thus appear as the embryos of the full-fledged state sponsored
genocides of the twentieth century—the Holocaust stands as the extreme man-
ifestation, or *apex,* of these processes.[1] As global citizens we can only hope
that the genocides in Cambodia, Rwanda, Darfur, Bosnia (the list could be
expanded) in the second half of the twentieth century will come to represent
the decline of the genocidal process. Perhaps the term *never again* will have the
limited meaning that a state sponsored genocide the scale of the Nazis will
never happen again. We can only hope.

 As our conception of the Holocaust has temporally expanded as part of
larger historical processes, it has spatially stretched as well. We now know the
center of the killing was in the so-called Bloodlands[2] of East Central Europe
and co-produced by both the Nazis and Soviets. Holocaust perception is also

becoming globalized as Nazi impact and policies in North Africa and the Middle East are unearthed.

Our conception of victim groups has also been transfigured. While the Holocaust remains *the* central event in modern Jewish history we have come to full realization that there were a number of other groups doomed for destruction, including the handicapped and insane, homosexuals, gypsies, and, according to the Nazi's *Generalplan Ost,* most of the Slavic peoples. It thus appears that the Final Solution to the Jewish Question was at the center of a larger project, perhaps best understood as serial genocide.

Finally the way we perceive the Holocaust experience has undergone significant changes. The original binary between perpetrators and victims no longer suffices. In his last work written shortly before he died in 1987, Primo Levi argued that it was time to confront a Gray Zone embedded in Holocaust experience where the categories of perpetrator and victim intermingle and collapse. Levi's primary concern was the collaboration of the *sonderkommando*[3] in Auschwitz which he framed as National Socialism's most "demonic crime."[4] Levi recognized that the "harsher the oppression, the more widespread among the oppressed is the willingness ... to collaborate."[5] Levi also described that although the motivations differed among prisoners the goal was "the wish to preserve and consolidate established privilege vis-à-vis those without privilege."[6] Levi was suggesting that in the inferno produced by the Nazis no one survived without some form of moral compromise—even himself. He stated, "it is naive, absurd, and historically false to believe that an infernal system such as National Socialism sanctifies its victims: on the contrary, it degrades them, it makes them resemble itself, and this all the more when they are available, blank, and lacking a political or moral armature."[7] Here was his last and perhaps most profound probing of the depth of victimization and human debasement created by Nazi oppression—an exploration of the subsequent shame one felt after such profound humiliation he initiated in 1946 with his masterful testimony originally titled *If this is a Man?*

Levi also warned against passing judgment on survivors—because that wasn't his point. He wanted us to confront and to stay connected to the insight that survival meant entering a Gray Zone where judgment had to be suspended. In the most extreme form this was the arena of dehumanizing *choiceless choices* where morality and conscience lost any moorings. As we have seen when confronted with Nazi oppression Frankl entered the Gray Zone in a variety of ways, because participation in the Gray Zone is one consequence of attempting to survive the nauseating, humiliating, victimization. But, following the critical view of Lawrence Langer, I have passed judgment on Frankl. Not a specifically moral judgment, but my opinion about his failure to get the full reality of the Holocaust experience, and in particular Auschwitz, correct. Frankl's version of survival does not make us confront and stay connected to the Gray Zone but rather in Langer's words he *preempts* the Holocaust by framing it as a manage-

able experience that was survivable. However, against Levi's injunction not to judge, I suggest that as historians we have to judge in order to stay true to reality, or at the very least to discern and try to comprehend the events—and that also implies some elements of a moral judgment.[8]

We can't know how Levi would respond to the claim that comprehension necessitates judgment, even if it is tempered judgment. But he might lightly chuckle and reply, "why would you expect Frankl to get the Auschwitz experience right?" It is well known that Levi engaged in a Herculean effort to remember and document in detail his experience in Auschwitz, a quest he carried on for years. He was still "working through" his experiences in his last book. Frankl, on the other hand, dictated his testimony in nine days in a white heat. Clearly he was not trying to get it right in the same sense as Levi, despite the tenor and scientific objectivity in his narrative voice. Arguably both Levi and Frankl shared a similar psychological need after their victimization at the hands of the Nazis—a need to restore some sense of dignity. Levi claimed he aimed his testimony at the Germans "like a gun."[9] Ashamed and angry, his testimony is profound sublimation of anger turned into a brilliant lashing out that required staying true to reality so he could hit the target. On the other hand, Frankl turned to his training as therapist and existential trends in psychology to create a heroic version of survival. The point is that Holocaust testimony is best understood not only as a need to testify, but perhaps more importantly, an attempt to restore one's humanity.[10] It is certainly possible that Frankl's spiritual heroism was reflective of a pervasive attitude among the educated privileged prisoners in the Theresienstadt ghetto, but the majority of Holocaust survivors and victims had a very different experience. When I interviewed Ernst Seinfeld, a fellow prisoner of Frankl in Dachau, he confided to me that when he met Frankl in the camps he wasn't preaching heroic survival but rather complaining about how he didn't take the opportunity to emigrate. Seinfeld's claim is unverifiable, but also likely what Frankl was feeling as he struggled to stay warm and survive Dachau during the hellish winter of 1944–1945. That Frankl was in those circumstances was his profound personal tragedy. But he was one of the millions of victims who were in dire straits or outright murdered during the war, and therefore is reflective of an unfathomable cultural tragedy that still reverberates. Once again, a remarkable, emblematic twentieth century life.

Notes

1. See Timothy Pytell, "Weighing Genocide," in *Hate Crimes: Understanding and Defining Hate Crime* V. 1, ed. Barbara Perry and Brian Levin (Westport: Praeger, 2009).
2. See Timothy Snyder, *Bloodlands: Europe Between Hitler and Stalin* (New York: Basic Books, 2012).
3. The *sonderkommando* were the special squads of Jewish prisoners that unloaded fellow victims from the trains and directed them to the gas chambers.

4. Primo Levi, *The Drowned and the Saved* (New York: Vintage Books, 1988), 53.

5. Ibid., 43.

6. Ibid., 43.

7. Ibid., 40.

8. Adam Brown, *Judging 'Privileged' Jews: Holocaust Ethics, Representation and the 'Grey Zone'* (New York, Berghahn Books, 2013).

9. Ibid., 168.

10. I make this case most forcefully in a comparison of Frankl and Bruno Bettelheim. See Timothy Pytell, "Extreme Experience, Psychological Insight and Holocaust Perception: Reflections on Bettelheim and Frankl," *Psychoanalytic Psychology* 24, no. 4 (2007). I also compare Levi and Frankl's version of survival in Timothy Pytell, "Typology of Gray Flowers: Levi and Frankl on Surviving Auschwitz," in *The Legacy of Primo Levi,* ed. Stanislao G. Pugliese (New York: Palgrave Macmillan, 2004).

Sources Consulted

Interviews

Lydia Marinelli. Interview. Vienna: 6/8/96.

Ernst Federn. Interview. Vienna: 6/12/96.

Rüdiger Stix. Interview. Vienna: 6/15/96.

Ernest Seinfeld. Interview. Connecticut: 7/9/96.

Else Pappenheim. Interview. New York City: 7/15/96.

Maurice Friedman. Interview. San Diego: 5/1/06.

Viktor Frankl. Interviewed by Tom Corrigan 1981 (audio tape), Vienna, Austria, 1981, Graduate Theological Union, Berkeley, California.

Viktor Frankl. Interviewed by Franz Ferdinand Wolf 11/1/1994 (video tape) Politische Akademie der Freiheitlichen Partei Öesterreichs, Vienna.

Viktor Frankl. Interviewed by Dr. Wolfgang Neugebauer and Dr. Elisabeth Klamper. 2/1/1993 Dokumentationsarchiv des Österreichischen Widerstandes no. 832.

Viktor Frankl. Interviewed by Giselherr Guttmann 6/29/1996 (audio tape) World Congress of Psychotherapy, Vienna.

Cohen, David. "The Frankl Meaning," *Human Behavior* 6, no. 7 (July 1977): 52–62.

Hall, Mary. "Conversation with V.E. Frankl of Vienna," *Psychology Today* no. 9 (February 1968): 56–63.

Schuller, Robert. "Dr. Robert Schuller Interviews Viktor Frankl: How to Find Meaning in Life," *Possibilities: The Magazine of Hope* (March/April 1991): 8–12.

Scully, Matthew. "Viktor Frankl at Ninety: An Interview," *First Things* 52 (April 1995): 39–43.

Newspapers and Periodicals

Ars Medici Germany: 1938–1942.
Journal of des Viktor Frankls Instituts Vienna: 1992–1998.
Münchner Medizinische Wochenschrift Germany: 1928–1938.
Neue Frei Presse. Vienna: 1936.
Neue Kronen Zeitung Vienna: 1996.
News Vienna: 1996.
Politik Vienna: 1993–1996.
profil Vienna: 1996.
Simon Wiesenthal Center News Release 29 June 1995.
Der Standard Vienna: 1996.
Wiener Medizinische Wochenschrift Vienna: 1934–1942.
Wiener Zeitschrift für Nervenheilkunde Vienna: 1934–1942.
Zentralblatt für Psychotherapie Germany: 1933–1942.

Published Documents

Alpenvereinsjahrbuch Berg 1992. Herausgegeben vom Deutschen und Österreichishen Alpenverein, Munich und Innsbruck (1992).
Bericht: über die Tätigkeit der seminaistische Arbeitgemeinschaft zwischen der Wiener psychologischen Schule (Führung Professor Dr. Karl Bühler) und der Wiener psychiatrisch-hirn-pathologischen Schule (Führung Professor Dr. Otto Poetzl) im Wintersemester 1934/35. Herausgegeben vom Auguste Flach and Karl Theodore Dussik. Vienna: Verlag von Moritz Perles, 1935.
Deabohe Gelehrtenkalender. Herausgegeben vom Kürschners. Berlin, New York: 1992.
Jüdische Schicksale. Herausgegeben vom Dokumentationsarchiv des Österreichischen Widerstandes. Vienna: Österreichischer Bundesverlag, 1992.
Das Recht Auf Das Eigene Leben, Document no. 14.385, Institute für Geschichte der Medezin (Vienna).
Sexualnot und Sexualreform: Verhandlungen der Weltliga für Sexualreform. IV Congress. Abgehalten zu Wien vom 16. bis 23. September 1930, ed. Herbert Steiner. Vienna: Elbemühl-Verlag, 1931.
Totenbuch Theresienstadt (Wien: 1971).

Unpublished Documents

Alfred Mauczka's Nazi Party file no. 002208184. Dokumentationsarchiv des Österreichischen Widerstandes.
Alfred Mauczka's Volksgericht no. 21866/45. Dokumentationsarchiv für Österreichischen Widerstandes.
Emil Tuchman's file no. 17142. Dokumentations archiv der Österreichischen Widerstandes, Wien.
Frankl's Emigration Questionnaire. Archiv der Israelistischen Kultusgemeinde Wien.
Frankl's Gauachten. Staatsarchiv, Vienna document PB 7223.
Frankl's Dermögensderzeichnis. Staatsarchiv Vienna documents no. 62/1068 and 62/1072.
Index of Psychiatric Krankenhaus Baumgartnerhöhe 1934-1938, Wien Landes Stadt Archiv.
Die National Socialist Beamtenschaft der Heilanstalt, Am Steinhof. Dokumentationsarchiv des Österreichischen Widerstandes.
Otto Pötzl's Nazi Party file. Dokumentationsarchiv des Österreichischen Widerstandes, Vienna.
Umschlagbogen 194 Otto Pötzl. Staatsarchiv Vienna.

Books by Frankl

Frankl, Viktor. *The Doctor on the Soul*. Translated by Richard Winston and Clara Winston. New York: Alfred A. Knopf, 1965.

———. *From Death-Camp to Existentialism: A Psychiatrist's Path to a New Therapy*. Translated by Ilse Lasch. Boston: Beacon Press, 1959.

———. *Frühe Schriften: 1923-1942*. Wien: Verlag Wilhelm Maudrich, 2005.

———. *Gesammelte Werke: ...trotzdem Ja zum Leben sagen und ausgewählte Briefe (1945-1945) Band 1.*, ed. A. Batthyany, K. Biller, and E. Fizzotti. Vienna: Böhlau Verlag, 2011.

———. *Homo patiens*. Vienna: Franz Deuticke, 1950.

———. *Logos und Existenz*. Vienna: Amandus-Verlag, 1951.

———. *Logotherapie und Existenzanalyse*. Munich: Piper, 1987.

———. *Man's Search for Meaning*. New York: Simon & Schuster, 1984.

———. *Man's Search for Ultimate Meaning*. New York: Insight Books, 1997.

———. *Psychotherapy and Existentialism: Selected Papers on Logotherapy*. New York: Washington Square Press, 1967.

———. *Die Sinnfrage in der Psychotherapie*. Munich: R. Piper, 1981.

———. "Synchronisation in Birkenwald: Eine metaphysische Conference," *Der Brenner*, Hrsg. Ludwig Ficker, Innsbruck 1948.

———. *Synchronization in Buchenwald*. Translated by Joseph Fabry. Berkeley: Institute of Logotherapy Press.

———. *Theorie und Therapie der Neurosen: Einführung in Logotherapie und Existenzanalyse*. Munich: Ernst Reinhardt Verlag, 1975.

———. *... trotzdem Ja zum Leben Sagen*. Vienna: Franz Deuticke, 1946.

———. *Der unbedingte Mensch*. Vienna: Franz Deuticke, 1949.

———. *Der unbewusste Gott*. Vienna: Amandus-Verlag, 1949.

———. *The Unconscious God: Psychotherapy and Theology*. New York: Simon and Schuster, 1975.

———. *The Unheard Cry for Meaning: Psychotherapy and Humanism*. New York: Simon & Schuster, 1978.

———. *Viktor Frankl—Recollections: An Autobiography*. Translated by Joseph Fabry and Judith Fabry. New York: Insight Books, Plenum Press, 1997.

———. *Was nicht in meinen Büchern steht*. Munich: Quintessenz, 1995.

———. *The Will to Meaning: Foundations and Applications of Logotherapy*. Cleveland, Ohio: World Publishing, 1969.

Articles by Frankl

Frankl, Viktor. "Der Alpinismus und die Pathologie des Zeitgeistes," *ÖAV-Mitteilungen* (June 1987).

———. "Aus der Praxis Jungendberatung," *Psychotherapeutic Praxis* no. 7 (1935): 155–159.

———. "Beyond Self-actualization and Self-expression," *Journal of Existential Psychology* 1, no. 1 (1960): 5–20.

———. "Collective Neuroses of the Present Day," *International Journal für prophylaktische Medizin und Socialhygiene* 2, no. 3 (June 1958): 1–5.

———. "Concept of Man in Psychotherapy," *Pastoral Psychology* 6 (1955): 16–26.

———. "Cosmos and the Mind, (How Far Can We Go?)," *Pace* 5, no. 8 (August 1969): 34–39.

———. "Encounter: The Concept and Its Vulgarization," *Journal of the American Academy of Psychoanalysis* 1, no. 1 (1973): 73–83.

———. "Existential Dynamics and Neurotic Escapism," *Journal of Existential Psychiatry* 4 (1963): 27–42.

———. "Facing the Transitoriness of Human Existence," *Generations: Aging and the Human Spirit* 14, no. 4 (Fall 1990).

————. "From Psychotherapy to Logotherapy," *Pastoral Psychology* 7 (1956): 56–60.

————. "Zur geistigen Problematik der Psychotherapie," *Zentralblatt für Psychotherapie* 10 (1937): 33–45.

————. "Gründet Jugendberatungsstellen," *Der Abend* 12, no. 200 (1926): 7.

————. "Ein Haüfiges Phänomen bei Schizophrenie," *Zeitschrift für Neurologie und Psychologie* no. 152 (1935): 161–162.

————. "Jungendberatung," *Der Mensch im Alltag* 1, no. 5/6 (1927): 5.

————. "Logos and Existence in Psychotherapy," *American Journal of Psychotherapy* 7 (1953): 8–15.

————. "Logotherapy and Existential Analysis—A Review," *American Journal of Psychotherapy* 20 (1966): 252–260.

————. "Logotherapy and Existentialism," *Psychotherapy: Theory, Research and Practice* 4, no. 3 (August 1967): 138–142.

————. "Logotherapy and the Challenge of Suffering," *Review of Existential Psychology and Psychiatry* 1, no. 1 (Winter 1961): 3–7.

————. "Zur medikamentösen Unterstützung der Psychotherapie bei Neurosen," *Schweizerisches Archiv für Neurologie und Psychiatrie* no. 43 (1939): 26–31.

————. "In Memorium," *The Jewish Echo: Periodical of Jewish Intellectuals* 5, no. 6 (1949).

————. "*Zur Mimischen Bejahung und Verneinung,*" *Internationale Zeitschrift für Psychoanalyse* no. 10 (1924): 437–438.

————. "Opening Address to the First World Congress: Logotherapy on Its Way to Degurufication," in *Analecta Frankliana: The Proceedings of the First World Congress of Logotherapy* (1980), ed. Sandra A. Wawrytko. Berkeley: Institute of Logotherapy Press, 1982.

————. "Paradoxical Intention," *American Journal of Psychotherapy* 14 no. 3 (July 1960): 8–15.

————. "Paradoxical Intention and Dereflection," *Psychotherapy: Theory, Research and Practice* 12, no. 3 (1975): 226–237.

————. "Pervtin Intrazisternal," *Ars Medici* no. 1 (1942): 58–60.

————. "Philosophical Foundations of Logotherapy." In *Phenomenology: Pure and Applied*, ed. Erwin Strauss. Pittsburgh Pennsylvania: Duquesne University Press, 1964.

————. "Philosophie und Psychotherpie, Zur Grundlegung einer Existenzanalyse," *Schweizerische medizinische Wochenschrift* no. 31 (1939): 24–28.

————. "Der Platz der Religion in der Welt von heute," *Mahnruf: Für Freiheit und Menschenrecht* no. 6 (July 1947): 1–2.

————. "The Pleasure Principle and Sexual Neurosis," *International Journal of Sexology* 5 (1952): 128–130.

————. "Psychiatry and Man's Quest for Meaning," *Journal of Religion and Health* 1, no. 2 (January 1962): 93–103.

————. "Psychohygiene im Notstand," *Hygiene* (October 1952).

————. "Zur Psychologie des Intellektualismus," *Internationale Zeitschrift für Individualpsychologie* (1926): 326–333.

————. "Psychotherapie und Weltanschauung," *International Zeitschrift für Individualpsychologie* no. 3 (1925): 250–252.

————. "Reductionism and Nihilism." In *Beyond Reductionism: New Perspectives in the Life Sciences*, ed. Arthur Koestler. New York: Macmillan, 1970.

————. "Response to May," *Journal of Humanistic Psychology* 18, no. 4 (Fall 1978): 57–58.

————. "Schafft Jungendberatungsstellen," *Die Mutter* 2, no. 39 (1926): 8.

————. "Seelenärtliche Selbstbesinnung," *Der Christliche Ständestaat* (30 January 1938): 72–74.

————. "Selbstmordprophylaxe und Jugendberatung," *Münchner Medizinische Wochenschrift* (4 October 1929): 1675.

————. "Self-transcendence as a Human Phenomenon," *Journal of Humanistic Psychology* 6, no. 2 (1966): 97–106.

————. "The Spiritual Dimension in Existential Analysis and Logotherapy," *Journal of Individual Psychology* 15, (Nov. 1959): 157–165.

————. "There is No Collective Guilt," *Austrian Information* 41, no. 6 (1988).

————. "Time and Responsibility," *Existential Psychiatry* 1 (1946): 361–366.

————. "Typische 'Faelle' aus der Jugendberatung," *Zeitschrift für Kinderschutz, Familien- und Berufsfuerssorge* no. 11 (1929): 163–164.

————. "Über die Notwendigkeit der Schaffung von Jungendberatungstellen," *Zeitschrift für Kinderschutz, Familien- und Berufsfuersorge* 18, no. 7 (1926): 130–132.

————. "Über Lehrbarkeit und Lernbarkeit der Psychotherapie." In *Festschrift: Zum 70. Geburtstag von Prof. Dr. Otto Pötzl*, Herausgegeben von Hurbert Urban. Innsbruck, Austria: Universitätsverlag Wagner, 1949.

————. "Viktor Frankl." In *Psychotherapie in Selbstdarstellung*, ed. Ludwig J. Pongratz. Vienna: Verlag Hans Huber, 1973.

————. "Was ist Jungendberatung?," *Der Mensch im Alltag* 1, no. 3 (1927): 5.

————. "What is Meant by Meaning?," *Journal of Existentialism* 7, no. 25 (Fall 1966): 21–28.

————. "Wien und die Seelenheilkunde," *Wiener Kurier* (23 March 1946): 11–13.

————. "Wille und Vernunft," *Wiener Medizinische Wochenschrfit* No. 13 (1927).

————. "The Will to Meaning," *Journal of Pastoral Care* 7 (Summer 1958): 82–88.

————. "Wirtschaftskrise und Seelenleben vom Standpunkte des Jungendberaters," *Sozialärtlich Rundschau* no. 3 (1933): 43–46.

Primary Sources: Books

Adler, Alfred. *The Individual Psychology of Alfred Adler*, ed. Heinz Ansbacher and Rowena Ansbacher. New York: Harper and Row, 1964.

Allers, Rudolf. *Essays in Order*. London: Sheed and Ward, 1932.

————. *What's Wrong With Freud: A Critical Study of Freudian Psychoanalysis*. Fort Collins, Co.: Roman Catholic Books, 1941.

Amstädter, R. *Der Alpinismus*. Vienna: WUV-Universitätsverlag, 1996.

Batthyány, Alexander. *Mythos Frankl? Geschichte der Logotherapie und Existenzanalyse 1925-1945, Entgegnung auf Timothy Pytell*. Wien; Berlin; Münster: 2008.

Bischof, Günter, and Pelinka, Anton, eds. *Austrian Historical Memory and National Identity. Contemporary Austrian Studies* 5. New Brunswick: Transaction Publishers, 1997.

Bukey, Evan. *Hitler's Austria: Popular Sentiment in the Nazi Era, 1938-1945*. University of North Carolina Press: 2000.

Bulka, Reuven. *The Quest for Ultimate Meaning*. New York: Philosophical Library, 1978.

Dandy, W.E. *Neurosurgery*. Hagerstown, Md.: 1945.

Fabry, Joesph. *The Pursuit of Meaning: Viktor Frankl, Logotherapy, and Life*. Boston: Beacon Press, 1968.

Gauger, Kurt. *Politische Medizin: Grundriss einer Deutchen Psychotherapie*. Hamburg: Hanseatische Verlagsanstalt, 1934.

Klingberg, Haddon Jr. *When Life Calls Out to Us: The Love and Lifework of Viktor and Elly Frankl*. Doubleday: New York, 2001.

Längle, Alfred. *Viktor Frankl Ein Porträt*. München: Piper, 1998.

Maslow, Abraham. *Farther Reaches of Human Nature*. New York: Viking, 1971.

————. *The Journals of A.H. Maslow*, ed. Richard Lowry. Monterey, California: Brooks/Cole Publishing Co., 1979.

Mühleitner, Elke. *Medizinische Psychologie und Psychotherapie in Österreich: 1900-1950* (unpublished).

Pytell, Timothy. *Viktor Frankl: Das Ende eines Mythos?* Wien: Studienverlag, 2005.

Rogers, Carl. *Carl Rogers on Encounter Groups*. New York: Harrow, 1970.

Schuller, Robert. *Prayer: My Soul's Adventure with God*. New York: Doubleday, 1995.

Tweedie, Donald. *The Christian and the Couch*. Michigan: Baker Book House, 1963.

Ungersma, Aron J. *The Search for Meaning: A New Approach in Psychotherapy and Pastoral Psychology*. Philadelphia: Westminster Press, 1961.

Urban, Hurbert. *Festschrift: Zum 70. Gerburtstag von Prof. Dr. Otto Pötzl*. Innsbruck, Austria: Universitätsverlag Wagner, 1949.

Weisskopf-Joelson. *Father, Have I kept My Promise? Madness as Seen from Within*. Indiana: Purdue University Press, 1988.

Primary Sources: Articles

Allers, Rudolf. "Die neue Zeit und die Heilerziehung," *Der Christliche Ständestaat* (4 March 1934).

Birnbaum, Ferdinand. "Frankl's Existential Psychology from the Viewpoint of Individual Psychology," *Journal of Individual Psychology* 17 (1961): 162–166.

Bulka, Reuven. "Death in Life—Talmudic and Logotherapeutic Affirmations," *Humanitas* 10, no. 1 (February 1974): 33–41.

———. "The Ecumenical Ingredient in Logotherapy," *Journal of Ecumenical Studies* (Winter 1974): 13–23.

———. "From Confusion to Fusion," in *The Other Side of the Couch*, ed. Mark Stern. New York: Pilgrim Press, 1981.

———. "Is Logotherapy a Spiritual Therapy?," *Association of Mental Health Clergy Forum* 30, no. 2 (January 1978): 83–88.

———. "Is Logotherapy Authoritarian?," *Journal of Humanistic Psychology* 18, no. 4 (Fall 1978): 46–54.

———. "Logotherapy and Judaism-Some Philosophical Comparisons," in *A Psychology-Judaism Reader*, ed. Reuven Bulka and Moshe Halevi Spero. Springfield, Mass.: Charles C. Thomas, 1982.

———. "Logotherapy as a Response to the Holocaust," *Tradition* 15 (1975): 89–96.

Dandy, W.E. "Ventriculography Following the Injection of Air into the Cerebral Ventricles," *The Annals of Surgery* (July 1918).

Eliasberg, Wladimir. "Allgemeine Ärztliche Gesellschaft für Psychotherapie, 1926-31," *American Journal of Psychiatry* 112 (1956): 738–740.

Fabry, Joseph, and Elisabeth Lukas, "In Pursuit of Logos: Correspondence with Viktor Frankl," translation of Prologue and first chapter of the book, *Auf den Spuren des Logos—Briefwechsel mit Viktor E. Frankl aus der Pionierzeit der Logotherapie, Journal des Viktor Frankl Instituts* 3, no. 1 (Spring 1995).

Fizzotti, Eugenio. "Prolegomena zu einer Psychotherapie mit menschlichen Antlitz in den Schriften des jungen Viktor E. Frankl 1923-1942," *Journal Des Viktor-Frankl-Instituts* 3, no. 1 (Spring 1995): 29–39.

Frankl, Viktor, and Otto Poetzl. "Analyse einer transitorischen temporalen Aphasia," *Wiener Zeitschrift Nervenheil* no. 11 (1955): 362–380.

Frankl, Viktor, and Otto Poetzl. "Über die seelischen Zustaende während des Absturzes: eine psycho-physiologische Studie," *Monatsschrift Psychiatrie und Neurologie* no. 123 (June 1952): 362–380.

Grollman, Earl. "The Logotherapy of Viktor Frankl," *Judaism* 8 (1965): 22–38.

Grossman, Nathan. "Rabbi and Doctor of the Soul," *Jewish Spectator* 34, no. 1 (January 1969): 8–12.

Gruber, Marianne. "Der Wille zum Sinn," *Die Pestsäule* (December 1974).

Häberlin, Carl. "Die Bedeutung Von Ludwig Klages und Hans Prinzhorn für die Deutsche Psychotherapie," *Zentralblatt für Psychotherapie* 7 (1934): 38–51.

Johnson, Paul. "Challenge of Logotherapy," *Journal of Religion and Health* 7 (1968): 122–130.

———. "Logotherapy: A Corrective for Determinism," *Christian Advocate* 5 (23 November 1961): 12–13.

Kalmar, Stephen. "A Brief History of Logotherapy," in *Analecta Frankliana*. Berkeley: Logotherapy Press, 1982.

Krauss, Karl (with Joseph Fabry). "My Most Famous Student," *NRTA Journal* no. 29 (November–December 1978).

Kubler-Ross, Elisabeth. "Behüt Dich Gott," *International Forum for Logotherapy* no. 3 (Spring 1980): 49–50.

Leslie, Robert. "The Story of a Bestseller," *International Forum for Logotherapy* 13, no. 1 (Spring 1990): 64–66.

Maslow, Abraham. "Comments on Dr. Frankl's Paper," *Journal of Humanistic Psychology* 6 (1966): 107–112.

May, Rollo. "Response to Bulka's Article," *Journal of Humanistic Psychology* 18, no. 4 (Fall 1978).

Polak, Paul. "Frankl's Existential Analysis," *American Journal of Psychotherapy* 3 (1949): 517–522.

Porter, Jack Nusan. "The Affirmation of Life After the Holocaust: The Contributions of Bettelheim, Lifton and Frankl," *Association for Humanistic Psychology Newsletter* (August–September 1980): 9–11.

Sahakian, William. "Logotherapy as Personality Theory," *Israel Annals of Psychiatry and Related Disciplines* 10 (1972): 230–244.

Sakel, Manfred. "Über die Einfüehrung der sogenannten Schocktherapie und Pötzl's Verdienst um ihre Einführung." In *Festschrift: Zum 70. Gerburtstag von Prof. Dr. Otto Poetzl*, ed. Hurbert Urban. Innsbruck, Austria: Universitätsverlag Wagner, 1949.

Schacter, Stanley. "Bettleheim and Frankl: Contradicting Views of the Holocaust," *Reconstructionist* 26, no. 20 (10 February 1961): 6–11.

Soffner, Von Heinrich. "Die Seelische Not unserer Jugend und ihre Bekampfung," *Die Bereitschaft* 7, no. 2 (1927): 17–18.

Weisskopf-Joelson, Edith. "Logotherapy and Existential Analysis," *Acta Psychotherapeutica: International Journal for Psychotherapy, Psychosomatics, Special Education* 4, no. 3 (1958): 193–204.

———. "Logotherapy: Science or Faith," *Psychotherapy: Theory, Research and Practice* 12, no. 3 (Fall 1975): 238–240.

———. "Paranoia and the Will to Meaning," *Existential Psychiatry* 1 (1966): 316–320.

———. "The Place of Logotherapy in the World Today," *International Forum for Logotherapy* no. 3 (Spring 1980): 3–7.

———. "Six Representative Approaches to Existential Therapy." In *Existential—Phenomenological Alternatives for Psychology*, ed. Ronald S. Valle and Mark King. New York: Oxford University Press, 1978.

———. "Some Comments on a Viennese School of Psychiatry," *The Journal of Abnormal and Social Psychology* 51, no. 3 (November 1955): 701–703.

———. "Some Suggestions Concerning the Concept of Awareness," *Psychotherapy: Theory, Research and Practice* 8, no. 1 (Fall 1971): 2–7.

Wolfram, Fritz. "Die Problematik einer weiteren Arbeitszeitverkürzung und Freizeitvermehrung," *freie argumente* no. 2 (January 1981): 26–31.

Secondary Sources

Adler, H.G. *Theresienstadt 1941-1945*. Tübingen: 1960.

Adorno, Theodor. *Negative Dialectics*. Translated by E.B. Ashton. New York: The Seabury Press, 1973.

Allport, Gordon. *The Individual and His Religion*. New York: Macmillan, 1960.

Baeck, Leo. "A People Stands Before Its God." In *We Survived*, ed. Eric Boettm. Santa Barbara: ABC info. service, 1975.

Barrett, William. *Irrational Man: A Study in Existential Philosophy*. New York: Doubleday, 1958.

Batthyany, Alexander, and Jay Levisnon eds. *Existential Psychotherapy of Meaning: Handbook of Logotherapy and Existential Analysis.* Phoenix: Zeig, Tucker and Theisen, 2009.

Berkley, George. *The Story of Theresienstadt*. Boston: Branden Books, 1993.

———. *Vienna and Its Jews: The Tragedy of Success*. Boston: Madison Books, 1988.

Berg, Manfred and Geoffrey Cocks. *Medicine and Modernity: Public Health and Medical Care in Nineteenth- and Twentieth-Century Germany*. Washington, D.C.: German Historical Institute and Cambridge University Press, 1996.

Bernstein, Micheal. *Foregone Conclusions: Against Apocalyptic History*. Berkeley: University of California Press, 1994.

Birken, Lawrence. *Consuming Desire: Sexual Science and the Emergence of a Culture of Abundance, 1871-1914*. New York: Cornell University Press, 1988.

Blackbourn, David, and Geoff Eley. *The Peculiarities of German History: Bourgeois Society and Politics in Nineteenth-Century Germany*. New York: Oxford University Press: 1984.

Bottome, Phyllis. *Alfred Adler: A Portrait from Life*. New York: GP Putnam's Sons, 1936.

Botz, Gerhard. *Kontroversen um Österreichs Zeitgeschichte: verdrängte Vergangenheit, Österreich-Identität, Waldheim und die Historiker*. New York: Campus Verlag, 1994.

Boyer, John. *Culture and Political Crisis in Vienna: Christian Socialism in Power, 1897-1918*. Chicago: University of Chicago Press, 1995.

Brecht, Karen, F. Volker, M.H. Ludger, J.I. Kaminer, and D.H. Jülich, eds. *Here Life Goes on in a Most Peculiar Way: Psychoanalysis before and after 1933*. Translated by Christine Trollope. Hamburg: Kellner, 1995.

Choron, Jacques. *Death and Western Thought*. New York: Macmillan, 1963.

Cocks, Geoffrey. *Psychotherapy in the Third Reich: The Göring Institute*. New York: Oxford University Press, 1985. New Jersey: Transaction, 1997.

———. *The State of Health: Illness in Nazi Germany*. New York: Oxford University Press, 2013.

Coser, Lewis. *Refugee Scholars in America*. New Haven: Yale University Press, 1984.

DeCarvalho, Roy Jose. *The Founders of Humanist Psychology*. New York: Praeger, 1991.

Dennet, Daniel. *Darwin's Dangerous Idea: Evolution and the Meanings of Life*. New York: Simon and Schuster, 1995.

Des Pres, Terence. *Writing into the World*. New York: Penguin, 1991.

Dickstein, Morris. *The Gates of Eden*. New York: Penguin, 1989.

Dienelt, Karl. *Von Freud zu Frankl*. Vienna: Österreichischer Bundesverlag, 1967.

Dreyfus, Herbert. *Being-in-the-World: A Commentary on Heidegger's Being and Time, Division I*. Cambridge, Mass.: MIT Press, 1991.

Eksteins, Modris. *Rites of Spring: The Great War and the Birth of the Modern Age*. New York: Doubleday, 1989.

Edmondson, C.E. *The Heimwehr and Austrian Politics, 1918-1936*. Athens, Ga.: University of Georgia Press, 1978.

Fallend, Karl. *Sonderlinge Träumer Senstitive: Psychoanalyse auf dem Weg zur Institution und Profession*. Veröffentlichungen des Ludwig-Boltman-Institutes für Geschichte und Gesellschaft, Band 26. Vienna: n.p., 1995.

Fallend, Karl. *Wilhelm Reich in Wien*. Wien: Geyer, 1998.

Faye, Emmanuel. *Heidegger: The Introduction of Nazism into Philosophy in Light of the Unpublished Seminars of 1933-1935*. New Haven: Yale University Press, 2011.

Fleming, Donald, ed. *The Intellectual Migration*. Cambridge, Mass.: Harvard University Press, 1969.

Fox, W.L. *Dandy of John Hopkins*. Baltimore, Md.: Williams and Wilkins, 1984.

Fraenkel, Josef. *The Jews of Austria*. London: Vallentine and Mitchell, 1970.

Freidenreich, Harriet Pass. *Jewish Politics in Vienna: 1918-1938*. Bloomington: Indiana University Press, 1991.

Freud, Sigmund. *Civilization and Its Discontents*. New York: Norton, 1961.

Friedlander, Albert. *Leo Baeck: Teacher of Theresienstadt*. New York: Holt, Rinehart and Winston, 1978.

Gardner, Sheldon, and Gwendolyn Stevens. *Red Vienna and the Golden Age of Psychology*. New York: Praeger, 1992.

Gay, Peter. *Freud: A Life for Our Time*. New York: Doubleday, 1988.

Gehl, Juergen. *Austria, Germany, and the Anschluss: 1931-1938*. London: Oxford University Press, 1963.

Glaser, Ernst. *Im Umfeld des Austromarxismus: Ein Beitrag zur Geistesgeschichte des Österreichischen Sozialismus*. Vienna: Europaverlag, 1981.

Goeschel, Christian. *Suicide in Nazi Germany*. London: Oxford University Press, 2009.

Gould, Stephen Jay. *Ever Since Darwin: Reflections in Natural History*. New York: Norton, 1977.

Gould, William Blair. *Viktor E. Frankl: Life with Meaning*. Belmont, California: Brooks/Cole, 1993.

Gruber, Helmut. *Red Vienna: Experiment in Working Class Culture 1919-1934*. New York: Oxford University Press, 1991.

Guignon, Charles. *The Cambridge Companion to Heidegger*. Boston: Cambridge University Press, 1996.

Haider, Jörg. *Die Freiheit die ich meine*. Vienna: Ulstein, 1993.

Halperin, Irving. *Messengers from the Dear*. Philadelphia: Westminister Press, 1972.

Hartman, Geoffrey. *Holocaust Remembrance: The Shapes of Memory*. Cambridge Mass.: Blackwell, 1994.

Martin Heidegger. *Being and Time*. Translated by John Macquarrie and Edward Robinson. New York: Harper and Row, 1962.

———. *Martin Heidegger: Basic Writings*. Edited and translated by David F. Krell. San Francisco: Harper, 1977.

———. *Nietzsche I*. Translated by David F. Krell. San Francisco: Harper, 1991.

———. *Poetry, Language, Thought*. Translated by Albert Hofstadter. New York: Harper and Row, 1971.

———. *The Question Concerning Technology and Other Essays*. Translated by William Lovitt. New York: Harper and Row, 1977.

Herf, Jeffrey. *Reactionary Modernism*. Cambridge, Mass.: Harvard University Press, 1984.

Hödl, Carl. *Leben ist nicht Zufall*. Vienna: n.p. 1990.

Hoffman, Edward. *The Drive for the Self: Alfred Adler and the Founding of Individual Psychology*. New York: Addison-Wesely, 1994.

Hubenstorf, Micheal. "Medizinische Fakultät 1938-1945," in *Willfärige Wissenschaft: Die Universität Wien 1938-1945*. Vienna: Verlag für Gesellschaftskritik, 1989.

Huber, Wolfgang. *Psychoanalyse in Österreich seit 1933*. Vienna: Geyer-edition, 1977.

Izenberg, Gerald. *The Existentialist Critique of Freud: The Crisis of Autonomy*. Princeton, New Jersey: Princeton University Press, 1976.

Janik, Allan, and Stephen Toulmin. *Wittgenstein's Vienna*. New York: Simon & Schuster, 1973.

Jaspers, Karl. *Karl Jaspers: Basic Philosophical Writings*. Edited and translated by Edith Ehrlich, Leonard H. Ehrlich, and George B. Pepper. New Jersey: Humanities Press, 1986.

Judt, Tony. *Postwar: A History of Europe Since 1945*. New York: Penguin Books, 2005.

Kaplan, Leonard, and Rudy Koshar, eds. *The Weimar Moment: Liberalism, Political Theology, and Law*. Lanham, Md.: Lexington Books, 2012.

Kaplan, Marion. *Between Dignity and Despair: Jewish Life in Nazi Germany*. New York: Oxford University Press, 1998.

Kaufmann, Walter. *Existentialism from Dostoevsky to Sartre*. New York: NAL Penguin, 1975.

Kershaw, Ian. *The Nazi Dictatorship*. London: Edward Arnold, 1985.

Kipling, Rudyard. *The Man Who Would Be King*. Edited by Louis Cornell. New York: Oxford University Press, 1987.

Koshar, Rudy. *Social Life, Local Politics and Nazism: Marburg, 1880-1935*. Chapel Hill: University of North Carolina Press, 1986.

Kubler-Ross, Elisabeth. *On Death and Dying*. New York: Macmillan, 1969.

LaCapra, Dominick. *Representing the Holocaust*. Ithaca: Cornell University Press, 1994.

Lang, Berel. *Writing and the Holocaust*. New York: Holmes and Meir, 1988.

Langer, Lawrence. *Admitting the Holocaust*. New York: Oxford University Press, 1995.

———. *Holocaust Testimonies*. New Haven: Yale University Press, 1991.

———. *Versions of Survival*. Albany: State University of New York Press, 1982.

Lasch, Christopher. *Psychic Survival in Troubled Times*. New York: Norton, 1984.

Lederer, Zdenek. *Ghetto Theresienstadt*. New York: Fertig, 1993.

Lehrer, Ronald. *Nietzsche's Presence in Freud's Life and Thought: On the Origins of a Psychology of Dynamic Unconscious Mental Functioning.* Albany: State University of New York Press, 1995.

Le Rider, Jacques. *Modernity and Crisis of Identity: Culture and Society in Fin-de-siècle Vienna.* New York: Continuum, 1993.

Levi, Primo. *Survival in Auschwitz.* Translated by Stuart Woolf. New York: Collier Books, 1961.

Lifton, Robert Jay. *Death in Life: Survivors of Hiroshima.* New York: Random House, 1967.

———. *The Nazi Doctors: Medical Killing and the Psychology of Genocide.* New York: Basic Books, 1986.

Low, Alfred. *The Anschluss Movement.* New York: Columbia University Press, 1985.

Maderegger, Sylvia. *Die Juden im Österreicheschen Ständestaat 1934-1938.* Vienna: Geyer-Edition, 1973.

May, Rollo. *Existence: A New Dimension in Psychiatry and Psychology.* New York: Basic Books, 1958.

———. *Existential Psychology.* New York: Random House, 1961.

———. *Love and Will.* New York: Norton, 1973.

———, ed. *Politics and Innocence.* Dallas, Texas: Saybrook, 1986.

McGrath, William. *Dionysian Art and Populist Politics in Austria.* New Haven: Yale University Press, 1974.

Megargee, Geoffrey, ed. 0315-0208 Dachau/Kaufering I-XI, *The United States Holocaust Memorial Museum Encyclopedia of Camps and Ghettos, 1933–1945—Volume I Early Camps, Youth Camps, and Concentration Camps and Subcamps under the SS-Business Administration Main Office.* Bloomington, Ind.: Indiana University Press, 2009.

Mitten, Richard. *The Politics of Antisemitic Prejudice.* Boulder, Co.: Westview, 1992.

Mitzman, Arthur. *The Iron Cage.* New Jersey: Transaction, 1985.

Molina, Ferdinand. *Existentialism as Philosophy.* Englewood Cliffs, New Jersey: Prentice-Hall, 1962.

Mosse, George. *The Crisis of German Ideology.* New York: Grossett and Dunlap, 1964.

———. *Nazi Culture.* Translated by Salvator Attanasio. New York: Grosset and Dunlap, 1966.

Musil, Robert. *The Man Without Qualities.* New York: Perigee Books, 1980.

Neske, Gunther, and Emil Kettering, eds. *Martin Heidegger Questions and Answers.* New York: Paragon House, 1990.

Nietzsche, Friedrich. *On the Genealogy of Morals.* Translated by Walter Kaufman. New York: Vintage Books, 1959.

———. *The Will to Power.* Translated by Walter Kaufman and R.J. Hollingdale. New York: Vintage Books, 1957.

O'Callaghan, M. *Psychosurgery.* New Jersey: Bogden and Son, 1982.

Parkinson, F. *Conquering the Past.* Detroit: Wayne State University, 1989.

Pauley, Bruce. *From Prejudice to Persecution: A History of Austrian Anti-Semitism.* Chapel Hill: The University of North Carolina Press, 1992.

———. *Hitler and the Forgotten Nazis: A History of Austrian National Socialism.* Chapel Hill: University of North Carolina Press, 1981.

Pfoser, Alfred. *Literatur und Austromarxismus.* Vienna: n.p., 1980.

Popper, Ludwig. *Soziale Medizin.* Bremerhaven: Wirtschaftsverlag NW, 1991.

Rabinbach, Anson. *The Austrian Socialist Experiment.* Boulder, Co.: Westview, 1985.

———. *The Crisis of Austrian Socialism: From Red Vienna to Civil War, 1927-1934.* Chicago: University of Chicago Press, 1983.

Rabinovici, Doron. *Eichmann's Jews: The Jewish Administration of Holocaust Vienna, 1938-1945.* Translated by Nick Somers. Cambridge: Polity Press, 2011.

Reich, Wilhelm. *People in Trouble.* New York: McGraw-Hill, 1976.

Ringer, Fritz *The Decline of the German Mandarins: The German Academic Community, 1890-1933.* Cambridge, Mass.: Harvard University Press, 1969.

Rosenkranz, Herbert. *Verfolgung und Selbstbehauptung: Die Juden in Österreich 1938-1945.* Vienna and Munich: Herald, 1978.

Rubenstein, Richard. *After Auschwitz: History, Theology, and Contemporary Judaism.* Baltimore, Md.: Johns Hopkins University Press, 1992.

Sartre, Jean Paul. *Existential Psychoanalysis*. New York: Gateway, 1962.

Schiff, Vera. *The Theresienstadt Deception*. New York: Mellen Press, 2013.

Schorske, Carl. *Fin-de-siècle Vienna: Politics and Culture*. New York: Knopf, 1981.

Shaffer, J. *Humanistic Psychology*. New Jersey: Prentice Hall, 1978.

Sichrovsky, Peter. *Born Guilty*. New York: Basic Books, 1993.

Silverman, Lisa. *Becoming Austrians: Jews and Culture between the World Wars*. New York: Oxford University Press, 2012.

Sperber, Manes. *The Unheeded Warning: 1918-1933*. Translated by Harry Zohn. New York: Holmes and Meyer, 1992.

Staude, John Rapheal. *Max Scheler 1874-1928*. New York: The Free Press, 1967.

Stern, Eric. *Die letzten 12 Jahre Rothschild-Spital Wien: 1931-1943*. Vienna: Europäischer Verlag, 1974.

Stern, Fritz. *The Failure of Illiberalism: Essays on the Political Culture of Modern Germany*. New York: Oxford University Press, 1961.

———. *The Politics of Cultural Despair*. New York: Doubleday, 1965.

Sternhell, Zeev. *The Birth of Fascist Ideology*. Translated by David Maisel. Princeton, N.J.: Princeton University Press, 1994.

———. *Neither Left nor Right: Fascist Ideology in France*. Translated by David Maisel. Berkeley: University of California Press, 1986.

Stevenson, Robert Louis. *Dr. Jekyll and Mr. Hyde*. New York: Vintage, 1991.

Sully, Melanie. *A Contemporary History of Austria*. New York: Routledge, 1990.

———. *Political Parties and Elections in Austria: The Search for Stability*. London: C Hurst and Co. Publishers 1981.

Sulloway, Frank. *Freud, Biologist of the Mind: Beyond the Psychoanalytic Legend*. New York: Basic Books, 1983.

Sutich, Anthony, and Miles Vich. *Readings in Humanistic Psychology*. New York: The Free Press, 1969.

Tweedie, Donald. *Logotherapy and the Christian Faith*. Grand Rapids, Mich.: Baker Book House, 1961.

Weber, Max. *From Max Weber: Essays in Sociology*. Edited and translated by C. Wright Mills and Hans Gerth. New York: Oxford University Press, 1958.

Weibel, Peter, and Friedrich Stadler, eds. *The Cultural Exodus from Austria*. Vienna: Loecker Verlag, 1993.

Weidenholzer, Josef. *Auf dem Weg zum "Neuen Menschen": Bildungs- und Kulturarbeit der Österreichischen Sozialdemokratie in der Ersten Republik*. Vienna and Munich: Europa Verlag, 1981.

Weinmann, Martin, ed. *Das nationalsozialistische Lagersystem*. Frankfurt: Zweitausendeins, 1990.

Wiesel, Elie. *Legends of Our Time*. New York: Schocken Books, 1982.

Wistrich, Robert. *Austrians and Jews in the Twentieth Century: From Franz Joseph to Waldheim*. New York: St. Martin's Press, 1992.

———. *Socialism and the Jews: The Dilemmas of Assimiliation in Germany and Austro-Hungary*. Rutherford, New Jersey: Farleigh Dickinson University Press, 1982.

Wolin, Richard. *The Heidegger Controversy*. New York: Columbia University Press, 1991.

———. *The Politics of Being: The Political Thought of Martin Heidegger*. New York: Columbia University Press, 1990.

Wyschogrod, Edith. *Spirit in the Ashes: Hegel, Heidegger, and Man-Made Mass Death*. New Haven: Yale University Press, 1985.

Zimmerman, Michael. *Heidegger's Confrontation with Modernity: Technology, Politics, and Art*. Bloomington: Indiana University Press, 1990.

Secondary Sources: Articles

Baudrillard, Jean. "Symbolic Exchange and Death," in *Jean Baudrillard: Selected Writings*, ed. Mark Poster. California: Stanford University Press, 1988.

Bentwich, Norman. "The Destruction of the Jewish Community in Austria 1938-1942," in *The Jews of Austria*, ed. Josef Fraenkel. London:Vallentine and Mitchell, 1970.

Bischof, Günter. "Victims? Perpetrators? 'Punching Bags' of European Historical Memory? The Austrians and Their World War II Legacies," *German Studies Review* 27 (Feb. 2004): 17–32.

Fellner, Fritz. "The Problem of the Austrian Nation after 1945," *Journal of Modern History* 60 (June 1988): 264–289.

Friedlander, Saul. "Trauma, Memory, Transference," in *Holocaust Remembrance: The Shapes of Memory*, ed. Geoffrey Hartmann. Cambridge, Mass.: Blackwell, 1994.

Fritzsche, Peter. "Nazi Modern," *Modernism/Modernity* 3.1 (1996): 1–22.

Geyer, Michael. "Resistance as Ongoing Project:Visions of Order, Obligations to Strangers, Struggles for Civil Society," *Journal of Modern History* 64 (December 1992): 1–8.

Gould, Stephen Jay. "The Confusion over Evolution," *New York Review of Books* (19 November 1992): 47–54.

Grosz, Paul. "A Jewish View of the Anschluss and the Second Republic," in *Austria, 1938-1988: Anschluss and Fifty Years*, ed. William Wright. Riverside, Calif.: Ariadne Press, 1995.

Gruber, Helmut. "Red Vienna and the Jewish Question" *Leo Baeck Yearbook* (1992): 99–118.

Hájková, Anna. "Sexual Barter in Times of Genocide: Negotiating the Sexual Economy of the Theresienstadt Ghetto," *Signs* 38, no. 3 (Spring 2013): 503–533.

Harrer, Von G., and H. Hoff. "Otto Pötzl zum Gedenken," *Wiener Klinische Wochenschrift* 80, no. 45/46 (8 November 1968): 826–827.

Howe, Irving. "Writing and the Holocaust," in *Writing and the Holocaust*, ed. Berl Lang. New York: Holmes and Meier, 1988.

Hughes, H. Stuart. "Social Theory in a New Context," in *The Muses Flee Hitler*, ed. Jarrel Jackman, Washington, D.C.: Smithsonian Institution Press, 1983.

Judt, Tony. "Austria and the Ghost of the New Europe," *New York Review* (15 February 1996): 22–25.

———. "The Past is Another Country: Myth and Memory in Postwar Europe," *Daedalus* (1992–1994): 83–118.

Kline, Arthur. "A Psychiatrist Discovers God: We are Born to Believe," *Women's Home Companion*, April 1954.

Kwiet, Konrad. "Suicide in the Jewish Community," *Leo Baeck Yearbook* 38 (1993): 135–167.

Langer, Walter. "An American Analyst in Vienna during the Anschluss," *Journal of the History of the Behavioral Sciences* no. 14 (1978): 37–54.

Lifton, Robert Jay. "Questions of Guilt," *Partisan Review* 39, no. 49 (Fall 1972): 514–534.

Pauley, Bruce. "The Social and Economic Background of Austria's *Lebensunfähigkeit*," in *The Austrian Socialist Experiment*, ed. Anson Rabinbach. Boulder, Co.: Westview, 1985.

———. "Fascism and the Führerprinzip," *Central European History* 12 (1979).

Piotrowski, Harry. "The Soviet Union and the Renner Government of Austria, April-November 1945," *Central European History* (1988): 247–279.

Pytell, Timothy. "Typology of Gray Flowers: Levi and Frankl on Surviving Auschwitz," in *The Legacy of Primo Levi*, ed. Stanislao G. Pugliese. New York: Palgrave Macmillan, 2004.

Rabinbach, Anson. "Politics and Pedagogy: The Austrian Social Democratic Youth Movement 1931-1932," *Journal of Contemporary History* 13, no. 2 (April 1978): 337–356.

Rosenkranz, Herbert. "The Anschluss and the Tragedy of Austrian Jewry 1938-1945," in *The Jews of Austria*, ed. Josef Fraenkel. London:Vallentine and Mitchell, 1970.

Schick, Alfred. "Die Judischen Ärzte und die Medizin in Wien," *Geschichte der Juden in Österreich*. Tel Aviv: Olamena, 1971.

Schlesinger, Arthur. "The Worst Corruption," *The Wall Street Journal* (22 November 1995).

Schorske, Carl. "Generational Tension and Cultural Change: Reflections on the Case of Vienna," *Daedalus* 107, no. 4 (Fall 1978): 111–122.

Schneider, Marius G. "The Existentialistic Concept of the Human Person in Viktor E. Frankl's Logotherapy," in *Heirs and Ancestors*, ed. John K. Ryan. Washington D.C.: Catholic University Press, 1973.

Spiegel, Rose. "Survival, Psychoanalysis and the Third Reich," *Journal of The American Academy of Psychoanalysis* 13, no. 4 (1985): 521–536.

Whiteside, Andrew. "Austria," in *The European Right*, ed. Hans Rogger and Eugen Weber. Berkeley: University of California Press, 1965.

Williams, Maurice. "German Imperialism and Austria, 1938," *Journal of Contemporary History* 14 (1979): 139–153.

Index